# Energy and Ethics?

# Journal of the Royal Anthropological Institute Special Issue Series

The *Journal of the Royal Anthropological Institute* is the principal journal of the oldest anthropological organization in the world. It has attracted and inspired some of the world's greatest thinkers. International in scope, it presents accessible papers aimed at a broad anthropological readership. All of the annual special issues are also available from the Wiley-Blackwell books catalogue.

Previous special issues of the *JRAI*:

*Dislocating Labour: Anthropological Reconfigurations*, edited by Penny Harvey and Christian Krohn-Hansen

*Meetings: Ethnographies of Organizational Process, Bureaucracy, and Assembly*, edited by Hannah Brown, Adam Reed, and Thomas Yarrow

*Environmental Futures*, edited by Jessica Barnes

*The Power of Example: Anthropological Explorations in Persuasion, Evocation, and Imitation*, edited by Andreas Bandak and Lars Højer

*Doubt, Conflict, Mediation: The Anthropology of Modern Time*, edited by Laura Bear

*Blood Will Out: Essays on Liquid Transfers and Flows*, edited by Janet Carsten

*The Return to Hospitality: Strangers, Guests, and Ambiguous Encounters*, edited by Matei Candea and Giovanni da Col

*The Aesthetics of Nations: Anthropological and Historical Approaches*, edited by Nayanika Mookherjee and Christopher Pinney

*Making Knowledge: Explorations of the Indissoluble Relation between Mind, Body and Environment*, edited by Trevor H.J. Marchand

*Islam, Politics, Anthropology*, edited by Filippo Osella and Benjamin Soares

*The Objects of Evidence: Anthropological Approaches to the Production of Knowledge*, edited by Matthew Engelke

*Wind, Life, Health: Anthropological and Historical Perspectives*, edited by Elisabeth Hsu and Chris Low

*Ethnobiology and the Science of Humankind*, edited by Roy Ellen

# ENERGY AND ETHICS?

EDITED BY METTE M. HIGH and
JESSICA M. SMITH

This edition first published 2019
© 2019 Royal Anthropological Institute

*Registered Office*
John Wiley & Sons Ltd, The Atrium, Southern Gate, Chichester, West Sussex PO19 8SQ, UK

Editorial Offices
350 Main Street, Malden, MA 02148-5020, USA
9600 Garsington Road, Oxford OX4 2DQ, UK
The Atrium, Southern Gate, Chichester, West Sussex PO19 8SQ, UK

For details of our global editorial offices, for customer services, and for information about how to apply for permission to reuse the copyright material in this book, please see our website at www.wiley.com/wiley-blackwell.

*Library of Congress Cataloging-in-Publication Data*

CIP data requested

9781119596998

A catalogue record for this book is available from the British Library.

Journal of the Royal Anthropological Institute.
Incorporating MAN
Print ISSN 1359-0987
All articles published within this special issue are included within the ISI Journal Citation Reports® Social Science Citation Index. Please cite the articles as volume 25(Supp) of the Journal of the Royal Anthropological Institute.

Cover image: 'Energy resources', copyright Seebest

Cover design by Ben Higgins

Set in 10 on 12pt Minion by Aptara Inc.

Printed in Singapore by C.O.S. Printers Pte Ltd

1 2019

# Contents

# Notes on contributors

**Hannah Appel** is Assistant Professor of Anthropology at University of California, Los Angeles (UCLA). She is the author of *Oil and the licit life of capitalism in Equatorial Guinea* (Duke University Press, 2019). Her current projects examine the rise of Pan-African banks on the African continent and the possibilities of debtors' unions under finance capitalism. *375 Portola Plaza, 341 Haines Hall, University of California, Los Angeles, Box 951553, Los Angeles, CA 90095, USA. happel@ucla.edu*

**Jamie Cross** is a Senior Lecturer in Social Anthropology at the University of Edinburgh. He is the author of *Dream zones: anticipating capitalism and development in India* (Pluto, 2014) and is currently completing work on a monograph about solar power, business, and development in South Asia. *Social Anthropology, Chrystal Macmillan Building, 15a George Square, University of Edinburgh, Edinburgh EH8 9LD, UK. jamie.cross@ed.ac.uk*

**Mette M. High** is a Reader in Social Anthropology at the University of St Andrews. She is author of *Fear and fortune: spirit worlds and emerging economies in the Mongolian gold rush* (Cornell University Press, 2017). Her current project examines money, oil, and climate change in global energy markets. *Department of Social Anthropology, University of St Andrews, 71 North Street, St Andrews KY16 9AL, UK. mmh4@st-andrews.ac.uk*

**Cymene Howe** is Associate Professor of Anthropology at Rice University and founding faculty of The Center for Energy and Environmental Research in the Human Sciences. She publishes widely on energy and the environment, co-hosts the Cultures of Energy podcast, and is author of *Ecologics: wind and power in the Anthropocene* (Duke University Press, 2019) and co-editor (with Anand Pandian) of *The Anthropocene unseen: a lexicon* (punctum books, 2019). *Department of Anthropology, Rice University, 6100 Main Street MS-20, Houston, TX 77005-1827, USA. cymene@rice.edu*

**Arthur Mason** is Associate Professor in the Department of Social Anthropology at the Norwegian University of Science and Technology. He is co-editor (with Hannah Appel and Michael Watts) of *Subterranean estates: life worlds of oil and gas* (Cornell University Press, 2015). His current work examines aesthetics and politics in energy imagery. *Department of Social Anthropology, Norwegian University of Science and Technology, Dragvoll, Trondheim 7491, Norway. arthur.l.mason@ntnu.no*

**Amy Penfield** is a Lecturer in Social Anthropology at the University of Bristol. Interested in material and ethical value in Amazonia, she is currently investigating economic livelihoods and imaginaries of the global in Peruvian prospector mining sites. *Department of Anthropology, University of Bristol, 43 Woodland Road, Clifton, Bristol BS8 1UU, UK. Amy.Penfield@bristol.ac.uk*

**Jessica M. Smith** is Associate Professor at the Colorado School of Mines. She is author of *Mining coal and undermining gender: rhythms of work and family in the American West* (Rutgers University Press, 2014). Her current project investigates engineering and social responsibility in mining and energy industries. *Engineering, Design & Society Division Colorado School of Mines, 1500 Illinois Street, Golden, CO 80401, USA. jmsmith@mines.edu*

**Andrew Walsh** is Associate Professor in the Department of Anthropology at the University of Western Ontario. He has conducted ethnographic research in northern Madagascar since 1992 and is the author of *Made in Madagascar: sapphires, ecotourism, and the global bazaar* (University of Toronto Press, 2012). *Department of Anthropology, University of Western Ontario, London, Ontario, N6A 5C2, Canada. awalsh33@uwo.ca*

**Caura Wood** is a corporate anthropologist working in the fields of governance, finance, and energy entrepreneurialism in Calgary, Alberta. Her research explores the nexus of oil and natural gas, finance capital, governance, and contested spatial practices. Her current research focus is on oil at the end of profit. *639-5th AVE SW, Suite 700, Calgary, Alberta, T2P 0M9, Canada. Caura.wood@gmail.com*

*Journal of the Royal Anthropological Institute (N.S.), 7-8*
© Royal Anthropological Institute 2019

# Introduction: The ethical constitution of energy dilemmas

METTE M. HIGH *University of St Andrews*

JESSICA M. SMITH *Colorado School of Mines*

Growing anthropological research on energy provides critical explorations into the cross-cultural ways in which people perceive and use this fundamental resource. We argue that two dominant frameworks animate that literature: a critique of corporate and state power, and advocacy for energy transitions to less carbon-intensive futures. These frameworks have narrowed the ethical questions and perspectives that the discipline has considered in relation to energy. This is because they are animated by judgements that can implicitly shape research agendas or sometimes result in strong accusations that obscure how our interlocutors themselves may consider the rightness and wrongness of energy resources and the societal infrastructures of which they form a part. We propose a more capacious approach to studying energy ethics that opens up energy dilemmas to ethnographic inquiry. As such, we show how energy dilemmas constitute important sites for the generation of anthropological knowledge, encouraging more insightful and inclusive discussions of the place of energy in human and more-than-human lives.

'Are you sure you aren't from the *New York Times*? Are you accompanied by a TV crew? Will I be reading my words in some undercover exposé?' Such were the words from an oil executive after his company had spent three days vetting one of us (High) ahead of our first meeting in Colorado. His initial distrust and expectation of impending criticism were palpable and far from unique in our experiences of doing ethnographic research on the oil, natural gas, and coal industries in the United States. The second author (Smith) received almost identical questions when conducting research in Wyoming, even when most of her interlocutors knew that she had grown up there and worked in the mines herself. Issues surrounding energy can divide people into starkly opposed camps between those supporting and those contesting the realization of different energy visions. Whether it is the construction of oil pipelines, liquefied natural gas (LNG) export terminals, or offshore wind farms, or it is the closure of coal mines or the burning of charcoal, these happenings crystallize and accentuate the difficult energy

*Journal of the Royal Anthropological Institute (N.S.), 9-28*
© 2019 The Authors. Journal of the Royal Anthropological Institute published by John Wiley & Sons Ltd on behalf of Royal Anthropological Institute

dilemmas that confront us today. Ethical criteria, ethical states, and ethical responses are brought to bear on the divergent paths that have been tried in the past and that can be pursued in the future. And with climate change becoming an increasingly urgent issue, the stakes involved in our energy practices are enormous and ever-rising. As a matter on which humanity and other beings depend for their livelihood, energy raises fundamental questions that involve judgements about our entangled *telos*. What is the place of energy in life? How are we to make sense of the ways in which energy is produced, distributed, used, and disposed of? And how do such actions relate to what we consider to be right or good? Questions about energy are intensely ethical as they encourage, if not demand, reflection on how we feel we ought to live. There is thus no 'neutral' ground on which to stand when judging the ways in which energy can contribute to or imperil the kinds of lives and societies that we desire for ourselves and our others.

This special issue attends ethnographically to these ethical questions as they emerge in encounters with and understandings of energy. However, given the geopolitics in natural resource extraction, the strong industry lobbies, and clear activist agendas, people's own ethical sensibility in relation to energy can easily disappear from view and be overshadowed by more vocal and vested voices. Indeed, as we will show in this introduction, much of the existing anthropological literature on energy has been framed by two overarching concerns: the first with critiquing state and corporate power; and the second with advocating energy transitions that cast fossil fuel resources as necessarily immoral and renewable resources as their assumed opposites. These frameworks are animated by ethical views that can implicitly shape research agendas or sometimes result in strong accusations that obscure how our interlocutors themselves may consider the rightness and wrongness of energy resources and the societal infrastructures of which they form a part. As such, these impositions hinder the anthropological project of understanding the diversity of living in the world by predefining how people ought to live, what kinds of societies they should want, and how they ought to relate to the environment and other forms of life.

Opening up these energy dilemmas to ethnographic inquiry, this special issue shows how they constitute important sites for the generation of anthropological knowledge, encouraging us to be curious and interested, puzzled and surprised by how others view and experience the world. Rather than approaching the recurring judgements that are made in the anthropological scholarship on energy as just reactions to, if not frustrations with, current political events, we show how they have been left strikingly unchallenged by anthropologists. This is despite numerous introspective critical turns and returns in anthropology. Given the way in which anthropology as a discipline has evolved, certain modes of inquiry have come to flourish. We will first consider this history and the role of judgement in anthropological argumentation and then offer a detailed examination of anthropological engagements with energy practices in order to show how a particular and problematic ethics of life runs through this scholarship. The essays that follow in this special issue then illustrate an array of ethical sensibilities and questions that arise in people's energy encounters. The essays present reflections and experiences, visions and failures, concords and conflicts, that 'gesture both to the supra-individual, supra-present contexts in which we all craft quotidian ethics, *and* to the expansive geographies and timescapes in which the effects of our ethical practices ramify', as Hannah Appel notes in her concluding piece (Appel, this volume, p. 179, our emphasis). These 'ethical worlds' are multiple and overlapping, sometimes in mutual

**Figure 1**. Energy generation from wind and oil coexists side-by-side in many places in the United States, as here in Texas. (Photo by Ben, courtesy of a Creative Commons licence, available at *https://tinyurl.com/ydz5kmev*.)

accordance and other times at odds, demonstrating why it is important to think of energy ethics in much more capacious ways. These ethical worlds present a plurality and complexity, idiosyncrasy if not inconsistency that current scholarship is poorly positioned to grasp.

As anthropological engagements with energy continue to grow (e.g. Boyer 2014; 2015; Love & Isenhour 2016; Smith & High 2017; Strauss, Rupp & Love 2013a), many scholars in this field seek to imagine transitions to new energy futures, as we illustrate below. We strongly argue that in order for this to be generative of new insights and deeper understandings of the complexities involved, we must start by giving greater recognition to how our interlocutors make sense of the world. As noted by Thomas Csordas, it is necessary to engage in 'a simultaneous consideration of the morality of anthropology and an anthropology of morality', demanding 'attention to how humans, including ourselves as anthropologists, can distinguish between right and wrong' (2013: 524). We thus suggest an analytical open-mindedness that allows for our interlocutors to not always share our views of how the world should and could be: that is, an analytical approach that allows for them to be social, situated, and unpredictable persons entangled in the politics of life. Ethical sensibility animates the everyday thoughts and practices of people, whether they work in renewables, nuclear energy, or fossil fuels; whether they work in industry, policy, or advocacy; whether they produce, distribute, or consume energy.

Yet it is important to note that this is not about defending the ethical worlds of energy actors (or anyone else for that matter) or about contesting the importance of those ethical worlds with which they intersect and contradict. As James Laidlaw has noted, '[T]he claim on which the anthropology of ethics rests is not an evaluative claim that people are good: It is a descriptive claim that they are evaluative' (2013: 3). In focusing on energy ethics, this special issue thus attends to 'a sort of grey territory that obliges us to rethink what we take for granted about the distinction between the bright side and the dark side of our moral world and about the separation of the ethical from the political' (Fassin 2013: 249). Rather than ignoring the political, we consider the pervasiveness of ethics in social life with a keen awareness that people do not necessarily meet their own or others' expectations or hopes. Questions of energy ethics are thus intensely ethical *and* political. And in order to get a sense of this and avoid the 'moral terrorism' that ensues when having an 'unacknowledged attachment to a given idea of truth' (Zylinska 2014: 82, 83), this special issue thus proposes to create an analytical space where we can attend to, take seriously, and seek to understand people's own experiences and evaluations without uncritically imposing our views of how we would like the world to be (see also Coleman 2015; Fassin 2008: 334), lest we risk energy becoming the latest chapter in the 'long history of global interventions based on unquestioned good' (Appel, this volume, p. 182).

We recognize how this is in itself not just an analytical call, but also an ethical and political one. And this is because it seeks to recognize *all* humans as ethical agents. Rather than drawing on and reproducing oppositions and tensions in society, it seeks to bring together people's multiple, differing, and interconnecting reflections and experiences. To ignore this not only produces a seriously distorted and simplified view of human and more-than-human life; it also jeopardizes our trust in each other's ethical capacities and the importance of bringing a diversity of perspectives to bear on energy dilemmas. At a time when we are confronted with deep questions about how we should live, what kinds of societies we want, and how we should relate to other forms of life, it is crucial to not miss this opportunity. Twenty years ago a group of economists considered the 'uncomfortable thought that they should ponder more fully the ethical foundations of their subject' (Groenewegen 1996: 12) – an admission that is also shared today by many leading economists of energy and climate change (Broome 2012; Stern 2014). But ultimately, our energy predicament is not simply about efficiency and other calculations that allude to notions of objectivity, but also importantly about values. And this puts us squarely in the domain of ethics.

## The promise and predicament of critique

In anthropology, the use of ethnography to draw critical attention to practices and institutions that readers may take for granted is as old as the discipline itself (Hart 2001; Holbraad 2012: 35). The practice of 'cultural critique' that unsettles and relativizes assumptions has been foundational to the establishment of anthropology and its ongoing intellectual project. As noted by Keith Hart, central to the practice of cultural critique is the practice of judgement: that is, 'the ability to form an opinion on the basis of careful consideration . . . of worth' (2001: 3037; see also Peters & Lankshear 1996: 54). Despite the challenge of awkward scales, if not the incommensurability of concepts, a deeply subjective process of translation, rescaling, and refocusing is necessary for the anthropologist in order to discern the worth of persons and things across 'contexts' (Feuchtwang 2010; Strathern 2010). How can charcoal be 'green'? To what extent can oil be a 'gift from God'? And what does it mean to say that your low return on gasoline is due to your family's misbehaviour? Categories of being have to be rendered intelligible and judged for their worth so that domains come to intersect and interrelate. Recognizing that we are not dealing with 'matters of fact' but 'matters of concern' (Latour 2004:

© 2019 The Authors. Journal of the Royal Anthropological Institute published by John Wiley & Sons Ltd on behalf of Royal Anthropological Institute

232), cultural critique renders explicit the emergence of what the anthropologist deems to be valued forms.

The intellectual practice of the discipline has been subject to intense scrutiny, introspection, and questioning since the establishment of anthropology as an academic discipline in the late nineteenth century. It has thus been commented that 'anthropology has been in crisis for as long as anyone can remember' (Grimshaw & Hart 1994: 227). What is interesting to note is that whilst these challenges have been numerous and far-reaching, none of them have put a serious question mark by the practice of cultural critique. Rather, it grew in prominence as emphasis shifted from life to text, from power to authority, from explanation to interpretation. And with these shifts came a greater analytical affordance for cultural critique and practices of judgement. Anthropologists could not claim to root their judgements in 'objective facts' or in supreme 'expert knowledge' accumulated through participant observation (Clifford 1986: 2). Instead, ethnography came to be understood as much as a literary endeavour as a scientific one, providing not facts but 'fictions in the sense of "something made or fashioned"' (Clifford 1986: 6). Language could be regarded not simply as descriptive but also as persuasive, while accounts could be regarded not as representative but only ever as partial and political. These critical introspections challenged the ethics of representation and the purpose of anthropology as they urged us to consider whom we write for and how we produce knowledge. While some saw this as a dangerous and dramatic path towards endless fragmentation and excessive relativism (Gellner 1992), it offered 'an invigorating stimulus' to the practice of cultural critique (Hart 2001: 3040).

Recognizing how cultural critique is rooted in judgement, some scholars have offered poignant self-reflexive accounts of how they deal with the difficult nature of making analytical judgements in anthropology: that is, a mode of reasoning that entails both knowing and valuing. Stephan Feuchtwang (2010) describes the difficult balancing act that he has experienced between his personal political persuasions and the realities of fieldwork and analysis. For him, it has required a bridging of multiple contexts and time lags in order to repeatedly correct his 'double vision'. And for Marilyn Strathern (2010), it has been a long process of learning when and how she judges in her personal and ethnographic experiences. She has come to realize moments in which worth can only be established when she takes a step back and suspends immediate judgement. These personal accounts of academic practice demonstrate how important, yet profoundly difficult, it is to know how we make judgements and assign value to that which and those whom we seek to understand. As noted by Susanne Brandtstädter and Karen Sykes,

> To distinguish between the moralist and the critical polemic is a matter of knowing what *judgement is, and is not* ... Passing judgement means combining the felt sense of what is a good decision with careful reasoning about the possibilities of ever knowing another person's 'true' intentions. Exerting judgement in order to correct wrongs and grievances suggests that anthropology might step too closely along the moralist's path (2010: 91-2, italics in original).

As we will show in the following section, anthropological studies of energy have been numerous and wide-ranging. However, they have often exerted unreflexive judgement on what the place of energy in human life *should* be, which energy sources are *good*, and whose conduct is *wrong*. While judgements are fundamental to our practice of cultural critique, we can learn much from those anthropologists who have come closer to knowing what judgement is. This is particularly crucial for research on energy, where

*Journal of the Royal Anthropological Institute (N.S.), 9-28*
© 2019 The Authors. Journal of the Royal Anthropological Institute published by John Wiley & Sons Ltd on behalf of Royal Anthropological Institute

personal political persuasions can so easily cause 'double vision' and where many energy actors have come to anticipate our hostile criticism.

## Thinking anthropologically about energy

Anthropologists have been working on issues of energy since Leslie White's (1943; 1959) early thesis that the 'cultural development' of societies could be correlated to their energy production. Since then, ethnographic studies of energy have contributed key perspectives to the discipline as a whole. Given its conceptually vexing status as material yet immaterial, near yet distant, potentially dangerous yet necessary to life, energy has offered a particularly rich arena from which to explore human social life. The dominant Western understanding of energy as 'the capacity to do work' emerged from a particular historical and cultural context in eighteenth-century Europe and with the particular aim of improving the efficiency of machines. This context of the Industrial Revolution resulted in 'norms, values, and principles' of energy deriving from 'the scientific control of the forces of nature through mathematical language and the application of the scientific method' (Frigo 2017: 7, 8). These particular assumptions do not hold across other understandings of energy, such as the Vedic concept of *agni*, the Chinese *qi*, the 'vital energy' animating agrarian communities in Panama and Colombia (Gudeman 2012), or a more diffuse force of life that many Americans believe is embedded in relationships among humans and other entities (Lennon 2017; Rupp 2016). Ethnography richly demonstrates the multiple and sometimes conflicting ways in which people understand and experience energy, from Alaskan Native communities and scientists weighing renewable and fossil fuel development (Chapman 2013) to citizens of São Tomé and Príncipe anticipating a future with oil (Weszkalnys 2011; 2014).

Ethnographic studies of electrification projects have been particularly evocative for illuminating the social construction of energy and processes of cultural change. These show that new technology is embedded in, but also transforms, its sociocultural, economic, and political contexts. In rural Zanzibar, people associated newly provisioned electricity with Islamic ideals of purity and safety, even as the ability to stay up watching television past sunset resulted in some people missing morning prayers. Religious restrictions there against men and women sharing social space relaxed but did not disappear in the context of newly lighted homes (Winther 2011). For Peruvian *campesinos*, off-grid electricity offered a welcomed sense of heightened connectivity with the wider world along with the ability to work locally in the village instead of migrating to the city (Love & Garwood 2013). Indian villagers with access to small solar electricity batteries drew on kinship idioms and expectations when sharing them with others in the vicinity (Singh, Strating, Herrera, van Dijk & Keyso 2017). These approaches depart from the cultural evolutionist framework, which Leslie White advocated during the discipline's first sustained interest in questions of energy.

Energy's infrastructural dimensions raise further methodological opportunities and challenges. As Dominic Boyer writes, the 'enabling power' in electricity is in some ways like other forms of infrastructures, being at once both a 'thing' and a 'relation between things' (2015: 532, quoting Larkin 2013: 329). Rather than interacting with energy directly, people often experience it indirectly through their use of objects, such as engaging with electricity through manipulating electronic devices or gasoline through driving cars. This dimension of energy lends it a certain invisible quality, which scholars and activists argue accustoms consumers to rely on more and more quantities of it without being aware of their consumption, thereby exacerbating social and environmental harms

*Journal of the Royal Anthropological Institute* (N.S.), 9-28
© 2019 The Authors. Journal of the Royal Anthropological Institute published by John Wiley & Sons Ltd on behalf of Royal Anthropological Institute

in the process (Huber 2013; Hughes 2017). Other research and the contributions to this special issue underscore that this invisibility relates particularly to people who are accustomed to its regular flows: while blackouts prompt New Yorkers to suddenly reflect on the energy on which they depend for their daily livelihood (Rupp 2016), energy is an everyday topic of conversation for those who lack regular access to it (Degani 2017; Kesselring 2017). As this special issue makes clear, the invisibility of energy for consumers does not extend to those who sell or produce it, such as the indigenous Sanema who sell gasoline to artisanal miners (Penfield); the Malagasy who make, trade, and use charcoal (Walsh); the Wyoming coal miners who ground their sense of national belonging in their status as energy providers (Smith); and the oil executives, experts, and other actors who imagine and bring about future development as well as the end of production (High, Mason, and Wood). Nor does it extend to the solar humanitarians who design, build, and sell solar photovoltaic technologies to those living in energy poverty (Cross) and to the species that attest to the harms of wind turbines (Howe). Collectively, our research asks for whom energy is invisible, when, and with what effects.

Even though energy is thus to some extent an abstract phenomenon, mostly experienced through its material mediation, it nonetheless deeply informs how people view and understand the world (Strauss *et al.* 2013a). Energy-based metaphors abound in the English language: we cure the fatigue of 'drained batteries' by 'recharging', we 'shed light' on ideas that can in turn be 'illuminating', and we praise attentiveness as being 'plugged in'. But beyond metaphors, energy also shapes how anthropologists have theorized that world. Boyer goes so far as to assert that electricity is the 'foundational apparatus upon which the experience of modernity has been constituted since the late nineteenth century', yet it 'hides in plain sight' (2015: 532). He argues that electrical thinking has shaped key paradigms and approaches in social theory, including Freudian metapsychology, cybernetic theory, and the decline of culture theory in favour of 'open systems' of operation, code, force, and flow. Perhaps more than any other area of scholarship, energy has seeped into anthropological theorizing that seeks to advance cultural critiques of corporate and state power.

### Critiques of corporate and state power

Ethnographic studies of energy have served as a backbone for the long-standing anthropological project of critiquing corporate and state power and their mutual imbrication. While this scholarship has generated productive theoretical paradigms and provided platforms for more engaged ethnography, it has also profoundly narrowed the kinds of ethical questions and perspectives that the discipline has considered in relation to energy. This trend is particularly evident in the ever-growing anthropology of oil (see Appel, Mason & Watts 2015a and Rogers 2015b for more detailed summaries). Anthropologists have documented and strongly criticized the troubling political, economic, and environmental effects of oil production around the world. They have done so by questioning the mainstream 'resource curse' theory that dominates policy-making and other social science research on oil (e.g. Appel, Mason & Watts 2015b; Gilberthorpe & Rajak 2017; Reyna & Behrends 2011; Weszkalnys 2011; see also Watts 2004). Rather than reproducing that framework by attributing blame to 'weak governance' by 'failed states', anthropologists have demonstrated that oil is central to the performativity of state power.[1] At the same time, anthropologists have documented the ways in which oil development intertwines the power of the state with that of transnational capital, especially in producing harm against already marginalized groups such as indigenous communities (e.g. Cepek 2012; Davidov 2013; Sawyer 2004). They have revealed how, through processes of abstraction, companies cultivate the appearance of separation between themselves and local populations, thereby disentangling themselves from and abdicating responsibility for any problems that may arise. Appel (2012) has powerfully demonstrated such processes in her research on Equatorial Guinea's offshore oil industry. Far from a monolith, the oil 'industry' emerges as a distributed assemblage of corporate forms as well as 'expansive and porous networks of labourers and technologies, representation and expertise, and the ways of life oil and gas produce at points of extraction, production, marketing, consumption, and combustion' (Appel *et al.* 2015*a*: 17; see also Ferguson 2005). This approach to oil is a key part of broader anthropological trajectories that theorize 'resource materialities': materials conventionally referred to as resources, such as oil and gas, exist in distributed assemblages of extractive infrastructures (such as pipelines, roads, and tanks), everyday practices, entities such as corporations, and discourses of the market, development, and nation (Richardson & Weszkalnys 2014).

Even a brief overview of the anthropology of oil makes clear that this area of scholarship shares the larger discipline's predilection for non-Western fieldsites. However, beginning in the mid-2000s, the boom in unconventional oil and gas onshore production brought anthropological questions about energy squarely back to locations such as the United States and Australia.[2] The vast majority of anthropologists working in these regions framed their work in terms of an explicit critique of corporate power. For instance, the editors of the book *ExtrACTION: impacts, engagements, and alternative futures* conclude their introduction by arguing:

> There is perhaps no other issue that threatens humankind as does unchecked industrial-scale resource extraction, and it is this dilemma that 'extr-ACTIVISTS' seek to resolve. Local communities, activist coalitions, and forward thinking governments are seeking to alter their fate as victims of extraction . . . leading the way to a post-extractivist future. The ultimate goal of this text is to share their stories and to encourage others to follow their path in building a world driven by principles other than those tied to legacies of exploitation and injustice (Jalbert, Willow, Casagrande & Paladino 2017: 11).

The contributing authors synthesize and amplify many of the existing trends in that literature, which document and critique the social and environmental dislocations and insecurities engendered by shale oil and gas production. They do this by studying the people who are critical of the industry, often because they are negatively impacted by it in some form (see also Hudgins 2013; Hudgins & Poole 2014; Paladino & Simonelli 2013; Pearson 2017; Willow 2018; Willow & Wylie 2014). Work by Kim de Rijke and colleagues (de Rijke 2013*a*; 2013*b*; Espig & de Rijke 2016) on coal seam gas conflicts in Australia stands out for its broadening of research questions and interlocutors to include people who work inside of the industry as well as those who oppose it. As such, this work builds on other research in the anthropology of oil that examines the knowledge, practices, and world-views of experts and executives (High, this volume; Hughes 2017; Mason, 2007; 2013; this volume; Rogers 2015*a*; Wood 2016; this volume).

As many anthropologists have heeded Laura Nader's (1980) early call to study energy experts and other professionals (see, e.g., McLeod & Nerlich 2017; Newberry 2013; Özden-Schilling 2015; 2016), it is important to note that far less attention has been directed towards rank-and-file labourers (see High, this volume; Smith, this volume; also Atabaki, Bini & Ehsani 2018; Ehsani 2018: 21). The critiques that have been advanced against corporate and state power have largely ignored the very people who make

*Journal of the Royal Anthropological Institute (N.S.), 9-28*

up these institutions. However, the little work that has been done in this area has been generative. Elana Shever (2012) shows that the kinship practices of oil workers accompanied and facilitated the privatization of the Argentine oil industry, while Diane Austin and her colleagues (Austin 2006; Austin & McGuire 2017; Austin, McGuire & Higgins 2006) have used their long-standing research with workers in the Gulf Coast region of the United States to illustrate the massive changes that accompanied the industry's movement into deeper offshore waters, presenting greater risks to workers and communities alike.

Anthropological engagements with coal have generated strong critiques of state and corporate power from the perspective of labour. However, it is only recently that a few scholars have begun to explicitly connect these critiques to issues of energy as such. Coal mining has been central to theories of class and capitalism (Gibson-Graham 2006: 208; Long 1989; Montgomery 1987),[3] and with the declining fortunes of the industry, coal mining towns have been key sites for studies of post-industrial decline (Charlesworth 2000; Kideckel 2008; Stewart 1996; Thorleifsson 2016). The gender dynamics of an industry (in)famous for its dominance by white men have generated rich studies of gender and work (Lahiri-Dutt 2012; Moore 1996; Rolston 2014; Scott 2010) and notions of 'race' (Brown, Murphy & Porcelli 2016). Jessica Smith (this volume) builds on this literature by considering the specific dimensions of coal as an energy source, showing how conceptions of energy provision and exchange undergird miners' sense of personhood, vocation, and national belonging. The energy-based dimensions of coal are also evident in ethnographic research on anti-coal activism, as over 90 per cent of coal is used to generate electricity. Bryan McNeil (2011) offers a textured account of the moral dilemmas that local people face when their mountains become targets for mountaintop removal mining (see also Witt 2016). Viewing morality as a 'social process people use to decide right from wrong in a complicated social world' (McNeil 2011: 65), McNeil explores the contestations over values and attachments to place that inform an environmental organization's criticisms of both coal companies and government at the state and federal levels. In New Mexico, the Navajo (Diné) Nation must also grapple with economic dependence on coal corporations and the federal government while criticizing the same sector's environmental impacts, as revealed by Dana Powell (2017; 2018). She argues that the defeat of the proposed Desert Rock coal plant was grounded in Navajo visions of autonomy and sovereignty that challenged state and corporate colonial histories while engaging with debates over global climate change.

Indigenous critiques of settler colonialism and intersection of land use and racism in the US Southwest figure particularly prominently in ethnographic studies of nuclear energy. Valerie Kuletz explores how scientists and Native Americans differently understand landscape: whereas many indigenous communities understood the desert as a 'geography of the sacred', scientists viewed it as an empty 'sacrifice zone' and 'expendable landscape' to be used for the development, testing, and waste storage of nuclear materials (1998: 12-13). Many Navajo went to work as uranium miners, suffering grave consequences to their health because the federal government and mining companies failed to inform them of the potential risks (Brugge, Benally & Yazzie-Lewis 2006). Traci Voyles (2015) ties the two histories together in her concept of 'wastelanding' in Navajo Country, a process whereby both the environment and the bodies of the people inhabiting it are rendered pollutable. Complementary work explores how communities come to accept the risks of nuclear waste disposal, from the New Mexican town that hosts the Waste Isolation Pilot Plant, the only active nuclear waste storage facility in the United States (Richter 2017), to the Skull Valley Band of Goshute Indians in Utah, who contemplated concepts of stewardship during their consideration of hosting a nuclear waste disposal facility in order to generate much-needed economic development (Clarke 2010; Hanson 2001). In a very different context, Françoise Zonabend's (2007) ethnography of a French nuclear waste processing plant shows how workers and local residents understood risks while enabling family life to go on as usual by disassociating the possibility that they could be affected by radiation and contamination.

One of the distinguishing features of anthropological and closely related work on nuclear energy is its long-standing and critical engagement with scientists and other industry experts. Indeed, one of the most enduring legacies of work done by anthropologists on energy in the late 1970s and early 1980s are Laura Nader's (1980, 1981) reflections on energy and expertise that stemmed from her serving on the US National Academy of Science's Committee on Nuclear and Alternative Energy Systems (CONAES). Her observations led her to identify the implicit cultural assumptions animating much policy-making, from 'group think' and a rejection of energy conservation and 'soft paths' like solar energy (1981) to an 'inevitability syndrome' that excluded from consideration models that did not rest on ever-expanding resource use (2004). These themes remained central for ethnographies of nuclear statecraft (Gusterson 1996; Hecht 2000; 2014; Masco 2006) as well as the growing anthropology of energy in general. Studies of oil highlight a similar 'inevitability syndrome' that assumes that the world will always need hydrocarbons (Chapman 2013; Huber 2013: 309; Hughes 2017: 90), and research with scientists producing biofuels likewise identifies the assumptions and contradictions animating their everyday practice and view of energy (McLeod & Nerlich 2017; Newberry 2013).

To a lesser extent than research on fossil fuels and nuclear energy, some research on renewable energy also advances critiques of corporate and state power, from the 'extractivist' logics of wind energy projects (Argenti & Knight 2015; Boyer & Howe 2019; Franquesa 2018) and rural resistance to 'Big Wind' and the marginalization of the public in siting decisions in the American West (Phadke 2011; 2013), to the harms shouldered by neighbourhoods cross-cut by massive transmission lines that carry renewable energy to urban consumers (Vandehey 2013; cf. Wuebben 2017). Dominic Boyer and Cymene Howe's (2019) research surrounding controversial wind park projects on the Isthmus of Tehuantepec in Oaxaca, Mexico, stands out in the anthropological literature on renewable energy for questioning the 'good' of wind power. They argue instead that wind power did not have a 'singular form or meaning' in their research but 'was a different ensemble of force, matter and desire; it seemed inherently multiple and turbulent involving both humans and non-humans' (2019: 4). Their critique inspired the concept of *energopower*, drawing attention to the multiple ways in which political power is exercised and contested through electricity and its concomitant infrastructure, such as grids (Boyer 2014; 2015; Boyer & Howe 2019; see also Mitchell 2011). Steeped in neoliberal development logics that aligned Mexican government agencies with renewable energy corporations, the project threw into sharp relief the fissures between, on the one hand, advocates for renewable energy transitions that would benefit the planet by reducing carbon emissions and, on the other, local community members who opposed the project on the grounds of its impacts on their fishing livelihoods and the lack of free, prior, and informed consent in approving it (Howe 2014). Howe troubles facile calls for clean energy transitions by revealing the competing ethical claims at play: '[L]ocal environmentally informed responses and those that purport to speak on

behalf of a global scale are often conflicted, and their sources of knowledge disparate'
(2014: 395). In this case, even endangered species whose existence is 'actively balanced
against a "greater good" for humanity' can 'speak' through their threatened status and
environmental management regimes (Howe, this volume, p. 161). The critique of state
and corporate power by Howe and others, as well as their research on the troubling
environmental effects occasioned by large-scale wind energy development, provide a
valuable counterweight to the tendency in anthropology to associate such negligence
primarily with fossil fuels while calling for increased energy generation from renewable
sources, as we discuss next.[4]

**Energy transitions**

In addition to this long-standing critique of corporate and state power through
ethnographic studies of various energy sources, a second and complementary
underlying theme of the anthropology of energy is a strong encouragement of energy
systems that are more environmentally sustainable at both local and global scales.
Much of the surge in anthropological studies of energy is tied to growing concerns
about the contribution of energy systems to climate change (Rogers 2015b: 366). We
argue here that the overarching frame of 'energy transitions' has narrowed the scope of
how anthropologists understand and engage with the ethical dilemmas posed by energy.
Calls to hasten a transition to less carbon-intensive forms of energy all too often cast
fossil fuels – and the people whose work and lives bring them into being – as immoral
(Smith, this volume). This precludes understanding the ethical logics at play in those
distributed assemblages and hinders our ability to engage with and respond to them.

   Almost without exception, anthropological research on energy either presumes or
advocates an energy transition. The 2014 special issue of *Anthropological Quarterly* puts
forward the concept of 'energopower' in the very context of a 'transition' (Boyer 2014).
The editors of the *Cultures of energy* volume likewise frame anthropology's contribution
to energy studies in a highly specific ethical register. For them, the use of fossil fuels must
and will decline in the coming transition towards more 'sensible and sustainable' energy
futures, with anthropologists assisting in that transition (Strauss, Rupp & Love 2013b:
11-12). The editors of the 2016 *Economic Anthropology* special issue on energy similarly
argue that because 'the postcarbon transition … is now inevitable', anthropologists
must encourage people to 'make room for the development of plausible postcarbon
narratives' (Love & Isenhour 2016: 8). And the introduction to Imre Szeman and
Dominic Boyer's *Energy humanities* anthology calls for a 'sociopolitical revolution that
is both necessary and unavoidable' in order to address 'the social, cultural, and political
challenges posed by global warming and environmental damage and destruction' (2017:
7, 1). We caution that this emphasis on transition casts particular sorts of energy sources
and energy futures as good or desirable, leaving little room to understand how people
themselves might consider the ethical dimensions of energy.

   The limitations when taking this kind of approach are made clear in David Hughes'
monograph *Energy without conscience: oil, climate change, and complicity* (2017). Starting
with the premise that the problem of oil is that it has not been made a moral issue –
an assertion that other scholars (e.g. Appel *et al.* 2015a; High, this volume; Watts
2008) would strongly resist – his aim is to correct a so-called 'ethical deficit' that is
said to facilitate the 'contemporary great evil of dumping carbon dioxide into the
skies' (Hughes 2017: 14). For Hughes, Trinidad and Tobago makes for an especially
compelling case as the island country stands to suffer from the sea-level rises induced

by climate change, yet depends on massive oil production and export for its economic growth. In addition to criticizing petroleum geologists for facilitating the continuation and expansion of oil production, he goes a step further to argue that Trinidadian environmental activists and ordinary citizens are also 'complicit'. This is because, in his judgement, they are 'collectively benefitting from the lethal hydrocarbon system and, in so doing, exacerbating climate change' (2017: 120). Hughes argues that a lack of sympathy for one's interlocutors is required for a 'militant anthropology of elites' that emphasizes 'responsibility more than care' (2017: 4). He believes that his duty – and the call for the social science of climate change – is to reveal the wider harms caused by his interlocutors rather than deferring to them with 'waiter-like … humility' (2017: 63, quoting Rabinow 1977: 45; see also Benson & Kirsch 2010). While acknowledging critiques of North Atlantic environmentalists acting imperialistically by imposing their agendas on the Global South (2017: 63), Hughes argues that the grave dangers posed by climate change necessitate such unsavoury interventions.

Hughes' agenda rests on and emphasizes a black-and-white ethical world where oil is immoral and his interlocutors are 'in the wrong and doing wrong' (2017: 4, 151). His book concludes with optimism, forecasting that 'people of good conscience will eventually strand conscienceless forms of energy. Oil will pass from inevitable to immoral to impossible' (2017: 148). In support of his view, he cites Barack Obama's blocking of the Keystone XL pipeline and the desires of an influential Trinidadian policy-maker to install wind turbines on the country's north coast (2017: 152). His conviction that 'virtually the whole world' is moving towards a low-carbon future and a 'rapid economic and political shift to sustainability' (2017: 152) seems anachronistic in the wake of Trump's actions approving controversial pipelines, extending support for the coal industry, and leaving the Paris accords.[5] This is not to mention the explosive growth in oil and natural gas production in the United States and other shale fields following the large-scale application of hydraulic fracturing and horizontal drilling over the last decade.

Hughes' work exemplifies a broader failure to understand the ethical sensibilities of others, judging them by the analyst's standards of right and wrong. This creates blind spots in our disciplinary understanding and thus in our ability to engage across difference (High, this volume; Howe, this volume; Smith, this volume) as we imagine 'new global energy arrangements' (Appel, this volume). While we do not need to *endorse* the ethical standpoints of our interlocutors, we do need to be able to understand them on their own terms in order to respond to them. Powell's (2018) nuanced exploration of the controversy surrounding the proposed Navajo Nation's Desert Rock coal-fired power plant provides one example of how to do so. She squarely situates her research within her own history as an activist ally for indigenous environmental justice movements. In making the 'dizzying' shift from 'activist to researcher' (2018: xiv), the complicated ethical positionings she came to recognize among the Diné in relation to coal and indigenous sovereignty prompted her to rethink 'the logics and allegories of global environmentalism' (2018: 14). She traces out a 'hybrid' ethical positioning among the Diné in which they can value coal as a source of financial security and as a symbol of anti-colonial resistance, at the same time as they criticize the 'intensification of large-scale extraction' that reshapes the landscape and climate that forms the basis for their way of life (2018: 147). Crucially for the purposes of this volume, the hybrid ethical positioning she recognizes in the Navajo Nation invites reconsideration of the 'universal motifs' underlying 'dominant projects in the energy humanities and social sciences' (2018: 14), opening up space in anthropological explorations of energy dilemmas to include the questions, desires, and concerns of humans and more-than-humans who inhabit 'ethical worlds' that are distinct yet interlinked with our own.

## Essays in the volume

As a whole, the special issue lays out a new approach to analysing the ethical worlds of energy as they are experienced by humans and more-than-humans, spanning a diversity of engagements with energy in a variety of geographical spaces. While we are attentive to the lived experiences of our interlocutors, we situate these within larger structures of power and longer political-economic histories in order to grasp the complexities involved in imagining energy futures. For example, Smith shows that the Wyoming miners' sense of vocation as energy providers comes to be only within larger trajectories of US energy policy, and Walsh argues that new renewable initiatives in Madagascar form part of a 'Regional Modernization Strategy' funded by international donors and viewed as 'pro-poor, pro-development, and a potential driver of sustainable economic growth' (Walsh, this volume, p. 118, quoting Ackerman, Kirtz, Andriamanantseheno & Sepp 2014: 38).

As a whole, the special issue seeks to make multiple interventions into the often unstated ethical paradigms that animate anthropological studies of energy. It opens by pairing Mette High's exploration of Colorado oil and natural gas industry actors' broader, cosmoeconomic understandings of oil as a force for good with Jamie Cross's analysis of 'solar philanthropists' who seek to use off-grid renewable energy to alleviate poverty in sub-Saharan Africa and South Asia. This pairing unsettles simplistic judgements of fossil fuels as necessarily party to immoral or amoral projects and renewables as the opposite. It also invites theorization across two energy sources that are usually considered separately. High illustrates how oil and gas exploration is informed by multiple projects and moral ambitions that require analytical attention to broader understandings of agency, responsibility, and devotion. She argues that although energy projects may appear like any formal company promotional pitch, the oilfield and corporate office actors' own ethical reflections reveal more-than-human visions of oil's potentiality. Her essay thus demonstrates how multiple and diverging ethical registers inform the valuation of oil and people's moral ambitions of doing good through oil. Cross also takes up the theme of doing good through energy, but does so by troubling the 'solar utopias' imagined by the people who design, build, and sell solar photovoltaic technologies to those living in energy poverty across sub-Saharan Africa and South Asia. These moral projects give rise to ethical tensions and ambiguities, as they require finding a balance between the gift of humanitarian aid and the logic of market transactions. Cross thus shows that the energy futures envisioned by the solar philanthropists reproduce forms of production and exchange, ownership and property that characterize capitalist economies, including the privileges of race, gender, and class.

The next set of essays, by Caura Wood and Jessica Smith, add further complexity to hasty portrayals of morally depraved fossil fuel energy worlds. They highlight the ethics of return that animate oil executives in Canada and coal miners in Wyoming, respectively, as they grapple with the decline of their livelihoods and the erosion of crucial relationships. Wood explores the ethical dilemmas of a Canadian oil and gas company on the verge of insolvency. She shows how debtors focus strictly on calculative regimes of recovery, with no moral regard for the consequences of 'market death' as experienced by executives who have obligations to families, employees, and known shareholders. Attention to the forms and conditions of such disentanglement with insider equity capital in times of loss highlights how ethical registers are at work in the flows of capital and oil. This is manifested evocatively through negotiations over the fate and ownership of 'orphaned' wells as it is decided that they will end their productive lives. The Wyoming miners who form the basis of Smith's essay have considerably less power to shape energy investments and infrastructures than do the elites studied by High, Cross, and Wood. But like Wood's executives, they, too, ground their senses of personhood and vocation in long-standing relationships of exchange which they keep in view between electricity consumers and themselves as energy producers. The miners lament denunciations of coal energy that cast blame on them rather than on the network as a whole, and call for energy transitions to begin with a recognition of the debts engendered by mutual dependence rather than the current unceremonial end to a long history of exchange.

While critiques of energy often focus on conflicts that emerge during production, as discussed earlier, the next set of essays, by Andrew Walsh and Arthur Mason, enter into the ordinary ethics of unexpected but crucial ethical worlds of energy. Focusing on charcoal, an energy source deceptively viewed to be 'mundane', Walsh illustrates the material, social, and ethical entanglements embedded in the making, trading, and use of this fuel in the lives of Malagasy people. He argues that charcoal, while good at being a commodity, is never fully alienated because Malagasy keep keen attention to how it links people with matter, markets, and one another – in ways that echo the Wyoming miners, though at smaller and more immediate scales. Western environmental organizations seeking to slow deforestation try to promote 'Green Charcoal' that is more efficient and sustainable, yet it is disruptive to the ordinary ethics of charcoal. The villagers' less than enthusiastic support for the programme thus underscores the potential for conflict between the ethical worlds of environmental organizations and the people they seek to serve. Mason also trains anthropological attention on ordinary ethics, but in the powerful 'energy salons' where the world's elite gathers to craft energy policy. He sketches out a broad transformation in the production of energy knowledge provisioning in the Global North, in which the consultants who dole out predictions inside of elite spaces have eclipsed more democratic mechanisms of deliberation and oversight. Analysing the importance of luxury for imbuing the information provided by the consultants with prestige and trustworthiness, Mason argues that a certain virtue ethics proliferates as clients look to the person-based qualities of energy consultants as guarantors of their ability to recommend a judicious course of action.

Finally, the essays by Amy Penfield and Cymene Howe argue that the anthropology of ethics has been strikingly human-centred and call for greater attention to how more-than-human beings figure in the ethical worlds of energy – as also argued by High in the context of psychic practitioners and devoted Christians in the US oilfields. Penfield's study of gasoline in the everyday lives of indigenous Venezuelan Sanema points to the composite nature of ethics and energy, as the Sanema recognize agency in gasoline itself. Increasingly drawn into gold mining activities, dilemmas of kinship, the animist world of vengeful spirit masters, and ethically infused rumours of disaster, gasoline is considered a vital but volatile substance to live with. As gasoline is variously entangled in Sanema social worlds, Penfield suggests a 'composite ethics', which is premised on collective personhood. Such an ethics does not depend on a notion of the bounded individual subject, which forms the basis of much anthropological scholarship on ethics. Howe also expands the collection's treatment of energy ethics to encompass other-than-human entities in her exploration of a controversial industrial-scale wind

*Journal of the Royal Anthropological Institute (N.S.), 9-28*
© 2019 The Authors. Journal of the Royal Anthropological Institute published by John Wiley & Sons Ltd on behalf of Royal Anthropological Institute

park in Mexico's Isthmus of Tehuantepec. Following Foucault, she proposes that there is a form of parrhesia – a Greek form of 'truth speaking' – at work in how nonhuman beings like birds, hares, and bats are enunciated in environmental management regimes that seek to synchronize human and nonhuman life in settings of both local and global ecological failures. The wind energy project thus weighs the 'greater good of the climatological commons' (Howe, this volume, p. 163) against particular places and species. Howe's research makes clear the inherent political dimensions of ethical dilemmas, pushing readers to consider the collision of competing (and sometimes mutually exclusive) notions of 'the good' across the varying scales at which ethical standpoints are articulated by humans and other-than-humans.

Finally, Hannah Appel's concluding synthesis explores the implications of such multiple and coexisting 'ethical worlds'. She invites reflection on how anthropologists can fruitfully bring textured accounts of deeply held ethical worlds to bear on the long-studied histories and power imbalances in which they take shape. As she notes, careful ethnographic attention to energy dilemmas is urgent and necessary in order to ensure that energy does not become yet another instance of global interventions based on an unquestioned good. It is an issue around which many vocal and vested voices congregate. And as such, it demands of us scholars a particularly close self-reflexive engagement and careful analytical commitment to ensure that all voices get heard – including those who might hold different ethical visions for themselves and their others. This special issue thus calls for attention to an energy ethics that recognizes the multiplicity and diversity, disparity and inequality in life today. It is by attending to and seeking to understand people's own judgements about the place of energy in our entangled lives that we can bring a better world into being.

NOTES

| This project has received funding from the European Research Council (ERC) under the European Union's Horizon 2020 research and innovation programme under grant agreement No 715146. |  |
|---|---|

We also gratefully acknowledge the funding we have received to carry out the research from the Leverhulme Trust (ECF-2013-177), the British Academy (EN150010 and VF1101988), the National Endowment for the Humanities, and the National Science Foundation (1540298). We also thank the participants in the Energy Ethics conference held at the University of St Andrews in March 2016 and the Energy Ethics retreat held at The Burn in October 2016. These events have provided stimulating environments in which to discuss and reflect on the nature of and challenges in our energy dilemmas. We would finally also like to thank the anonymous *JRAI* reviewers for their insightful comments and the production team at Wiley, in particular Justin Dyer, who have so carefully and expertly led the manuscript to its completion. However, any shortcomings of this essay are entirely our own responsibility.

[1] This has been shown by Apter (2005) for Nigeria; Breglia (2013) for Mexico; Coronil (1997) and Penfield (this volume) for Venezuela; Limbert (2010) for Oman; Rogers (2015a) for Russia; and Shever (2012) for Argentina.

[2] This movement offered the opportunity to strengthen links between anthropology and the long-standing scholarship on energy boomtowns in sociology and rural studies (e.g. Jacquet 2014, though see Tauxe 1993 for an earlier bridging of these theoretical perspectives for energy development in North Dakota).

[3] This literature is heavily dominated by the United States and United Kingdom, though compare Allen (2009) on Japan and Simeon (1996) on India.

[4] Research on urban renewable energy projects in Washington, D.C., also complicates this trend by showing that these efforts are subject to and reinforce neoliberal logics (Morris 2013).

[5] Although Hughes' book was published in 2017, the manuscript was likely completed before the US election of November 2016.

## REFERENCES

ACKERMAN, K., L. KIRTZ, C. ANDRIAMANANTSEHENO & S. SEPP 2014. The Green Charcoal chain. Rural 21, News (available on-line: *http://www.rural21.com/english/news/detail/article/the-green-charcoal-chain-00001053/*, accessed 16 January 2019).

ALLEN, M. 2009. *Undermining the Japanese miracle: work and conflict in a Japanese coal-mining community.* Cambridge: University Press.

APPEL, H.C. 2012. Walls and white elephants: oil extraction, responsibility, and infrastructural violence in Equatorial Guinea. *Ethnography* 13, 439-65.

———, A. MASON & M. WATTS 2015a. Introduction: Oil talk. In *Subterranean estates: life worlds of oil and gas* (eds) H. Appel, A. Mason & M. Watts, 1-26. Ithaca, N.Y.: Cornell University Press.

———, ——— & ——— (eds) 2015b. *Subterranean estates: life worlds of oil and gas.* Ithaca, N.Y.: Cornell University Press.

APTER, A.H. 2005. *The Pan-African nation: oil and the spectacle of culture in Nigeria.* Chicago: University Press.

ARGENTI, N. & D.M. KNIGHT 2015. Sun, wind, and the rebirth of extractive economies: renewable energy investment and metanarratives of crisis in Greece. *Journal of the Royal Anthropological Institute (N.S.)* 21, 781-802.

ATABAKI, T., E. BINI & K. EHSANI (eds) 2018. *Working for oil: comparative social histories of labor in the global oil industry.* Basingstoke: Palgrave Macmillan.

AUSTIN, D. 2006. Women's work and lives in offshore oil. In *Markets and market liberalization: ethnographic reflections* (eds) N. Dannhaeuser & C.A. Werner, 163-204. Bradford: Emerald Group Publishing.

———, T. MCGUIRE 2017. The great crew change? Structuring work in the oilfield. In *ExtrACTION: impacts, engagements, and alternative futures* (eds) K. Jalbert, A. Willow, D. Casagrande & S. Paladino, 17-30. New York: Routledge.

———, ——— & R. HIGGINS 2006. Work and change in the Gulf of Mexico offshore petroleum industry. In *Markets and market liberalization: ethnographic reflections* (eds) N. Dannhaeuser & C.A. Werner, 89-122. Bradford: Emerald Group Publishing.

BENSON, P. & S. KIRSCH 2010. Capitalism and the politics of resignation. *Current Anthropology* 51, 459-86.

BOYER, D. 2014. Energopower: an introduction. *Anthropological Quarterly* 87, 309-33.

——— 2015. Anthropology electric. *Cultural Anthropology* 30, 531-9.

——— & C. HOWE 2019. *Wind and power in the Anthropocene.* Durham, N.C.: Duke University Press.

BRANDTSTÄDTER, S. & K. SYKES 2010. Prickly pear polemics – Introduction to Feuchtwang and Strathern: judgement, commensurability and double vision. *Critique of Anthropology* 30, 91-3.

BREGLIA, L. 2013. *Living with oil: promises, peaks, and declines on Mexico's Gulf Coast.* Austin: University of Texas Press.

BROOME, J. 2012. *Climate matters: ethics in a warming world.* London: Norton.

BROWN, K.L., M.W. MURPHY & A.M. PORCELLI 2016. Ruin's progeny: race, environment, and Appalachia's coal camp Blacks. *Du Bois Review: Social Science Research on Race* 13, 327-44.

BRUGGE, D., T. BENALLY & E. YAZZIE-LEWIS 2006. *The Navajo people and uranium mining.* Albuquerque: University of New Mexico Press.

CEPEK, M. 2012. The loss of oil: constituting disaster in Amazonian Ecuador. *Journal of Latin American and Caribbean Anthropology* 17, 393-412.

CHAPMAN, C. 2013. Multinatural resources: ontologies of energy and the politics of inevitability in Alaska. In *Cultures of energy: power, practices, technologies* (eds) S. Strauss, S. Rupp & T. Love, 96-109. Walnut Creek, Calif.: Left Coast Press.

CHARLESWORTH, S.J. 2000. *A phenomenology of working-class experience.* Cambridge: University Press.

CLARKE, T. 2010. Goshute Native American tribe and nuclear waste: complexities and contradictions of a bounded-constitutive relationship. *Environmental Communication: A Journal of Nature and Culture* 4, 387-405.

CLIFFORD, J. 1986. Introduction: Partial truths. In *Writing culture: the poetics and politics of ethnography* (eds) J. Clifford & G.E. Marcus, 1-26. Berkeley: University of California Press.

*Journal of the Royal Anthropological Institute (N.S.), 9-28*
© 2019 The Authors. Journal of the Royal Anthropological Institute published by John Wiley & Sons Ltd on behalf of Royal Anthropological Institute

COLEMAN, S. 2015. Borderlands: ethics, ethnography, and 'repugnant' Christianity. *Hau: Journal of Ethnographic Theory* **5**:2, 275-300.

CORONIL, F. 1997. *The magical state: nature, money, and modernity in Venezuela.* Chicago: University Press.

CSORDAS, T.J. 2013. Morality as a cultural system? *Current Anthropology* **54**, 523-46.

DAVIDOV, V. 2013. *Ecotourism and cultural production: an anthropology of indigenous spaces in Ecuador.* New York: Palgrave Macmillan.

DE RIJKE, K. 2013*a*. The agri-gas fields of Australia: black soil, food, and unconventional gas. *Culture, Agriculture, Food and Environment* **35**, 41-53.

——— 2013*b*. Hydraulically fractured: unconventional gas and anthropology. *Anthropology Today* **29**, 13-17.

DEGANI, M. 2017. Modal reasoning in Dar es Salaam's power network. *American Ethnologist* **44**, 300-14.

EHSANI, K. 2018. Disappearing the workers: how labor in the oil complex has been made invisible. In *Working for oil: comparative social histories of labor in the global oil industry* (eds) T. Atabaki, E. Bini & K. Ehsani, 11-34. Basingstoke: Palgrave Macmillan.

ESPIG, M. & K. DE RIJKE 2016. Unconventional gas developments and the politics of risk and knowledge in Australia. *Energy Research & Social Science* **20**, 82-90.

FASSIN, D. 2008. Beyond good and evil? Questioning the anthropological discomfort with morals. *Anthropological Theory* **8**, 333-44.

——— 2013. On resentment and ressentiment: the politics and ethics of moral emotions. *Current Anthropology* **54**, 249-67.

FERGUSON, J. 2005. Seeing like an oil company: space, security, and global capital in neoliberal Africa. *American Anthropologist* **107**, 377-82.

FEUCHTWANG, S. 2010. Corrections of double vision. *Critique of Anthropology* **30**, 94-101.

FRANQUESA, J. 2018. *Power struggles: dignity, value, and the renewable energy frontier in Spain.* Bloomington: Indiana University Press.

FRIGO, G. 2017. Energy ethics, homogenization, and hegemony: a reflection on the traditional energy paradigm. *Energy Research and Social Science* **30**, 7-17.

GELLNER, E. 1992. *Postmodernism, reason and religion.* London: Routledge.

GIBSON-GRAHAM, J.K. 2006. *The end of capitalism (as we knew it): a feminist critique of political economy.* Minneapolis: University of Minnesota Press.

GILBERTHORPE, E. & D. RAJAK 2017. The anthropology of extraction: critical perspectives on the resource curse. *Journal of Development Studies* **53**, 186-204.

GRIMSHAW, A. & K. HART 1994. Anthropology and the crisis of the intellectuals. *Critique of Anthropology* **14**, 227-61.

GROENEWEGEN, P. 1996. Introduction. In *Economics and ethics?* (ed.) P. Groenewegen, 1-14. London: Routledge.

GUDEMAN, S. 2012. Vital energy: the current of relations. *Social Analysis* **56**, 57-73.

GUSTERSON, H. 1996. *Nuclear rites: a weapons laboratory at the end of the Cold War.* Berkeley: University of California Press.

HANSON, R.D. 2001. An experiment in (toxic) Indian capitalism?: The Skull Valley Goshutes, New Capitalism, and nuclear waste. *PoLAR: Political and Legal Anthropology Review* **24**, 25-38.

HART, K. 2001. Cultural critique in anthropology. *International Encyclopedia of the Social and Behavioral Sciences* **5**, 3037-41.

HECHT, G. 2006. *The radiance of France: nuclear power and national identity after World War II.* Cambridge, Mass.: MIT Press.

——— 2014. *Being nuclear: Africans and the global uranium trade.* Cambridge, Mass.: MIT Press.

HOLBRAAD, M. 2012. *Truth in motion: the recursive anthropology of Cuban divination.* Chicago: University Press.

HOWE, C. 2014. Anthropocenic ecoauthority: the winds of Oaxaca. *Anthropological Quarterly* **87**, 381-404.

HUBER, M.T. 2013. *Lifeblood: oil, freedom, and the forces of capital.* Minneapolis: University of Minnesota Press.

HUDGINS, A. 2013. Fracking's future in a coal mining past: subjectivity undermined. *Culture, Agriculture, Food and Environment* **35**, 54-9.

——— & A. POOLE 2014. Framing fracking: private property, common resources, and regimes of governance. *Journal of Political Ecology* **21**, 303-19.

HUGHES, D.M. 2017. *Energy without conscience: oil, climate change, and complicity.* Durham, N.C.: Duke University Press.

*Journal of the Royal Anthropological Institute (N.S.), 9-28*

JACQUET, J.B. 2014. Review of risks to communities from shale energy development. *Environmental Science & Technology (on-line first)* **48**, 8321–33.

JALBERT, K., A. WILLOW, D. CASAGRANDE & S. PALADINO 2017. Introduction: Confronting extraction, taking action. In *ExtrACTION: impacts, engagements, and alternative futures* (eds) K. Jalbert, A. Willow, D. Casagrande & S. Paladino, 1-16. New York: Routledge.

KESSELRING, R. 2017. The electricity crisis in Zambia: blackouts and social stratification in new mining towns. *Energy Research & Social Science* **30**, 94-102.

KIDECKEL, D.A. 2008. *Getting by in postsocialist Romania: labor, the body and working-class culture.* Bloomington: Indiana University Press.

KULETZ, V. 1998. *The tainted desert: environmental and social ruin in the American West.* New York: Routledge.

LAHIRI-DUTT, K. 2012. The shifting gender of coal: feminist musings on women's work in Indian collieries. *South Asia: Journal of South Asian Studies* **35**, 456-76.

LAIDLAW, J. 2013. *The subject of virtue: an anthropology of ethics and freedom.* Cambridge: University Press.

LARKIN, B. 2013. The politics and poetics of infrastructure. *Annual Review of Anthropology* **42**, 327-43.

LATOUR, B. 2004. Why has critique run out of steam? From matters of fact to matters of concern. *Critical Inquiry* **30**, 225-48.

LENNON, M. 2017. Decolonizing energy: social movements and expertise at the intersections of Black Lives Matter and energy democracy. *Energy Research & Social Science* **30**, 18-27.

LIMBERT, M.E. 2010. *In the time of oil: piety, memory, and social life in an Omani town.* Stanford: University Press.

LONG, P. 1989. *Where the sun never shines: a history of America's bloody coal industry.* New York: Paragon House.

LOVE, T. & A. GARWOOD 2013. Electrifying transitions: power and culture in rural Cajamarca, Peru. In *Cultures of energy: power, practices, technologies* (eds) S. Strauss, S. Rupp & T. Love, 147-63. Walnut Creek, Calif.: Left Coast Press.

——— & C. ISENHOUR 2016. Energy and economy: recognizing high-energy modernity as a historical period. *Economic Anthropology* **3**, 6-16.

MCLEOD, C. & B. NERLICH 2017. Working with bacteria and putting bacteria to work: the biopolitics of synthetic biology for energy in the United Kingdom. *Energy Research & Social Science* **30**, 35-42.

MCNEIL, B.T. 2011. *Combating mountaintop removal: new directions in the fight against Big Coal.* Urbana: University of Illinois Press.

MASCO, J. 2006. *The nuclear borderlands: the Manhattan Project in post-Cold War New Mexico.* Princeton: University Press.

MASON, A. 2007. The rise of consultant forecasting in liberalized natural gas markets. *Public Culture* **19**, 367-79.

——— 2013. Cartel consciousness and horizontal integration in the energy industry. In *Cultures of energy: power, practices, technologies* (eds) S. Strauss, S. Rupp & T. Love, 126-38. Walnut Creek, Calif.: Left Coast Press.

MITCHELL, T. 2011. *Carbon democracy: political power in the age of oil.* New York: Verso.

MONTGOMERY, D. 1987. *The fall of the house of labor: the workplace, the state and American labor activism, 1865-1925.* Cambridge: University Press.

MOORE, M. 1996. *Women in the mines: stories of life and work.* New York: Twayne Publishers.

MORRIS, J. 2013. The evolving localism (and neoliberalism) of urban renewable energy projects. *Culture, Agriculture, Food and Environment* **35**, 16-29.

NADER, L. 1980. *Energy choices in a democratic society.* Washington, D.C.: National Academy of Sciences.

——— 1981. Barriers to thinking new about energy. *Physics Today* **34**, 99-104.

——— 2004. The harder path: shifting gears. *Anthropological Quarterly* **77**, 771-91.

NEWBERRY, D. 2013. Energy effects and affects: on contested representations of Brazilian biofuel sustainability and their invisible proximity. In *Cultures of energy: power, practices, technologies* (eds) S. Strauss, S. Rupp & T. Love, 228-42. Walnut Creek, Calif.: Left Coast Press.

ÖZDEN-SCHILLING, C. 2015. Economy electric. *Cultural Anthropology* **30**, 578-88.

——— 2016. The infrastructure of markets: from electric power to electronic data: infrastructure of markets. *Economic Anthropology* **3**, 68-80.

PALADINO, S. & J. SIMONELLI 2013. Hazards so grave: anthropology and energy. *Culture, Agriculture, Food and Environment* **35**, 1-3.

PEARSON, T.W. 2017. *When the hills are gone: frac sand mining and the struggle for community.* Minneapolis: University of Minnesota Press.

*Journal of the Royal Anthropological Institute (N.S.), 9-28*

PETERS, M. & C. LANKSHEAR 1996. Critical literacy and digital texts. *Educational Theory* **46**, 51-70.

PHADKE, R. 2011. Resisting and reconciling Big Wind: middle landscape politics in the New American West. *Antipode* **43**, 754-76.

——— 2013. Public deliberation and the geographies of wind justice. *Science as Culture* **22**, 247-55.

POWELL, D.E. 2017. Toward transition? Challenging extractivism and the politics of the inevitable on the Navajo Nation. In *ExtrACTION: impacts, engagements and alternative futures* (eds) K. Jalbert, A. Willow, D. Casagrande & S. Paladino, 211-26. New York: Routledge.

——— 2018. *Landscapes of power: politics of energy in the Navajo Nation*. Durham, N.C.: Duke University Press.

RABINOW, P. 1977. *Reflections on fieldwork in Morocco*. Berkeley: University of California Press.

REYNA, S.P. & A. BEHRENDS 2011. The crazy curse and crude domination: towards an anthropology of oil. In *Crude domination: an anthropology of oil* (eds) A. Behrends, S.P. Reyna & G. Schlee, 3-29. New York: Berghahn Books.

RICHARDSON, T. & G. WESZKALNYS 2014. Introduction: Resource materialities. *Anthropological Quarterly* **87**, 5-30.

RICHTER, J. 2017. Energopolitics and nuclear waste: containing the threat of radioactivity. *Energy Research & Social Science* **30**, 61-70.

ROGERS, D. 2015*a*. *The depths of Russia: oil, power, and culture after socialism*. Ithaca, N.Y.: Cornell University Press.

——— 2015*b*. Oil and anthropology. *Annual Review of Anthropology* **44**, 365-80.

ROLSTON, J.S. 2014. *Mining coal and undermining gender: rhythms of work and family in the American West*. New Brunswick, N.J.: Rutgers University Press.

RUPP, S. 2016. Circuits and currents: dynamics of disruption in New York City blackouts. *Economic Anthropology* **3**, 106-18.

SAWYER, S. 2004. *Crude chronicles: indigenous politics, multinational oil, and neoliberalism in Ecuador*. Durham, N.C.: Duke University Press.

SCOTT, R. 2010. *Removing mountains: extracting nature and identity in the Appalachian coalfields*. Minneapolis: University of Minnesota Press.

SHEVER, E. 2012. *Resources for reform: oil and neoliberalism in Argentina*. Stanford: University Press.

SIMEON, D. 1996. Coal and colonialism: production relations in an Indian coalfield, 1895-1947. *International Review of Social History* **41**, 83-108.

SINGH, A., A. STRATING, N. HERRERA, H. VAN DIJK & D. KEYSO 2017. Beyond rational choice perspective in energy trading: an ethnography of inter-household energy exchanges in rural India. *Energy Research & Social Science* **30**, 103-15.

SMITH, J. & M.M. HIGH 2017. Exploring the anthropology of energy: ethnography, energy and ethics. *Energy Research & Social Science* **30**, 1-6.

STERN, N. 2014. Ethics, equity and the economics of climate change. Paper 1: Science and philosophy. *Economics and Philosophy* **30**, 397-444.

STEWART, K. 1996. *A space on the side of the road*. Princeton: University Press.

STRATHERN, M. 2010. Learning. *Critique of Antyhropology* **30**, 102-9.

STRAUSS, S., S. RUPP & T. LOVE (eds) 2013*a*. *Cultures of energy: power, practices, technologies*. Walnut Creek, Calif.: Left Coast Press.

——— , ——— & ——— 2013*b*. Introduction: Powerlines: cultures of energy in the twenty-first century. In *Cultures of energy: power, practices, technologies* (eds) S. Strauss, S. Rupp & T. Love, 10-38. Walnut Creek, Calif.: Left Coast Press.

SZEMAN, I. & D. BOYER 2017. Introduction: On the energy humanities. In *Energy humanities: an anthology* (eds) I. Szeman & D. Boyer, 1-13. Baltimore, Md: Johns Hopkins University Press.

TAUXE, C. 1993. *Farms, mines and main streets: uneven development in a Dakota county*. Philadelphia: Temple University Press.

THORLEIFSSON, C. 2016. From coal to Ukip: the struggle over identity in post-industrial Doncaster. *History and Anthropology* **27**, 555-68.

VANDEHEY, S. 2013. Local power: harnessing nimbyism for sustainable suburban energy production. In *Cultures of energy: power, practices, technologies* (eds) S. Strauss, S. Rupp & T. Love, 243-56. Walnut Creek, Calif.: Left Coast Press.

VOYLES, T.B. 2015. *Wastelanding: legacies of uranium mining in Navajo country*. Minneapolis: University of Minnesota Press.

Watts, M. 2004. Resource curse? Governmentality, oil and power in the Niger Delta, Nigeria. *Geopolitics* **9**, 50-80.

———— 2008. Blood oil: the anatomy of a petro-insurgency in the Niger delta. *Focaal: Journal of Global and Historical Anthropology* **52**, 18-38.

Weszkalnys, G. 2011. Cursed resources, or articulations of economic theory in the Gulf of Guinea. *Economy and Society* **40**, 345-72.

———— 2014. Anticipating oil: the temporal politics of a disaster yet to come. *Sociological Review* **62**, 211-35.

White, L. 1943. Energy and the evolution of culture. *American Anthropologist* **45**, 335-56.

———— 1959. *The evolution of culture*. New York: McGraw Hill.

Willow, A.J. 2018. *Understanding extrACTIVISM: culture and power in natural resource disputes*. New York: Routledge.

———— & S. Wylie 2014. Politics, ecology, and the new anthropology of energy: exploring the emerging frontiers of hydraulic fracking. *Journal of Political Ecology* **21**, 222-36.

Winther, T. 2011. *The impact of electricity: development, desires and dilemmas*. New York: Berghahn Books.

Witt, J.D. 2016. *Religion and resistance in Appalachia: faith and the fight against mountaintop removal coal mining*. Lexington: University Press of Kentucky.

Wood, C.L. 2016. Inside the halo zone: geology, finance, and the corporate performance of profit in a deep tight oil formation. *Economic Anthropology* **3**, 43-56.

Wuebben, D. 2017. From wire evil to power line poetics: the ethics and aesthetics of renewable transmission. *Energy Research & Social Science* **30**, 53-60.

Zonabend, F. 2007. *The nuclear peninsula*. Cambridge: University Press.

Zylinska, J. 2014. *Minimal ethics for the Anthropocene*. Ann Arbor, Mich.: Open Humanities Press.

## Introduction : la constitution éthique de dilemmes énergétiques

*Résumé*

Le corpus de plus en plus conséquent de recherches anthropologiques consacrées à l'énergie permet des explorations critiques des perceptions et utilisations de cette ressource fondamentale entre différentes cultures. Nous affirmons que deux cadres dominants sous-tendent cette littérature : d'une part, une critique du pouvoir des entreprises et des États et, d'autre part, un plaidoyer pour la transition énergétique vers un futur moins chargé en carbone. Ces cadres ont restreint le champ des questions et points de vue éthiques abordés par l'anthropologie à propos de l'énergie parce qu'ils s'appuient sur des jugements qui peuvent, implicitement, dicter les agendas de la recherche ou, parfois, donner lieu à des accusations violentes qui occultent la manière dont nos interlocuteurs eux-mêmes considèrent le caractère bon ou mauvais des ressources énergétiques et les infrastructures sociétales dont elles font partie. Nous proposons une approche plus large et l'étude d'une éthique de l'énergie qui ouvre les dilemmes énergétiques à l'exploration ethnographique. En l'espèce, nous montrons comment ces dilemmes constituent d'importantes sources de connaissances anthropologiques en encourageant des discussions plus éclairées et inclusives sur la place de l'énergie dans les vies humaines et l'existence des autres espèces.

# 1

# Projects of devotion: energy exploration and moral ambition in the cosmoeconomy of oil and gas in the Western United States

Mᴇᴛᴛᴇ M. Hɪɢʜ *University of St Andrews*

This essay considers how people working in the oil and gas industry in Colorado perceive their involvement in energy exploration in relation to broader practices of devotion, compassion, and outreach. I argue that although their energy projects may appear to merely echo companies' formal promotional pitches, the oilfield and corporate actors' own moral ambitions reveal more-than-human cosmoeconomic visions of oil's potentiality. This essay thus demonstrates how multiple and diverging ethical registers intersect and inform the valuation of oil.

> The LORD himself goes before you and will be with you; he will never leave you nor forsake you. Do not be afraid; do not be discouraged.
>
> Deuteronomy 31:8

> If we do find oil here, this community of yours will not only survive. It will flourish.
>
> Daniel Plainview in *There will be blood*

The oil and gas industry in the United States is predicated on a precarious relationship between hope and knowledge. At times the commodity markets are strong and oil producers compete zealously to acquire leases to land, negotiate contracts for drilling rigs and crews, and secure financial backing for their new ambitious plans. At other times prices fall and widespread pessimism reverberates through the industry as many producers and service companies lay off workers, sell assets, and consolidate their debts.[1] Such ups and downs are dramatic, if not also 'utterly confusing' and 'mind-boggling' (Appel, Mason & Watts 2015: 8). These volatile cycles with periodic booms and busts characterize the oil industry, yet they often exceed simple explanations for their occurrence (Mitchell 2010: 201; see also Mabro 1992).[2] When rationalizing the past, optimizing the present, and, not least, attempting to predict the future, industry actors draw on multiple scales that encompass the globality of geopolitics, transnational investment agendas, and devastating environmental catastrophes as well as immediate interventions of individual CEOs, boards of directors, and particular investors. It is

*Journal of the Royal Anthropological Institute (N.S.)*, 29-46
© 2019 The Authors. Journal of the Royal Anthropological Institute published by John Wiley & Sons Ltd on behalf of Royal Anthropological Institute

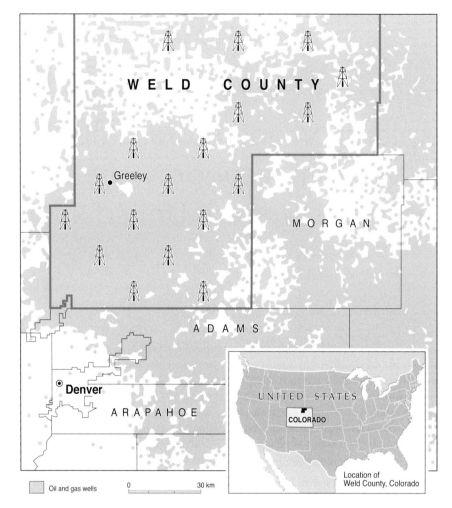

**Figure 1**. Map of Weld County, Colorado, which has the largest concentration of oil and gas wells in the state, numbering more than 22,000 active wells (see *https://www.weldgov.com/ departments/planning_and_zoning/oil_gas/*, accessed 7 January 2019). (G.F. Sandeman, School of Geography and Sustainable Development, University of St Andrews).

an industry that thus encapsulates the empirical conjuncture of 'awkward scales' that simultaneously construct and escape the dizzying reality of life (Comaroff & Comaroff 2003: 151; see also Atabaki, Bini & Ehsani 2018: 2). It is an industry where uncertainty is produced through the specific challenges that are involved in extracting subterranean resources, as well as through events and dynamics that take place at a very grand scale.

In this essay I draw on ethnographic fieldwork that I have carried out since 2013 in Colorado, United States, among people working in the oilfields and executive offices. This fieldwork has taken me out on the rigs in Weld County, into the drilling crew's 'shops' with equipment and trucks located a few hours' drive from the jobs, to the producing operators' 'field offices' in the county seat of Greeley, and into the executive headquarters in Denver where technical, sales, and executive teams are based (see Fig. 1). My hosts have let me into their workplaces and to the events that occur there. Sometimes

*Journal of the Royal Anthropological Institute (N.S.), 29-46*
© 2019 The Authors. Journal of the Royal Anthropological Institute published by John Wiley & Sons Ltd on behalf of Royal Anthropological Institute

they have given me an office, other times they have let me shadow them as they go about their workday. Fieldwork has thus taken me to corporate events, such as pre-planning meetings, investor meetings, and in-house client presentations, as well as to informal get-togethers after work at local bars. My hosts have also let me into their homes, joining them for family barbecues, dinners with friends, dog walks in the evening, church services on Sundays, and whatever else forms part of their everyday lives. In this essay I attend to the hopes and dreams, concerns and fears that inform people's actions as they go through the ups and downs of the oil industry. Examining how they seek to pave the way for their own ethical projects, I focus on those who 'try to do something serious, something big' (MacFarquhar 2015: xv; cf. Boyer 2008: 43). That is, those who try, often in their own discrete ways, to enact their 'moral ambitions' (Elisha 2011). Overall, I am thus interested in how industry actors confronted with the fundamental and structural uncertainty of the oil economy pursue projects of devotion, negotiating 'the human predicament of trying to live a life that one is somehow responsible for but is in many respects out of one's control' (Mattingly 2012: 179).

Moral philosophers Glen Pettigrove and Michael Meyer have remarked that the notion of 'moral ambition' conjoins 'two ideas that are fatally in tension with each other' (2009: 285). On the one hand, the morally ambitious can strive so determinedly for moral excellence that it makes the person aggrandize his or her own accomplishments while also dismissing or harbouring contempt for the accomplishments of others.[3] As such, it can become an example of what Thomas Hill has referred to as 'moral snobbery' (1991: 166), whereby a person's inflated sense of self becomes interrelated with a lack of respect for and a lack of recognition of others. On the other hand, if morality, in its broadest sense, is understood as a desire for life to flourish (Hursthouse 1999: 173), the morally ambitious can be caught in an insatiable state of constantly seeking something better. As Kant has put it, 'the state in which he now is will always remain an ill compared with a better one which he always stands ready to enter' (1996 [1794]: 227). Satisfaction and contentment can thus become frustratingly unachievable for the morally ambitious as the object of ambition is relative, fleeting, and only ever partial. As a result, the person is bound to be perpetually and deeply dissatisfied with life, consumed with disappointment. Considering these two aspects, moral ambition emerges as more of a vice than a virtue and is fundamentally self-defeating.

This view of moral ambition hinges on a particular and abstracted conceptualization of the striving individual (Long & Moore 2013: 4). Philosophers such as Bernard Williams identify this rationalized sovereign individual as historically and socioculturally contingent anchored in 'modern Western culture' (2006: 6). While also described as a 'fiction of . . . capitalist ideology' (Rigi 2018: 160; see also Kapferer & Gold 2018), it does not, however, resonate with my interlocutors, who can be seen as key exponents of 'oil capitalism' (Szeman 2007). That is, my interlocutors, who participate in and embrace the oil and gas industry as enacted in the American West today, pursue their personal ethical projects through a different understanding of moral ambition. Rather than being grounded in individual autonomy, they undertake their projects 'as a matter of relations that reach both into and beyond the individual' (Laidlaw 2010: 163). Motivated by diverse Christian-inspired outlooks, which proliferate in the oilfields, moral ambition here gives rise to a different dynamic than that which is envisioned by Pettigrove and Meyer. In an industry that many of my interlocutors associate geographically with a broad expansion of the so-called 'Bible belt', extending across and far beyond the oilfields, they emphasize how newcomers to the industry can readily and more or less explicitly be introduced to Christian faiths. Informed by the aspirational nature of Christian thought and action (Elisha 2011: 220), they conceptualize their oil work significantly in terms of spiritual servitude.[4] As they engage in practices of devotion, compassion, and outreach, they bring broader cosmoeconomic understandings of life to bear on their work in the industry. By using the notion of 'cosmoeconomy' (see also High 2017), my intention is to elucidate the articulations between beings who exist in a more-than-human world that is both expansive and inclusive, yet not necessarily calm and peaceful.[5] I am thus making an analytical move that signals from the very start that the 'we' of any argument is also already posited as a question, if not a problem, opening up an unknown and dynamic world of human and nonhuman beings and processes.

### Oil and gas as financial objects

When oil producers and service companies navigate the volatility of the oil economy, they are quick to point towards their well-assorted inventory of financial tools and techniques that they use to calculate matters such as cash flow, collateral, and liabilities.[6] With a keen eye on global energy prices, they construct what-if scenarios that simulate 'asset performances' under varying conditions in an attempt to 'facilitate high-level optimization and decision support' (Zhang, Orangi, Bakshi, Da Sie & Prasanna 2006: 1). Individual wells, recognized for their specific oil and gas recovery rates, production targets, and surface facilities, are conjoined with fiscal variables such as current spot prices and futures strip pricing. Assembled into larger units of proven reserves, net acreage, and asset packages, individual wells become disentangled from their localities and come to acquire a 'modular' (Appel 2012a: 693) existence in today's 'digital oil fields' (Carvajal, Maucec & Cullick 2018).[7] Described as 'knowledge management' (Soma, Bakshi & Prasanna 2007: 119), oilfield operations thus undergo a process of 'redomaining' (Shever 2012: 78) where, in this case, people work to transform an energy resource from a physical and idiosyncratic entity towards a digital and statistically pliable financial object. This performativity of everyday technocratic knowledge fills the spaces of corporate corridors and endless pages in industry magazines and media reports. It travels through the industry, enveloping all echelons from rig workers through to executives, foregrounding a conceptualization of oil and gas as, first and foremost, matters of finance (Ehsani 2018: 27; see also Labban 2008: 5).

This 'redomaining' of oil and gas into financial objects has fundamental implications for the social, political, and economic contours of the industry. While it downplays the significance of contested labour relations and spatial arrangements (see, e.g., Austin & McGuire 2017; Priest 2018), it also accentuates an 'infrastructure of calculability' and associated forms of risk and expertise (Beunza & Ferraro 2018: 2; Cabantous & Gond 2011). As Caura Wood (this volume) shows, the calculation of debt and the shouldering of risk have become fundamental to current practices of 'balance sheet cleaning' and the circulation of assets among corporate executives in the oil and gas industry. Also, Arthur Mason (this volume; see also 2007) demonstrates how the oil and gas industry employs the language of risk in its forecasting practices, contributing to the elevation of energy consultants into experts with the perceived knowledge to ascertain and manage those risks. Moreover, in the context of insurance practices and actuarial imaginaries of the oil and gas industry, Leigh Johnson (2015) has demonstrated how the calculation of risk in upstream production, compounded by increasingly adverse weather conditions, has now turned the industry into an 'unviable insurance class', increasingly underwritten by futures and options markets. This relationship between calculation and judgement, also known as 'qualculation' (Cochoy 2002; see also Callon & Law 2005), has received great scholarly attention beyond the specifics of the oil and gas industry (see, e.g., Çalişkan & Callon 2009; 2010; Callon & Muniesa 2005; Holmes 2013; Riles 2004). Examining the ways in which risk and expertise are co-produced, scholars have demonstrated how conviction rather than certainty, judgement rather than enumeration, emerge in and through these fiscal practices (Chong & Tuckett 2015; Millo & MacKenzie 2009; Zaloom 2004). And as such, they are animated by personal, interpersonal, and collective states that entail not only mathematical but also ethical, and increasingly private, projects (see Maurer 2002; Riles 2011; Striphas 2015).

In order to understand how these personal ethical projects underlie, inform, and perhaps motivate people's actions, I suggest it is necessary to apply a new analytical approach to the oil and gas industry. Up until now, a major area of scholarship has offered important insights into how oil and gas production is experienced by communities located near production sites (see Introduction, this volume). Scholars have examined how local inhabitants, both human and nonhuman, have felt or have been treated as marginal and voiceless, if not endangered, in confrontations with companies and governmental institutions (see Howe, this volume, for an example in the context of wind parks). This literature approaches oil and gas production as causing harm to humans as part of its ordinary functioning (Benson & Kirsch 2010: 465), and it focuses on some of the industry's strongest critics, namely those who are directly affected by but not necessarily directly benefiting from it. It concerns local inhabitants whose lands and lives have become intertwined with the activities of industry workers, drilling rigs, heavy trucks, as well as much that is unfamiliar and unknown. Focusing on the so-called 'brute realities of extraction' (Jalbert, Willow, Casagrande & Paladino 2017: 3), this literature brings attention to those affected or angered by energy production. Yet in doing so, scholars have rendered people working in the oil and gas industry noticeably absent from their accounts. As Kaveh Ehsani has noted, '[T]his literature predominantly treats the oil sector as a black box that has a significant impact (often negative) on the world around it, yet excludes its internal tensions and dynamics from the story' (2018: 22). By simplifying the messy reality of life, this black boxing of the industry can lead to the uncritical foregrounding of scholars' own value judgements. David Hughes, for example, has recently commented how oil industry actors 'are in the wrong', should be consigned 'to an ash heap, worthy of condescension and worse', and 'as an industry . . . should go extinct' (2017: 152, 4). I understand how the urgency surrounding issues of energy production can encourage such views, especially at a time when climate change is becoming an increasingly urgent challenge for humanity. However, this challenge makes it even more crucial that we correct our 'double vision' (Feuchtwang 2010) if we want to understand our others; that we keep a focus on our interlocutors', rather than our own, understandings and experiences (see also Zylinska 2014: 83). As Susanne Brandtstädter and Karen Sykes have remarked, '[Ex]xerting judgement in order to correct wrongs and grievances suggests that anthropology might step too closely along the moralist's path' (2010: 92; see also Holbraad 2018). Recognizing how our interlocutors' and our own personal ethical projects are not necessarily shared and similar, I will now turn to the cosmoeconomic understandings that underlie the public-facing fiscal practices of risk management and expertise building in the oil and gas industry.

*Journal of the Royal Anthropological Institute (N.S.), 29-46*
© 2019 The Authors. Journal of the Royal Anthropological Institute published by John Wiley & Sons Ltd on behalf of Royal Anthropological Institute

## Oil is everything

The production of oil has been part of Colorado's history for a very long time. The first oil well was drilled during the 1860s in the semi-desert high arid lands of Florence in Southern Colorado and it was the second oldest commercial oilfield in the United States (Scamehorn 2002: 43). Located along the Denver and Rio Grande Western railroad, the Florence oilfield was a booming success that spurred the search for oil across the region and led to the establishment of an industry that became an important part of the state economy and many people's everyday life. With the large-scale use of hydraulic fracturing and directional drilling, Colorado is today among the ten most oil-productive states in the country and thousands of people make a living in the industry.[8]

Drilling rigs tower high above the ranches and can be seen across the plains (Fig. 2). Oil and gas pipes, which a few years ago had to be laid quickly to keep up with the rapid pace of production, run above ground along roads teeming with huge trucks hauling sand and water to and from well sites. Steel storage tanks cluster in the corners of the cornfields while large production batteries and compressor stations for natural gas leave an almost futuristic industrial mark on the landscape. In this oil- and gas-rich state, it is hard to ignore the 'lifeblood' of these fossil fuels (Huber 2013). Yet they have an uncanny invisibility (see also B. Johnson 2014: 159; Szeman & Boyer 2017: 6). Despite their physical presence in the drilling rigs and pipelines, trucks and tanks, it is as if their presence is only commented on by those who oppose oil and gas. A recurring lament among people in the industry is thus that they feel that others do not see and recognize just how important fossil fuels are in their everyday lives. This proliferation of petroleum and petrochemical products[9] in how we presently organize human life prompted Stephanie,[10] in her late fifties and highly successful in the oil industry, to propose the following scenario for a commercial:

> A man and a woman are driving on a city road into Denver. The woman is heavily pregnant and they are rushing to the hospital. But suddenly everything starts to change: The car runs out of gas … It comes to a halt, can't go any further. Then the tyres slowly evaporate – they disappear. Then the plastic steering wheel disappears. Then the seats, the safety belts, even their clothes. The woman is just lying there on the ground, going to give birth. There's *nothing* without oil! Nothing! There's no hospital. No bed. No car. Nothing! People think that it's just about gas. But it isn't. Oil is everything!! This commercial might make people think twice before criticizing us for the work we do.

This story-line has already been promoted by the American oil industry's trade association, the American Petroleum Institute. Among other activities, they create and freely distribute teaching materials to schoolchildren and educators. In these teaching materials, they communicate to school children how their lifestyles are 'fuelled by oil and natural gas products'.[11] Their accompanying film, entitled *Energizing life*, is not about 'energy' in its plurality, but about oil and gas exclusively. Showing how oil and gas 'support an American way of life', it concludes that 'American Energy is America's Progress' (see also B. Johnson 2014: 146; LeMenager 2014). You certainly get the sense that 'oil is everything'. But while this trade association explicitly and strategically advances the interests of the US oil and gas industry, company employees like Stephanie are not mere mouthpieces. They are not automatons, acting in the absence of their own motive force. When they accuse and receive accusation, when they act on and are acted upon, they are navigating ethical registers that are not limited to and bound by corporate interests. Although they work for oil producers, their own values and interests may thus exceed those of the corporation.

**Figure 2.** Drilling for oil in Weld County, Colorado. (Photograph by milehightraveler).

'Can I make a confession?', Naomi asked me. 'Of course', I replied, slightly nervous as to what lay ahead. She worked for a drilling company that carries out 'frack jobs' – that is, the actual hydraulic fracturing that breaks apart the hard shale and releases the oil and gas contained within. She was young and new to the industry but navigated it very confidently. With parents and siblings all working in oil and gas, she commented how 'it's kind of like my family' and she knew the industry better than most. She had introduced me to everything and everyone, from the field offices where we wore our hard hats and protective gear to the folks she knew in Denver. She looked at me cautiously and began: 'Some of my friends are upset with me for getting into oil and gas . . .'. She told me how she had come to the industry without a petroleum engineering degree or other related qualification. She had worked in public communications and had had to learn everything from scratch. It had been a very steep learning curve.

> But I love it. I love the vibe, the drive, and the passion. You never get bored!! The company wants to make sure that I can succeed and I'm lucky to have great mentors. It's a really good industry. But my company recently lost about 40 per cent or so of its people. Last week several of my best friends have been let go. Men I respect and who helped me become who I am.

I asked her how she was doing when confronted with these kinds of severe job cuts, which were triggered by the recent drop in the oil price when this conversation took place in 2016.[12] Although many of her friends had been fortunate enough to find other jobs, she emphasized how they would have wanted to stay with the company if the choice had been theirs. Experiencing so many people getting laid off and wondering every day if it were going to be her turn next was intense, especially as her husband was out of work and they had two small children to care for. Yet, to my surprise, she elaborated:

> Truth be told, there is so much going on in the world right now. There are many problems … If I was so self-obsessed that I was only concerned about my job, then …

She paused and looked away before saying: 'I have much bigger issues. I am grateful to have a job'. As we nodded in unison, she continued:

> I know more than I should about people. I sometimes know more about you than you know yourself. I know stuff that will happen to other people before it happens. I know stuff that will be important before other people know. Are you alright with that?

And Naomi then began telling me about how she was having premonitions – so terrifying and confusing that she has only recently recognized and accepted her abilities. When some of her friends were furious at her for working in the oil and gas industry, it was not for the reasons that I had suspected. It was not primarily because they perceived fossil fuels as morally problematic: finite resources on which people have become too dependent; pollutants that contribute to the contamination of land, air, and water resources; or factors in anthropogenic climate change. It was also not primarily because they were critical of the oil and gas industry: an industry that often appears in headlines on environmental damage, local conflicts, and wealth disparities. Rather, it was because they thought that she should use her abilities in much better ways. 'Working in oil' was for them a waste of unique talent and insights. And Naomi was torn. She wanted to devote herself fully to this calling – 'a calling to do good, to help others', as she put it. Indeed, she was actively involved in helping the homeless in her town. She volunteered at a homeless shelter and prayed for their souls. She was keen to find other ways to do more, especially for impoverished children facing a future that was far from as bright and fortunate as her own. But she felt that there were also ways of 'doing good' within the industry; that it did not have to be a clash or a moral breakdown if she stayed in oil and gas (cf. Robbins 2004; Walsh 2006; Zigon 2007). For her, being involved in oil and gas was, just like sharing her premonitory insights, precisely 'to do good'. It was part of a mission to provide abundant and affordable energy to others. By working in oil and gas, she felt that she did 'her bit' to keep the production going and ensure energy independence and lower prices. The harder she worked in the industry, the better off she believed the less fortunate would be. Understanding energy as more than what we usually associate with an oil and gas company, she smilingly said: 'I believe in the truth of energy. We all need energy. It is vital to our existence'.

   Over the years I have come to know many people who work in both oilfields and executive offices who have personal psychic advisers, if not psychic abilities themselves.[13] They share experiences of a world in misery where life seems to be getting increasingly worse. Every day another war, another earthquake, another landslide, another epidemic is revealed. The desperation, hunger, and pain are felt intensely by them as if it were their own bodies directly experiencing the misery. By opening up energy channels and

*Journal of the Royal Anthropological Institute (N.S.), 29-46*
© 2019 The Authors. Journal of the Royal Anthropological Institute published by John Wiley & Sons Ltd on behalf of Royal Anthropological Institute

receiving communication, they seek to better understand themselves and their others. For some, it is an enormous, burdensome, and compassionate project that propels them into helping those in need. When Stephanie commented that 'oil is everything', a statement that resonates so well with the American oil industry's trade association, we thus cannot assume that this is just 'corporate speak', that it is an echo of the 'promotion pitch'. For Naomi, it was part of a larger cosmoeconomic understanding that sees hydrocarbons and communication channels as distinct, yet interrelated. In her experience, they offer complementary ways of enabling humans to live better lives. For her, we are all souls in bodily vessels and as such we live through different but connected forms of energy. You cannot create energy and you cannot destroy it. It merely changes form. Conversions, transformations, changes between one state and another are fundamental to our existence. This was Newton's first law of thermodynamics but also Naomi's personal experience. This does not mean that she sees an 'energy-just world' (Sovacool 2014: 21). This is not a world of rights, a world of fairness, a world of justice. In the absence of harmonious balance and peace, it is a world that feeds clashing and conflicting interests *because* energy is limited. This is an intensely political battleground, in particular for this industry actor.

## God has a plan for you

It is not only industry actors involved in spiritual battles and premonitions who see oil work as intimately interrelated with ambitious projects of 'doing good'. Particularly in the oilfields, the proactive Houston-headquartered nondenominational Oilfield Christian Fellowship (OCF) is fast-growing and dedicated to spreading the Word of God to men and women in the industry. With news reports about crime-crippled 'man camps' in oil-rich North Dakota eclipsing the more familiar accounts of workers' drinking sprees during leaves from offshore oil platforms, the oilfield today appears a prime location for evangelizing activities. In the words of Steve, one of the members of the OCF in the Denver chapter:

> The OCF is very evangelical. It looks at the rigs as a fertile field for ministry, which it is. It's probably just a step up from evangelizing at brothels! It's a rough lifestyle with some rough guys. It has always been that way. They have always been itinerant people, whether they were in California or Louisiana. It is a very target-rich environment. So they [OCF] felt like it was a good place to jump into people's lives and encourage them to go for higher goals rather than just immediate gratification and with some money in your pockets.

In order to reach out to these workers (Fig. 3), the OCF has produced its own custom-made oilfield Bible entitled *God's word for the oil patch, fuel for the soul*. Containing the Old and New Testaments in the New Living Translation version along with numerous testimonies and commentaries from CEOs to rig hands, 250,000 Oil Patch Bibles have apparently now been distributed to more than sixty countries in thirty languages – this is in addition to the OCF's freely available digital version.[14] Encouraging people to take Bibles with them on their next work trip, if not also undertake training to become an Oil Patch Chaplain, the OCF offers outreach which is as global as the oil and gas industry itself. Testimonies from workers travel across borders and along the vast range of job roles. Suddenly powerful testimonies from roustabouts intersect with those of sales executives, and any industry actor is welcomed to join their OCF prayer breakfasts, luncheons, and dinners. People are invited to come forth and give their testimony, sharing life experiences like this one:

**Figure 3.** Roughnecks on a drilling rig in Greeley. (Photograph by NIOSH).

'But God showed his great love for us by sending Christ to die for us while we were still sinners.' – Romans 5:8

Prior to 1983, I was addicted to drugs and alcohol. I was married and had two children and another on the way. I had recently lost my job and we had no place to live. We were offered a small house near the hometown of my wife's parents. The house was next door to a Baptist church. The pastor of the church came to visit us every Sunday for several months. Never once did he criticize me ... He just told me that he sure would love for me to come to a church service. He said, 'God has a message for you'.

One Sunday morning I decided to take the preacher up on his invitation. That Sunday, as he ended his message, he extended an invitation to those who wanted to know Christ as their Saviour. I could barely see the front of the church because of the tears in my eyes, but somehow I made my way to the front. I just could not get to the front fast enough. I took hold of the pastor's hand, laid my head on his shoulder, and cried like a baby. That Sunday, Jesus changed my life forever!

My wife and I teach prayer in prisons and churches, and we minister in the workplace. We founded the Oil and Gas Prayer Centre along with Be Free Prison Ministry. The Oil and Gas Prayer Centre partners with thousands of prayer warriors to pray for the needs of men and women working in oil, gas, and related businesses. It all started with a pastor who loved me right where I was. He prayed for me, invited me to church, and never gave up on me. Thank you reverend and thank you Jesus!

A large part of the OCF mission is thus as an outreach Bible Ministry enabled by people's oil and gas careers: that is, a partnership between people's spiritual calling and their work in the industry. When the oil patch is looked at as a fertile field for evangelizing, oil appears as a gift from God that can enable many to come to Christ. As people are experiencing the hardships of the industry, their hearts and minds might soften, preparing them to embrace God's goodness, omnipotence, and omniscience. Turning the pain and suffering into an intimate learning opportunity, the 'prayer warriors' hope that workers in the oil patch will draw closer to God. However, for some, their path will remain turbulent and ruinous. Indeed, for them, the future is likely to become gloomier than it was before they started their careers. As such, the oil patch raises the stakes for all, challenging people with profound trials and tribulations. With a God who loves unconditionally, oil thus becomes a potential catalyst for leaving the darkness and embracing conversion to a life in faith. Indeed, for some, the pain and challenges of life in the oilfield are considered a chance to experience the life of Christ by suffering in some small way as he did (see also Luhrmann 2012: 283). The greater gift of God in oil and gas is thus not just their mundane usage as energy sources, but also, as Steve, mentioned earlier, put it, their ability to 'turn oil workers over to Christ'. The fossil fuels and the hard reality of their extraction offer a path for people to experience the plan that God has for them, and that, for the fellowship, is the deep and powerful significance of oil and gas.

## Glorifying God through oil and gas business

While the OCF is primarily concerned with evangelical outreach activities in the oilfields, Tim, who is a member of its Denver chapter, has sought to 'channel the goodness of oil and gas' in a very different way. As a geophysicist, he used to work for an exploration and production company in North Dakota. But with the downturn in oil prices in 2014, he was laid off along with thousands of others in the industry. Married and with three children, he was the main breadwinner in the family. He described it as a 'freefall from the best ever to the worst of my career'. Tim reminded me of a bumper sticker that said: 'Please God, Just Give Me One More Oil Boom. I Promise Not To Blow It Next Time'; a humorous take on the industry's periodic downturns, which are difficult for many. However, he had been in the industry for many decades and it was not the first time he and his family experienced a downturn in oil prices. While they had become used to his sizeable earnings, they had managed to save up over the years and knew how to weather the commodity cycle. This time he and some close friends had been talking increasingly seriously about an idea that he was passionate about: they wanted to start their own oil and gas production company. This was his dream, and this particular moment felt like the right time to realize it.[15] They began to hold countless meetings with private equity fund managers and told them about their business plan, which was to acquire acreage in Wyoming where they had a high degree of familiarity and experience.[16] As Tim said:

> They [private equity fund managers] evaluate your team, your skill set, your reputation, your business plan, and they might commit a $150 million equity commitment or a $500 million equity commitment, which means you get a salary. You get money to pay for your office, overhead expenses, and you're supposed to go buy some acreage, acquire mineral leases, or buy some producing assets and then create value by making them a lot better by drilling. It was a relatively easy path to go down for people with our degree of experience and reputation. But what we discovered was that in the last year and a half it has been an exceptionally difficult road to go down. The private equity guys' response to the cycle is to sit back and watch, very, very cautiously. Very few teams like us would get funded. This past year, maybe only ten in the whole country. We thought we were excellent enough to get funded and what we discovered was that we were in the top 10 per cent. We know the numbers on this; we are just not in the top 1 per cent. It's really difficult. It's a very, very competitive acquisition world.

It was a hard reality for him to face. He was absolutely committed, not just because he had an entrepreneur's deep enthusiasm but also because he felt that he had God's mandate to do this. The contours of the company's ethos had come to him as a vision from God at a point when he sought divine comfort and reassurance. Having networked frenetically for months and felt lost in the process, he had retreated to a friend's holiday house in the mountains. The snow fell thick and deep. Eventually he was snowed in and had to extend his stay. Equipped with the Bible and various Christian books, he engrossed himself in the study when suddenly 'I felt like God was calling me to do this. That I had the skills and that there was a purpose for it. *This* was the purpose'. Rather than setting up an oil and gas production company that was motivated by a desire to increase profits for its shareholders, he felt that he was meant to reimagine the industry. His vision was to set up a company that was motivated by 'proselytizing'. It was going to be a 'force of good' but not in an evangelizing sense. His vision did not necessarily involve Bible distribution, prayer groups, or religious conversion. Highlighting the huge potential for profits in oil and gas, he envisioned the company as a vehicle for the redistribution of wealth, both through direct employment and through charitable donations. It was going to be a 'social entrepreneurship'. As he said one day in-between his meetings with equity fund managers, 'My dream is to do this oil and gas business in a way that really glorifies God'.

But his entrepreneurial journey was not straightforward, and after almost three years of trying he had to shelve the project, at least for the moment. Reflecting back on his path, he remembered the stay at his friend's holiday house in the mountains:

> One of the books I read had the theme of 'moving from a life of success to a life of significance'. There was an exercise that was about identifying the things that hold you back from doing what you really feel you should do. And I realized without question that it was fear. It was fear of two things: it was the fear of failure and it was the fear of finances. So guess what I got ... I took a very big step backward financially and I failed. And guess what ... It's not great but it's OK.
>
> It's possible that the reason why I was supposed to do this was so that I would learn that I'd be OK. After we threw in the towel on the business, I thought, 'OK, I'm going to have to look for a job but in the meantime I need some cash flow'. So I started driving Uber. The business failure, the financial setback, and the driving were so humbling to me. The whole driving thing, which I did for seven months, was a deeply spiritual experience for me of just humbling myself and connecting. So I think maybe God said 'this is what you should do' because I can be prideful. But I'm not greater than anybody else. It was an amazing experience and education.
>
> I now have this deep peace that it was what we were supposed to do. The reason why God wanted us to do this was that he had a different outcome in mind. What he had in mind required of us to start the company and for it to not be a success. Instead of accomplishing some grand reimagining of the oil and gas industry, which is really nothing less than what I have in my head still, maybe what I'm supposed to do is just be a great dad, a great husband, a great co-worker, a great non-profit board member, and a great volunteer. And touch a few hundred people that way. Maybe that's more radical than the other thing, really. I don't know.

Tim's work in the oil and gas industry offered him multiple routes for glorifying God, and although the start-up company did not succeed, he felt that he was able to find meaning in that process. He now works for a service company in the industry and hopes that perhaps one day God's plan will come to involve the successful launch of his production company. 'Throwing in the towel' thus did not lead to distrust either in the oil and gas industry or in God. Indeed, Tim's personal crisis became an important moment of reassurance for him as it demonstrated not just that God mattered as an abstract principle fundamental to the universe, but also that God was present for him in the particular (Elisha 2011; Luhrmann 2012: 127). Rather than asking God why his bids failed, he relied on his years of experience and well-versed technocratic knowledge to explain this. He shared with me detailed insights into the various financial models he had pursued and presented a 'conviction narrative' (Chong & Tuckett 2015) of his failure. But in an industry of ups and downs, where people are keenly aware of the limits to their knowledge with regard both to the future of the industry and to the future of their own careers, hope becomes an important mode of orientation. Rather than dwelling on the specific, be it a commodity cycle, a company merger, or a local community protest, hope has a propensity, if not an ability, to slip away from the immediate realm (Miyazaki 2006: 149; cf. Narotzky & Besnier 2014). Looking towards the future, Tim's faith in God made it possible for him to hope that opportunities would emerge so that one day he could pursue the oil and gas business in a way that he felt was compassionate.

## Conclusion

This essay has examined how some of the people working in the oil and gas industry pursue morally ambitious projects through the production, distribution, and consumption of these fossil fuels. For them, these hydrocarbons are resources that can bring about fundamental changes in people's lives; changes that go far beyond those commonly identified by the oil and gas industry itself. Implicated in relationships with various human and nonhuman beings, oil and gas become for them catalysts, if not proselytizers, of human flourishing.[17] They are regarded as 'forces of good' in spiritual battles against darker forces, in conversions to a life in faith, and in tortuous paths towards finding one's calling. These conceptualizations of oil and gas as 'forces of good' are not challenged or diminished by concerns about climate change. While some see the opportunities provided by fossil fuels as far outweighing negative consequences, others see 'change' as an inherent dynamic in the earth system as created by God. My interlocutors thus share a mode of knowing that places immense faith in spiritual worlds and that questions the nature and motivations of human actions (see also Gardiner 2010). Their moral outlooks raise personal and political questions about inequalities of access and what it might mean to flourish. Encouraging a reimagination of the role of energy in human life, they urge us to (re)consider the extent to which oil and gas can be forces of good.

But although these industry actors are employed by oil and gas companies, their insights into the place of energy in human life are far removed from the usual territories of corporate ethics. Often referred to as 'corporate social responsibility' or 'corporate conscience', this twinning of the corporate and the social, the market and morality, subsumes ethics within highly particular value regimes that are first and foremost related to marketing, advertising, and pricing (see also Dolan & Rajak 2011). As Hannah Appel has shown in her work on oil extraction in Equatorial Guinea, for transnational oil companies, corporate social responsibility is central to companies' involvement in zonal capitalism, to their disentanglement from what goes on outside the company gates. The separation, although partial and never complete, is strategic and performative, with 'many people doing a tremendous amount of work to maintain its boundaries' (Appel 2012b: 450; see also Cross 2011). It is a detachment that never succeeds. Attending to the practices of corporate social responsibility can thus yield insights into how 'the good' and 'the desirable' are mobilized and used instrumentally and strategically to help make companies financially viable and attractive entities to investors (see also Foster 2010). However, they tell us very little about how the various corporate actors who individually and collectively constitute these companies (Welker 2014) conceptualize and act on the ethical.

'Human flourishing', as recognized by Aristotle in the *Nicomachean ethics*, is not a meta-ontological category. It depends on how each of us defines the ultimate goal for a good life, enabling us to experience and make sense of our actions accordingly (Cooper 1975: 98). People in the oil and gas industry who pursue their various projects of devotion underscore how ethics are embedded squarely in the realm of action rather than (only) abstract reason (see also High 2018: 83; Lambek 2010: 14). Inspired by their moral ambitions and mobilized into what they see as compassionate action, these

*Journal of the Royal Anthropological Institute (N.S.), 29-46*
© 2019 The Authors. Journal of the Royal Anthropological Institute published by John Wiley & Sons
Ltd on behalf of Royal Anthropological Institute

projects seem to showcase an individual's ethical capacity. Indeed, in the literature on charity work, such individuals require much explanation. Why do they do it? How far would they go? What do they expect in return? Basically, what propels compassionate individuals into action? (see Allahyari 2000; MacFarquhar 2015; Miller 1999; Wuthnow 2012). But, as poignantly noted by Cheryl Mattingly (2012), this elevated and abstracted individualism that cultivates a virtuous character through self-care and agency has been central to not only Aristotle's practical (ethical) philosophy but also particular strands of anthropological theory that have presumed the efficacious individual to be more empowered, liberated, and creative (see also Laidlaw 2010).

Since I have highlighted how these industry actors have values and interests that may exceed those of oil and gas companies, they risk emerging as precisely such supercharged individuals who autonomously and abstractly bring about change. And this is how some of them may appear when you first meet them during fieldwork. The oilfields are host to many individuals who have left friends and family behind; who work for one company before working for another; who work on a rig in one site before relocating to another site; who treasure their independence and freedom; and who see the ups and downs of the industry as challenges they can and will overcome. The 'awkward scales' of the industry become a backdrop to the proclamation of an individual's strength and invincibility. However, by attending to their moral ambitions in a world in which the ultimate goal for a good life is often difficult to discern and even harder to achieve, I have sought to show how they pursue ambitious projects through their contingent relations and interactions with others. By recognizing these multiple and dynamic relational ties that exist within the cosmoeconomy of oil and gas, we can see the expansive and inclusive world within which people mobilize ethical action, sometimes in ways that we might not expect.

## NOTES

 This project has received funding from the European Research Council (ERC) under the European Union's Horizon 2020 research and innovation programme under grant agreement No 715146.

I also gratefully acknowledge the funding I have received to carry out this research from the Leverhulme Trust (ECF-2013-177) and the British Academy (EN150010). I thank my friends and interlocutors in Colorado who have let me into their lives and shared their thoughts and experiences so generously with me. I further thank my students and colleagues, especially Adam Reed and Aimee Joyce, as well as my Energy Ethics research team and my collaborator Jessica Smith, for their invaluable discussions and comments on earlier drafts of this essay. Thanks are also due to the participants in the Energy Ethics conference held at the University of St Andrews in March 2016, the Energy Ethics retreat held at The Burn in October 2016, the Centre for Ethics, Philosophy and Public Affairs (CEPPA) seminar held at the University of St Andrews in October 2018, and the Department of Social Anthropology research seminar held at the University of Bergen in December 2018. These events have provided ideal environments in which to discuss and reflect on the nature of and challenges in our energy dilemmas. I would finally also like to thank the anonymous *JRAI* reviewers for their perceptive comments and the production team at Wiley, in particular Justin Dyer, who have so carefully and expertly led the manuscript to its completion. However, any shortcomings of this essay are entirely my own.

[1] This special issue contains several ethnographic examples of how 'down periods' give rise to reassessments of responsibility and accountability, for example in the context of 'mature' oil assets in Canada (see

Wood, this volume) or coal as unacknowledged 'gifts' from miners in Wyoming (see Smith, this volume).

[2] As a convenient shorthand, in the rest of the essay I will sometimes refer to the oil and gas industry as simply the 'oil industry'. I do so not to ignore the importance of natural gas or to exaggerate the importance of oil in these contexts but rather to render the text more readable.

[3] I am here drawing on Pettigrove's (2007) work on ambition, especially his reflections on the dynamics of motivation and desire in relation to what he calls 'the value of ambition'.

[4] The notion of 'ambition' holds an important place in not only philosophical but also theological debates. In Saint Augustine of Hippo's own account of how he converted to Christianity after living a life in sin, he denounces the vice of ambition. Presenting it as a desire for the honour and glory that should only be accorded to God, he advises his followers to 'renounce worldly ambition' (1997: 198). As such, Augustine admonishes against a particular mode of ambition associated with the sins of the self. There are interesting parallels between the theologians' and philosophers' concerns about human ambition, but they would be too extensive to discuss here.

[5] Although the notion of cosmoeconomy emerged from my research on the Mongolian gold rush (High 2017), I have found it useful more generally when contemplating the vast world within which people conceptualize and mobilize economic life.

[6] See Mason (this volume) for a discussion of how this kind of technocratic knowledge is produced by energy consultants and received by government actors in the context of a natural gas pipeline in Alaska.

[7] Within the oil and gas industry, the notion of 'digital oil fields' refers primarily to upstream operations: that is, the extraction of oil and gas. It refers specifically to the integration of digital technology such as sensors and automated well mechanics, enabling the collection of high-volume data in real time, remote operations, automation, and visualizations. As I argue here, digitalization is part of a broader process of knowledge transformation and valuation in the industry.

[8] For more detailed information about the oil and gas industry in Colorado, including industry perspectives on issues surrounding hydraulic fracturing (also known as 'fracking'), see the Colorado Oil and Gas Association's website at *http://www.coga.org*. Also see de Rijke (2013) for a discussion of anthropology and hydraulic fracturing as well as Loomis (2017) for an account of the world-wide boom in unconventional oil and natural gas.

[9] Petroleum products include various grades of fuel oil and gasoline, while petrochemical products include chemical compounds used in plastics, fibres, adhesives, lubricants, and gels. According to the British Plastics Federation, '4% of global oil production is used for plastics. 87% is used for transport, energy and heating' (see *http://www.bpf.co.uk/press/oil_consumption.aspx*, accessed 7 January 2019).

[10] In this essay I use pseudonyms to protect the identity of my interlocutors. I have also altered other potential personal identifiers to further respect and ensure their anonymity.

[11] Their website (*http://www.api.org*) outlines their online educational resources and 'consumer information' for the classroom.

[12] Over the course of my research so far, the price for West Texas Intermediate crude oil has gone from a high of $111 per barrel in June 2014 to a low of $29 per barrel in January 2016. The volatility is thus dramatic and can happen over short periods.

[13] Their spiritual practices and affiliations are varied, but for reasons of confidentiality, I do not disclose any particular groups in this essay.

[14] The New Living Translation is a present-day rendition of the ancient Hebrew and Greek texts, intended to appeal to readers through its semantic translation rather than prioritizing the equivalence of words. As such, it is easy to read and in July 2008 apparently became the most popular English version of the Bible based on unit sales (see *https://www.gotquestions.org/New-Living-Translation-NLT.html*, accessed 7 January 2019).

[15] Trying to establish an oil production company is a relatively common aspiration for senior workers, especially at times of redundancy. However, the odds of success are low in any commodity cycle, and at this particular time it was apparent that only about 1 per cent of the start-up attempts managed to acquire sufficient investment.

[16] In a forthcoming article, I examine how private equity finance relates to oil entrepreneurs' visions in the circulation of finance capital.

[17] Paul Thomas Anderson's 2017 film *There will be blood* captures this potency of oil, which initially offers the lure and promise of flourishing wealth.

## REFERENCES

ALLAHYARI, R.A. 2000. *Visions of charity: volunteer workers and moral community*. Berkeley: University of California Press.

APPEL, H. 2012*a*. Offshore work: oil, modularity, and the how of capitalism in Equatorial Guinea. *American Ethnologist* **39**, 692-709.

———— 2012*b*. Walls and white elephants: oil extraction, responsibility, and infrastructural violence in Equatorial Guinea. *Ethnography* **13**, 439-65.

————, A. MASON & M. WATTS 2015. Introduction: Oil talk. In *Subterranean estates: life worlds of oil and gas* (eds) H. Appel, A. Mason & M. Watts, 1-26. Ithaca, N.Y.: Cornell University Press.

ATABAKI, T., E. BINI & K. EHSANI 2018. Introduction. In *Working for oil: comparative social histories of labor in the global oil industry* (eds) T. Atabaki, E. Bini & K. Ehsani, 1-10. Basingstoke: Palgrave Macmillan.

AUGUSTINE, SAINT 1997. *The confessions*, vol. **1** (trans. M. Boulding). Augustinian Heritage Institute. New York City: New City Press.

AUSTIN, D.E. & T.R. McGUIRE 2017. The great crew change? Structuring work in the oilfield. In *ExtrACTION: impacts, engagements, and alternative futures* (eds.) K. Jalbert, A. Willow, D. Casagrande & S. Paladino, 17-30. Abingdon, Oxon: Routledge.

BENSON, P. & S. KIRSCH 2010. Capitalism and the politics of resignation. *Current Anthropology* **51**, 459-86.

BEUNZA, D. & F. FERRARO 2018. Performative work: bridging performativity and institutional theory in the responsible investment field. *Organization Studies* (on-line first), 1-29. https://doi.org/10.1177/017084061 7747917.

BOYER, D. 2008. Thinking through the anthropology of experts. *Anthropology in Action* **15**: 2, 38-46.

BRANDTSTÄDTER, S. & K. SYKES 2010. Prickly pear polemics – Introduction to Feuchtwang and Strathern: judgement, commensurability and double vision. *Critique of Anthropology* **30**, 91-3.

CABANTOUS, L. & J.P. GOND 2011. Rational decision making as performative praxis: explaining rationality's *Éternel Retour*. *Organization Science* **22**, 573-86.

ÇALIŞKAN, K. & M. CALLON 2009. Economization, part 1: Shifting attention from the economy towards processes of economization. *Economy and Society* **38**, 369-98.

———— & ———— 2010. Economization, part 2: A research programme for the study of markets. *Economy and Society* **39**, 1-32.

CALLON, M. & J. LAW 2005. On qualculation, agency, and otherness. *Environment and Planning D: Society and Space* **23**, 717-33.

———— & F. MUNIESA 2005. Peripheral vision: economic markets as calculative collective devices. *Organization Studies* **26**, 1229-50.

CARVAJAL, G., M. MAUCEC & S. CULLICK 2018. *Intelligent digital oil and gas fields: concepts, collaboration and right-time decisions*. Oxford: Elsevier.

CHONG, K. & D. TUCKETT 2015. Constructing conviction through action and narrative: how money managers manage uncertainty and the consequence for financial market functioning. *Socio-Economic Review* **13**, 309-30.

COCHOY, F. 2002. *Une sociologie du packaging ou l'âne de Buridan face au marché: les emballages et le choix du consommateur*. Paris: Presses Universitaires de France.

COMAROFF, J. & J. COMAROFF 2003. Ethnography on an awkward scale: postcolonial anthropology and the violence of abstraction. *Ethnography* **4**, 147-79.

COOPER, J.M. 1975. *Reason and human good in Aristotle*. Indianapolis: Hackett.

CROSS, J. 2011. Detachment as a corporate ethic. *Focaal: Journal of Global and Historical Anthropology* **60**, 34-46.

DE RIJKE, K. 2013. Hydraulically fractured: unconventional gas and anthropology. *Anthropology Today* **29**: 2, 13-17.

DOLAN, C. & D. RAJAK 2011. Introduction: Ethnographies of corporate ethicizing. *Focaal: Journal of Global and Historical Anthropology* **60**, 3-8.

EHSANI, K. 2018. Disappearing the workers: how labor in the oil complex has been made invisible. In *Working for oil: comparative social histories of labor in the global oil industry* (eds) T. Atabaki, E. Bini & K. Ehsani, 11-34. Basingstoke: Palgrave Macmillan.

ELISHA, O. 2011. *Moral ambition: mobilization and social outreach in evangelical megachurches*. Berkeley: University of California Press.

FEUCHTWANG, S. 2010. Corrections of double vision. *Critique of Anthropology* **30**, 94-101.

FOSTER, R.J. 2010. Corporate oxymorons and the anthropology of corporations. *Dialectical Anthropology* **34**, 95-102.

GARDINER, S.M. 2010. Is arming the future with geoengineering really the lesser evil? In *Climate ethics: essential readings* (eds) S.M. Gardiner, S. Caney, D. Jamieson & H. Shue, 284-314. Oxford: University Press.

HIGH, M.M. 2017. *Fear and fortune: spirit worlds and emerging economies in the Mongolian gold rush*. Ithaca, N.Y.: Cornell University Press.

———— 2018. A question of ethics: the creative orthodoxy of Buddhist monks in the Mongolian gold rush. *Ethnos* **83**, 80-99.

HILL, T.E. 1991. *Autonomy and self-respect*. Cambridge: University Press.

HOLBRAAD, M. 2018. Steps away from moralism. In *Moral anthropology: a critique* (eds) B. Kapferer & M. Gold, 27-48. New York: Berghahn Books.

HOLMES, D.R. 2013. *Economy of words: communicative imperatives in central banks*. Chicago: University Press.

HUBER, M.T. 2013. *Lifeblood: oil, freedom, and the forces of capital*. Minneapolis: University of Minnesota Press.

HUGHES, D.M. 2017. *Energy without conscience: oil, climate change, and complicity*. Durham, N.C.: Duke University Press.

HURSTHOUSE, R. 1999. *On virtue ethics*. Oxford: University Press.

JALBERT, K., A. WILLOW, D. CASAGRANDE & S. PALADINO 2017. Introduction: Confronting extraction, taking action. In *ExtrACTION: impacts, engagements, and alternative futures* (eds) K. Jalbert, A. Willow, D. Casagrande & S. Paladino, 1-13. Abingdon, Oxon: Routledge.

JOHNSON, B. 2014. *Carbon nation: fossil fuels in the making of American culture*. Lawrence: University Press of Kansas.

JOHNSON, L. 2015. Near futures and perfect hedges in the Gulf of Mexico. In *Subterranean estates: life worlds of oil and gas* (eds) H. Appel, A. Mason & M. Watts, 193-210. Ithaca, N.Y.: Cornell University Press.

KANT, I. 1996 [1794]. *Religion and rational theology* (trans. & ed. A.W. Wood & G. di Giovanni). Cambridge: University Press.

KAPFERER, B. & M. GOLD 2018. Introduction: Reconceptualizing the discipline. In *Moral anthropology: a critique* (eds) B. Kapferer & M. Gold, 1-24. New York: Berghahn Books.

LABBAN, M. 2008. *Space, oil and capital*. Abingdon, Oxon: Routledge.

LAIDLAW, J. 2010. Agency and responsibility: perhaps you can have too much of a good thing. In *Ordinary ethics: anthropology, language, and action* (ed.) M. Lambek, 143-64. New York: Fordham University Press.

LAMBEK, M. 2010. Introduction. In *Ordinary ethics: anthropology, language, and action* (ed.) M. Lambek, 1-36. New York: Fordham University Press.

LEMENAGER, S. 2014. *Living oil: petroleum culture in the American century*. Oxford: University Press.

LONG, N.J. & H.L. MOORE 2013. Introduction: Achievement and its social life. In *The social life of achievement* (eds) N.J. Long & H.L. Moore, 1-30. Oxford: Berghahn Books.

LOOMIS, T.M. 2017. *Petroleum development and environmental conflict in Aotearoa New Zealand: Texas of the South Pacific*. Lanham, Md: Lexington Books.

LUHRMANN, T.M. 2012. *When God talks back: understanding the American evangelical relationship with God*. London: Vintage.

MABRO, R. 1992. OPEC and the price of oil. *The Energy Journal* **13**: **2**, 1-17.

MACFARQUHAR, L. 2015. *Strangers drowning: voyages to the brink of moral extremity*. London: Penguin.

MASON, A. 2007. The rise of consultant forecasting in liberalized natural gas markets. *Public Culture* **19**, 367-79.

MATTINGLY, C. 2012. Two virtue ethics and the anthropology of morality. *Anthropological Theory* **12**, 161-84.

MAURER, B. 2002. Repressed futures: financial derivatives' theological unconscious. *Economy and Society* **31**, 15-36.

MILLER, D.T. 1999. The norm of self-interest. *American Psychologist* **54**, 1053-60.

MILLO, Y. & D. MACKENZIE 2009. The usefulness of inaccurate models: towards an understanding of the emergence of financial risk management. *Accounting, Organizations and Society* **34**, 638-53.

MITCHELL, T. 2010. The resources of economics: making the 1973 oil crisis. *Journal of Cultural Economy* **3**, 189-204.

MIYAZAKI, H. 2006. Economy of dreams: hope in global capitalism and its critiques. *Cultural Anthropology* **21**, 147-72.

NAROTZKY, S. & N. BESNIER 2014. Crisis, value, and hope: rethinking the economy. *Current Anthropology* **55**: **S9**, 4-16.

PETTIGROVE, G.A. 2007. Ambitions. *Ethical Theory and Moral Practice* **10**, 53-68.

———— & M.J. MEYER 2009. Moral ambition. *Australasian Journal of Philosophy* **87**, 285-99.

*Journal of the Royal Anthropological Institute (N.S.)*, 29-46

Priest, T. 2018. Cat crackers and picket lines: organized labour in US Gulf Coast oil refining. In *Working for oil: comparative social histories of labor in the global oil industry* (eds) T. Atabaki, E. Bini & K. Ehsani, 227-56. Basingstoke: Palgrave Macmillan.

Rigi, J. 2018. The horizon of freedom and ethics of singularity: the social individual and the necessity of reloading the spirit of 1968. In *Moral anthropology: a critique* (eds) B. Kapferer & M. Gold, 155-68. New York: Berghahn Books.

Riles, A. 2004. Real time: unwinding technocratic and anthropological knowledge. *American Ethnologist* 31, 392-405.

——— 2011. *Collateral knowledge: legal reasoning in the global financial markets.* Chicago: University Press.

Robbins, J. 2004. *Becoming sinners: Christianity and moral torment in a Papua New Guinea society.* Berkeley: University of California Press.

Scamehorn, H.L. 2002. *High-altitude energy: a history of fossil fuels in Colorado.* Boulder: University Press of Colorado.

Shever, E. 2012. *Resources for reform: oil and neoliberalism in Argentina.* Stanford: University Press.

Soma, R., A. Bakshi & V.K. Prasanna 2007. A semantic framework for integrated asset management in smart oilfields. *Seventh IEEE International Symposium on Cluster Computing and the Grid*, 119-26.

Sovacool, B.K. 2014. What are we doing here? Analyzing fifteen years of energy scholarship and proposing a social science research agenda. *Energy Research & Social Science* 1, 1-29.

Striphas, T. 2015. Algorithmic culture. *European Journal of Cultural Studies* 18, 395-412.

Szeman, I. 2007. System failure: oil, futurity, and the anticipation of disaster. *South Atlantic Quarterly* 104, 805-23.

——— & D. Boyer 2017. Introduction: On the energy humanities. In *Energy humanities: an anthology* (eds) I. Szeman & D. Boyer, 1-13. Baltimore, Md: Johns Hopkins University Press.

Walsh, A. 2006. 'Nobody has a money taboo': situating ethics in a northern Malagasy sapphire mining town. *Anthropology Today* 22: 4, 4-8.

Welker, M. 2014. *Enacting the corporation: an American mining firm in post-authoritarian Indonesia.* Berkeley: University of California Press.

Williams, B. 2006. *Ethics and the limits of philosophy.* London: Routledge.

Wuthnow, R. 2012. *Acts of compassion: caring for others and helping ourselves.* Princeton: University Press.

Zaloom, C. 2004. The productive life of risk. *Cultural Anthropology* 19, 365-91.

Zhang, C., A. Orangi, A. Bakshi, W.J. Da Sie & V.K. Prasanna 2006. Model-based framework for oil production forecasting and optimization: a case study in integrated asset management. Intelligent Energy Conference and Exhibition, Society of Petroleum Engineers, Amsterdam, 11-13 April.

Zigon, J. 2007. Moral breakdown and the ethical demand: a theoretical framework for an anthropology of moralities. *Anthropological Theory* 7, 131-50.

Zylinska, J. 2014. *Minimal ethics for the Anthropocene.* Ann Arbor, Mich.: Open Humanities Press.

## Projets de dévotion : prospection énergétique et ambition morale dans la cosmoéconomie du pétrole et du gaz dans l'Ouest des États-Unis

*Résumé*

Cet essai examine la manière dont les travailleurs du pétrole et du gaz au Colorado perçoivent leur implication dans la prospection énergétique en relation avec des pratiques plus larges de dévotion, de compassion et de relations de proximité. Bien que leurs projets énergétiques semblent uniquement faire écho aux éléments de langage promus par les entreprises, les ambitions morales personnelles des acteurs sur les gisements et dans les entreprises révèlent des visions cosmoéconomiques des potentialités du pétrole qui vont au-delà de l'humain. L'auteure montre ainsi comment de multiples registres éthiques divergents se recoupent et entrent en compte dans la valorisation du pétrole.

*Journal of the Royal Anthropological Institute (N.S.), 29-46*

# 2

# The solar good: energy ethics in poor markets

Jamie Cross *University of Edinburgh*

What are the ethical commitments of people who design, build, and sell solar photovoltaic technologies to those living in energy poverty across sub-Saharan Africa and South Asia? Over the past decade, dramatic falls in the cost of solar photovoltaics have seen our increased capacity to convert sunlight into electricity married to projects of governance, social or moral reform, and expressions of care for distant others. Tracing these projects across the floor of an international trade fair in Dubai and a social enterprise in India, this essay shows that the pursuit of the solar good hinges on the knowable ground that is capitalism today.

## Doing well by doing good

In June 2008, Bill Gates resigned as CEO of Microsoft to focus his attention on the work of the Gates Foundation. The Foundation had become a vehicle for Gates' philanthropic work and was pioneering the application of business and marketing strategies to the provision of food, water, sanitation, and nutrition in contexts of chronic global poverty and humanitarian emergencies. To coincide with his resignation, Gates wrote an article for *Time* magazine, part of a series titled 'Doing well by doing good' (Gates 2008). In the article, Gates argued that our moral concerns with global poverty would be better focused by channelling them into the creation of new markets for manufactured goods. 'We see inequity as a business problem,' Gates wrote.

> It's not just about doing more corporate philanthropy or asking companies to be more virtuous ... It's about giving them a real incentive to apply their expertise in new ways while serving the people who have been left out ... It's about harnessing 'self-interest' to 'an ethic of care for others'.

The challenge, Gates argued, is finding 'markets all over the world that businesses have missed, studying the needs of the poorest two billion people in the world, and selling them goods and services that meet their unmet needs'. 'There are critics', he continued. 'There are sceptics. There are those that doubt such markets can be found, or that they have not yet been discovered'. But, he wrote, 'I disagree'.

*Journal of the Royal Anthropological Institute (N.S.)*, 47-66
© Royal Anthropological Institute 2019

[Critics] assume that businesses have already studied every possible market for their products. It's like that old joke about the economist walking down the street with his friend. The economist steps over a $10 bill that is lying on the ground. His friend asks him why he didn't pick it up. It can't possibly be there, the economist replies, because if it was somebody else would have picked it up already. All those people who decry the potential for doing business with the global poor, they think that all the $10 bills have already been picked up (Gates 2008: 26).

Such arguments circulate globally. Just as concepts that extend our critiques of corporate or financial capitalism have come to act as beacons of hope for scholars, as well as social and environmental activists (e.g. Graeber 2013; Kirsch 2018), arguments that present markets for new goods and services as engines of improvement have also come to act as sources of hope 'within' capitalism (e.g. Miyazaki 2006). Over the past decade, Bill Gates and others, like the management guru C.K. Prahalhad (Cross & Street 2009; Elyachar 2012), have done much to assert the promise that for-profit businesses can 'do well by doing good', establishing the terrain of humanitarian intervention and chronic global poverty as legitimate arenas for entrepreneurship and corporate activity. By presenting an explicit ideological defence of what has been called 'compassionate capitalism' (Benioff & Southwick 2004) and 'philanthrocapitalism' (Bishop & Green 2008), or what we might also call 'humanitarian capitalism', such ideas create new problems and questions for anthropology (e.g. Collier, Cross, Redfield & Street 2018; Schwittay 2011).

One arena in which attempts to 'do well by doing good' have flourished sits at the intersection of global poverty and solar energy. Efforts to provide a minimum, sustainable level of electrically powered lighting, refrigeration, and charging to the estimated 1.2 billion people who live without access to reliable mains electricity coincide with the interests of solar manufacturers and distributors, as they seek to accelerate the growth of markets for off-grid solar power. Between 2010 and 2018, global sales of 'off-grid' solar technologies that generate power for energy services in the absence of any connection to a mains electricity grid reached 130 million units, with the total sales value generated by the off-grid solar sector reported to have exceeded $3.9 billion (World Bank/Dalberg 2018). For many management and business executives in off-grid solar companies, selling solar power to people living in chronic energy poverty presents itself as an ethical-economic utopia: the opportunity to express care for others and the environment at the same time as fulfilling a fiduciary duty of care to investors and shareholders.

How are such ethical commitments articulated in the everyday life and work of solar markets? What are the 'ordinary ethics' (Lambek 2010) of the off-grid solar industry? If ethical projects always include values or commitments that compete with or support each other (Laidlaw 2002; 2013; Robbins 2013), then what kinds of overlapping or competing ethical projects underpin the growth of the global solar industry? How do solar executives and entrepreneurs articulate the pursuit of market goods – freedom, profit, growth, expansion, property – with an ethics of care to people and planet?

As Mette High and Jessica Smith write in the introduction to this volume, the everyday ethics of people employed in energy industries – whether fossil fuel, nuclear, or renewable – are frequently marked by 'plurality and complexity, idiosyncrasy if not inconsistency' (High & Smith, this volume, p. 11). The ethnographic challenge, they propose, is to take seriously how these people make sense of the world rather than move immediately to a position of critique or advocacy. This essay sets out to attempt such a

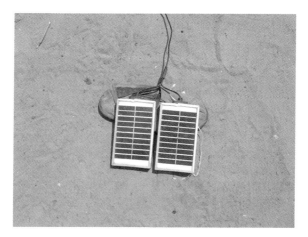

**Figure 1.** Solar panels charging a portable lamp in Goudoubou Refugee Camp, Burkina Faso, 2017.
(Photo: Adolphe Yentim/Jamie Cross.)

task in the context of the global off-grid solar industry, a uniquely rich site from which
to examine ethical commitments to people and the environment.

Solar energy has been morally encoded with a spirit of social and ecological
entrepreneurialism since the invention of the modern, silicon-based photovoltaic cell
in 1953. As I explore in the first section of this essay, the ethical commitments of the
solar industry have always had a humanitarian impulse or an orientation towards distant
others, underpinned by rhetorics of collectivity and sustainability as well as commercial
promise. In the mid-twentieth century, the ecological and market commitments – or
'ecologics' (Howe 2014; Howe & Boyer 2016) – of solar energy across sub-Saharan Africa
and South Asia were firmly tied to the logics and imaginaries of 'development' (Escobar
2011; Ferguson 1990; Li 2007). For the past half-century, the deployment of decentralized
solar energy technologies in countries from Mali to India have brought solar power into
alignment with programmes of 'improvement' in health and well-being, education,
livelihoods, and productivity (Cross 2013; 2018).

Yet attempts to engineer transitions to a low-carbon, solar economy also come with
costs (Newell & Mulvaney 2013). As Cymene Howe outlines in this volume, whilst the
dramatic expansion of renewable energy infrastructures world-wide is ethically laudable
and necessary, it also necessitates a tipping of 'value scales', with the deleterious effects
of wind or solar on communities, the environment, and nonhuman lives balanced
against humanity's 'greater good'. Nowhere is this more apparent than in the global
solar industry.

Our ability to convert sunlight into electricity depends upon the same extractive
industries, globalized production networks, and electronic waste flows that have
characterized the industrial exploitation of resources, land, and labour in the
Anthropocene, or what we might better call the Capitalocene (Haraway 2015;
Moore 2015). The exponential growth in the installed global capacity of solar over the
past decade and the dramatic fall in the cost of solar modules is often framed by clean
energy champions as a ubiquitous good (e.g. Sivaram 2018). Yet the accelerated growth
of global demand for solar energy is producing new economic inequities, ecological
harms, and forms of precarity.

The solar industry is a silicon-based microelectronic industry. The falling prices of solar modules have seen smaller margins for solar manufacturers, leading to pinch points across global supply chains. Sustained demand for solar power, for example, will depend on continued access to and exploitation of rare earths and mineral resources – including the silver, copper, bauxite, lithium, and silicon which are used to produce photovoltaic modules, rechargeable batteries, and electronic circuitry – at sites across Latin America, Central and Southern Africa, and South and Southeast Asia (Bazilian 2018; Revette 2017). The continued manufacturing and assembly of monocrystalline and polycrystalline silicon solar modules, electronic components, and batteries in off-grid solar technologies will hinge on efficiencies in the labour process at sites of offshore subcontracting in China and Malaysia akin to those at any other sites of global electronic production (e.g. Ngai 2005; Cross 2014). Finally, when solar systems break, fail, or reach the end of their working lives, they produce new flows of discarded electronic components and materials, as well as new questions about what to do with e-waste (Cross & Murray 2018; Lepawsky 2018). Like other microelectronic industries, the solar industry frequently conceals the conditions under which its solar goods are produced through forms of obfuscation, misdirection, or greenwashing, 'the glare from solar blind[ing] us to better alternatives' (Zehner 2012: 27). Rather than presenting an untroubled solution to our global energy challenges, then, the growth of the solar industry also signals the 'rebirth' of extractive and exploitative energy economies (Argenti & Knight 2015).

Seen in this light, any attempt to do good *and* do well by harnessing the power of the sun to generate electricity in contexts of global poverty involves compromises or trade-offs. In the shadow of such photovoltaic realism, the prospect that there might be something uniquely ethical about solar power is just another 'corporate oxymoron' (Benson & Kirsch 2010). But does this analysis do justice to the moral commitments of people running or employed by solar companies?

One risk of a purely political economic analysis of the solar industry, as Mette High writes of the oil industry (this volume), is that human actors are noticeable by their absence, rendered invisible by the moral authority of critique. Current critical engagements with the solar industry leave us with little understanding of what moves solar entrepreneurs to action, how people make sense of or articulate their ethical commitments in everyday working life, or how people balance costs and benefits in pursuit of a greater, common good.

My contribution to this special issue attempts to redress the imbalance by drawing from ethnographic research carried out since 2010 across the off-grid solar value chain. This has included fieldwork with designers and manufacturers of off-grid solar systems in corporate offices as well as fieldwork with the distributors and users of solar equipment in unelectrified parts of India, Kenya, Tanzania, and Burkina Faso (Cross 2016*a*; 2016*b*; 2018; Cross, Douglas, Martin, Ray & Verhoeven 2018). If executives in the off-grid solar industry engage with social anthropologists, it is usually with the aim of better understanding market conditions or the behaviour of poor consumers. They want to know why people adopt solar power or what the social impact of their technologies is in particular places. This essay reverses the ethnographic gaze. Moving from an international trade fair for the off-grid solar industry in Dubai to a small solar start-up in Hyderabad, India, I turn the focus away from consumers to the people whose business is selling solar technology to the poor.

*Journal of the Royal Anthropological Institute (N.S.), 47-66*
© Royal Anthropological Institute 2019

Corporate managers and executives in the off-grid solar industry are deeply committed to the idea that making consumer markets for solar goods is ethical. In the solar industry, making markets is a way of 'being ecological' (Morton 2018), of caring for distant others (Bornstein & Redfield 2011), and of creating corporate value (Foster 2007). I propose, building on the work of Joel Robbins (2012; 2013) and Frederic Jameson (2005), that we take these commitments seriously.

In his call for an anthropology of the good, Joel Robbins encouraged anthropologists to 'explore the ways in which people organize their personal and collective lives in order to foster what they think of as good, and to study what it is like to live at least some of the time in light of such a project' (2013: 457). We must not dismiss people's investments in realizing the good as mere utopianism, Robbins argues, or set out to smother their hopes with wet-blanket realism (2013: 458), but rather should give these idealizing aspects of their lives a place in our accounts. It is in this vein that I approach the solar industry.

All ethical and utopian visions need a knowable ground. In the off-grid solar industry, I propose, the pursuit of social and environmental goods, perhaps even the very possibility of being good, hinges on the knowable ground that is constituted by relationships and systems of market exchange.

This argument takes the 'anthropology of energy in the Global South' beyond the study of infrastructures of electricity and electrification (e.g. Gupta 2015) to the study of moral economy (see, e.g., Smith & High 2017). Furthering anthropological knowledge is not the only endpoint, however. As solar energy becomes a more significant part of our energy systems, I propose that a deeper understanding of practical ethics in the global solar industry can extend our critical engagement with the material politics of solar corporations, solar supply chains, and solar goods.

I begin by tracing the contours of ethical action in the brief modern history of photovoltaics. As I show, the search for new markets defined how the solar industry came to care.

### How the solar industry came to care

The specific content and contours of care in today's off-grid solar industry are shaped by a history of ideas about the relationship between electricity and humanity. The increased significance of electricity in mid-eighteenth-century programmes of social or moral reform (which saw the first experimental use of electrical machines to heal diseased bodies) was accompanied by a new 'electrical humanitarianism' that presented electricity as the basis for sustaining human life (Delbourgo 2006). At the beginning of the twentieth century, these ideas were an inextricable feature of modernist projects of electrification, from the United States and the Soviet Union to India (e.g. Buck-Morss 2002; Coleman 2017; Nye 1990). In the 1950s, with the invention of a technology that could convert sunlight into a clean, renewable source of electrical power, electricity and the notion of humanity were tied together in new ways.

On 25 April 1954, the US research and development company Bell Laboratories publicly announced that three of its scientists – Daryl Chapin, Gerald Pearson, and Calvin Fuller – had invented a silicon photovoltaic cell capable of converting enough of the sun's energy into power to run everyday electronic equipment. The *New York Times* heralded the invention on its front page, echoing Bell Laboratories' claims for its new technology that the solar cell 'may mark the beginning of a new era, leading eventually to the realization of one of mankind's most cherished dreams – the harnessing of the almost limitless power of the sun for the uses of civilization'. These

*Journal of the Royal Anthropological Institute (N.S.), 47-66*
© Royal Anthropological Institute 2019

**Figure 2.** Photovoltaic realism: 1950s advertisement for the Bell solar battery superimposed on street-side electronics traders in rural India in 2012. (Photo: Jamie Cross/Jenny Littlejohn.)

sentiments, with their emphasis on the potentially universal benefit of photovoltaics, were to become a mainstay of self-representation and corporate story-telling in the solar industry.

In the 1950s, there was little question that the price of electricity generated by silicon photovoltaic cells might immediately be competitive with the cost of grid-connected electricity generated by coal power plants or big dams. Instead, as US-based scientists and engineers struggled to find viable applications for the silicon-based solar cell, they embraced a post-war idea of 'development'. In the developing or 'disconnected world', they saw not just an unmet need for modern forms of energy but also vast potential markets for their technology. The search for these opportunities was to fuse an ecological-utopian vision to the commercial interests of the nascent solar industry.

In 1955, Bell Laboratories sold the first licence for the commercial manufacture of silicon solar modules to a US-based company, National Fabricated Products. National Fabricated Products was exploring the potential for solar power outside of Europe and America, driven not just by the idea of providing cheap power in parts of the world where power was not readily available but also by the untapped commercial value of new markets in Africa and Asia (Perlin 1999). In the mid-1950s, however, the costs of mass-producing solar modules remained high, and National Fabricated Products was unable to realize its ambitions. It was not until the early 1970s, when Exxon's Solar Power Corporation pioneered the mass production of silicon wafers, that the cost of photovoltaic solar cells dropped enough for them to have viable applications outside the military or the space industry.

The first field trials of a modern solar-powered technology designed for sub-Saharan Africa did not take place until 1977, when a French missionary, Bernard Verspieren, installed a water pump in the drought-ridden Sahel. 'Solar power is the answer', Verspieren told people in the village of Nabasso, Mali. 'It will be your salvation. You've seen it, touched it, listened to it – not in a laboratory but in your own backyard' (Perlin 1999: 111).

In the 1980s, the French and US governments funded further trials of solar power across West Africa, financing efforts to deploy their own solar photovoltaic kits to power irrigation systems, community electricity supplies, and communications (e.g. Akrich 1994). In the Global South as in the Global North, photovoltaic technologies allowed policy-makers and planners to imagine a decentralized solar future, with solar energy producing electricity for communities and households at the point of consumption.

During the 1980s and 1990s, these efforts often coincided with structural adjustment policies that rendered the building or expansion of large-scale electricity infrastructures economically unviable. Across the Global South, state energy utilities were restructured or privatized. Meanwhile, post-industrial, green visions of future energy infrastructures turned large-scale grids into ecological problems and championed decentralized or micro-level energy infrastructures. In the mid-1990s, amidst growing recognition that access to energy was critical for many development indicators, attempts to increase access to energy in contexts of international development shifted away from the extension of large-scale public infrastructure for electricity towards support for small-scale renewable energy technologies that generate electricity off the grid. Against this backdrop, international financial institutions led by the World Bank and the International Monetary Fund began to fund projects and programmes aimed at creating consumer markets for renewable energy technologies.

South Asia emerged as a testing ground for policies and business models that aimed at creating new consumer markets for off-grid solar systems. In the 1990s, the World Bank supported solar entrepreneurs in India, Indonesia, and Sri Lanka, setting up small businesses that would allow people to 'sell solar like Coca-Cola', in the expectation that they would have a demonstration effect, revealing a market to future businesses and larger competitors (Miller 2009: 114). By the end of the 1990s, these trends in international development assistance coincided with a transformation of the global solar photovoltaic industry. New developments in the production and manufacturing of photovoltaic materials and the diversification of Taiwanese and Japanese microelectronic companies into the sector saw a dramatic fall in the cost and a dramatic rise in the efficiency of solar cells or modules. As a small-scale technology that could provide decentralized electrical services to individual households or even single appliances, the photovoltaic solar cell proved enormously compatible with neoliberal policies that emphasized the role of the market in the delivery of energy services to people living off the grid (Jacobson 2007: 145-6).

Since the 1950s, the catalogue of photovoltaic appliances designed to do good in places with no or limited access to electricity has expanded exponentially. Alongside solar-powered water pumps, you can now find solar-powered desalination systems and purification kits; solar-powered medical packs, diagnostic devices, and vaccine refrigerators; and solar-powered chargers, mobile phones, and routers. Out of all this burgeoning solar array, it is the simple solar lantern that has become the most ubiquitous application for solar energy off the grid in the Global South.

Like the clean charcoal described by Andrew Walsh or the wind infrastructure project described by Cymene Howe in their contributions to this volume, the solar lantern has been designed with an expansive, even all-encompassing, capacity to care. This small-scale solar technology has reworked the connections between electricity and human life, tying solar power to new biopolitical projects of governance and reform in the Global South (Boyer 2011; Gupta 2015; Szeman 2014). Solar-powered lanterns designed in the United States, manufactured in China, and distributed in rural India or post-earthquake Haiti, for example, are celebrated for simultaneously delivering cheap and clean energy,

*Journal of the Royal Anthropological Institute (N.S.), 47-66*
© Royal Anthropological Institute 2019

safeguarding health, reducing carbon emissions, improving educational outcomes, and fostering economic productivity. Across sub-Saharan Africa and South Asia, these small solar objects fuse ecological, social, and economic imperatives, mandates of sustainability, and mantras of growth and gain.

Like other kinds of small-scale devices designed and built for people living in conditions of global poverty (Collier *et al.* 2018; Cross 2013), solar-powered lanterns emerged as a response to the perceived failures of states to care for or safeguard the health of their populations. In places where large-scale infrastructures for the delivery of energy do not reach or have collapsed, they are designed to provide a minimalist level of care (Redfield 2012). Access to a solar lantern – a small portable solar lighting device comprised of a solar photovoltaic cell, batteries, and LEDs (light-emitting diodes), often with mobile phone charging capabilities – has become the most basic measure of life with electricity. Under the auspices of the UN's Sustainable Development Goals, policy-makers have revised measurements and indices of poverty to accommodate the view that modern, efficient forms of electricity are essential for human well-being (Cross 2018). Electric illumination, equivalent to that provided by a solar-powered lantern, is now an internationally agreed minimum level of access to 'modern energy services' (Cross 2018). Such definitions have made small portable solar-powered devices a vital part of emergency responses to humanitarian crisis; mandating governments, international agencies, and solar companies to make them available to people as part of post-disaster relief efforts as well as to people living in chronic global poverty.

As they respond to human need by distributing solar technology, many organizations find themselves striving to strike the right balance between the gift of humanitarian assistance and the logic of market exchange. In April 2015, for example, the US agency Mercy Corp distributed 10,000 solar lanterns to families affected by a series of earthquakes that struck Nepal, adding solar lanterns to its critical basic non-food relief item kits. Mercy Corp determined that this was exactly the kind of crisis in which the short-term free distribution of energy technologies was needed and appropriate. In the aftermath, Mercy Corp created guidance for other programme teams responding to people's basic energy needs in acute emergencies. Its position on the relationship between energy, safety, health, and well-being in emergencies was summarized succinctly in the title of a report documenting the lessons of its intervention, 'With light there is more life'. As the report stated:

> In emergency response contexts, we must strike a balance between maintaining the core humanitarian principles and taking measures to not undermine the long term stability of clean energy markets by flooding healthy markets with free or heavily subsidised goods. This requires taking a nuanced approach to defining our humanitarian context, assessing market availability of goods and services, and choosing appropriate response mechanisms (e.g. results based financing agreements with local banks, government, or private sector, direct cash transfers to households, vouchers through local vendors, distributions of food or non-food items etc.) (Dworschak & Kleiman 2016: 5)

The design and distribution of solar-powered lanterns for the 'un-electrified poor' has seen technical support, start-up capital, equity investment, and grants flow into social enterprises from social investment funds and international development organizations. Between 2016 and 2018, off-grid solar companies operating in South Asia and sub-Saharan Africa raised $US500 million in investment to sell products ranging from small solar-powered lanterns and mobile charging devices to solar home systems capable of powering televisions and fans (World Bank/Dalberg 2018).

How are we to apprehend the good in these solar goods? In many respects, the social lives of solar goods in the Global South reproduce familiar stories of technological or commodity fetishism. Coming to the solar industry afresh, cynics might be forgiven for the suspicion that 'there is nothing new under the sun'. But, as Joel Robbins (2013) reminds us, there are other ways to think about 'the good' in 'the solar good'.

What would an anthropology of the good look like when it encounters the work of ecologically minded humanitarian capitalists? What might an anthropology of the good mean when it encounters a green, humanitarian ethic attached to the commodity form? And what might it mean to pursue an anthropology of the good in this double sense, by focusing both on the attempts by people to fashion and pursue the good in their practices of care for others and on the ways that these ideals are inscribed or materialized in a mass-produced commodity?

In the following sections, I explore these questions in two different locations: first, on the floor of a global trade fair for the off-grid solar industry held in Dubai, United Arab Emirates; and, second, on the floor of an off-grid solar sales company in Hyderabad, India. These two field settings offer insight into the ways that people located within the solar industry express their ethical commitments and work to establish the commensurability of 'doing well' and 'doing good'.

### Perpetual sunlight

In November 2015, I travelled to Dubai to attend an international trade conference organized by the Global Off-Grid Lighting Association (GOGLA), a body established to promote the interests of solar lighting companies in sub-Saharan Africa and South Asia. The growth of the off-grid solar lighting business in sub-Saharan Africa and South Asia has been reflected in the association's increased membership and prominence. The first meeting was held in a Senegal hotel in 2008. 'At that time if we sold 1,000 units that was a big deal', the co-founder of d.light, a leading off-grid solar company, told delegates. 'Back then there were just a few of us. Nobody really'. Seven years and four annual meetings later his company boasted sales of 6 million units, and the annual trade event occupied a suite of gigantic conference rooms across the Dubai World Trade Centre. The change in the off-grid solar industry's profile was signalled not just by the venue but also by the delegate list, which included the chief executives of global oil companies and government ministers. As d.light's co-founder put it in his opening address, 'Now, policy-makers are using our language'.

The trade fair took place in a vast hall at the end of a gigantic plaza packed with pizza parlours and sandwich and coffee joints. Entering the solar industry event meant leaving the plaza – with its shopping malls, t-shirts, and jeans – and entering a world that brought together global finance and solar humanitarianism. By contrast with the plaza beyond, the global off-grid lighting event was a sober affair, the challenges of global energy poverty both serious and contained, kept within the confines of its pre-booked hall, out of sight.

The venue was carefully choreographed to facilitate business. Unobtrusively placed white leather sofas allowed participants to conduct out-of-session discussions, sharing corporate gossip, investment success opportunities, broker potential partnerships and launch products. People worked on laptops, tablets, or phones or threw themselves into performances of entrepreneurialism, with ostentatious and self-conscious finger-clicking eureka moments. The event was dominated by young, white, English-speaking men, many with MBAs or graduate degrees in international development, who had founded off-grid solar companies, or were employed as industry analysts and financiers. Collectively, they worked the crowds, establishing themselves as leaders of this, the golden age of solar photovoltaics.

Some noticed my University of Edinburgh name badge and introduced themselves. Two men remembered their days as students in Edinburgh, where they had taken introductory classes in social anthropology before becoming, respectively, a lawyer and a financial broker. One had joined a firm working in the carbon-offset market with trading offices in Nairobi, the other a company with mining interests in Mozambique and Tanzania. Both were looking to get a foothold in sub-Saharan Africa's emerging off-grid solar industry, seeking out contacts and links.

If these delegates imagined market exchange as a natural, universal, trans-historical, and trans-cultural relationship, they did not assume that markets themselves were a given. Instead, many delegates appeared to share the view – familiar to economic anthropologists and sociologists – that markets must be made (e.g. Callon 2007; Callon, Meadel & Rabeharisoa 2002; Callon, Millo & Muniesa 2007; Foster 2007; Mackenzie 2007). To this end, the conference was resolutely focused on the practicality and materiality of market making. Across panels and roundtable sessions, the conference delegates reflected on the role of government regulation, business models, product standards, consumer warranties, market research data, and mobile phones as 'market devices' (Callon 2007): that is, as material technologies which, in their operation and use, had a role in making and expanding markets for off-grid solar technology in the Global South.

Even the most basic or entry-level solar-powered lamp – like those distributed as a humanitarian response to crisis or sold as a replacement for kerosene-fuelled lighting – had a part to play, inviting consumers into the solar industry's consumer economy. As one industry analyst put it to me, 'Eradicating kerosene is just the first step. Solar energy – decentralized power – allows people to leapfrog the grid, and as you get an ecosystem of products available, the market can really unlock'. As another industry analyst explained, 'If you want to face the harsh economies of competition, you've got to go multi-appliance. There is lots of opportunity to capitalize on the sun'.

The conference formally opened with a short film that showcased the solar industry's values and impact.

The film was produced by the World Bank's International Finance Corporation and told the story of two young girls: 'Anisha from India' and 'Adina from Nigeria'. Watching it on the big screen, I was struck by a parallel with the oil industry. Big oil companies often open annual meetings or trade events with films that highlight their investments in renewable energy or corporate social responsibility – films that display their commitments to social values – before turning to focus on their investments in and returns from fossil fuel (e.g. Appel, Mason & Watts 2015). For a moment, I was taken aback to see a similar film at a solar industry conference, where I assumed all delegates were familiar with the 'social story' of solar. But over the next few days, I came to see that it was incumbent upon solar industry executives to showcase their social and moral commitments before getting down to business. By reiterating the industry's ethical commitments and reinscribing these in its most iconic technology, the film established the parameters of the event, offering a unifying theme and a common message to the participants. 'From these films', one of the speakers told the gathering, 'we get a glimpse of what it is like to have solar-powered light … education … health … the ability to lead productive lives … jobs … it is about much more than light'.

The symbolism of these solar stories reworks the associations between electricity and human life, like those discussed in the previous section. Solar-powered lighting systems are presented as a palliative for people living in chronic energy poverty: a technological fix that will offer relief from darkness and improvements in the quality of life. Moving around the conference floor, I rubbed up against what Bhrigupati Singh has called the 'confident solar assumptions of modernizing scientific educators': people who like to pronounce on the significance of the candle, or the flame or the lamp in the darkness, and whose words express the kinds of 'Victorian physics' and pedagogic moralities that are 'etched into modernity' (Singh 2015: 294). Over four days in Dubai, I listened to solar entrepreneurs hold forth on the inevitable upward movement of the global poor from 'less' to 'more' sophisticated technologies. These transitions from fuel wood, dung, and crop waste to solar power, they argued, in speeches and PowerPoint presentations, would drive incremental gains in household income, well-being, and 'social development'. Across genres of corporate writing about solar energy – from the press releases put out by companies and social enterprises to the good news stories written by technology, business, and environmental journalists – the same tropes, assumptions, and utopian aspirations appear. Here, solar energy constitutes an unblemished form of the good. Similar sentiments can be heard around other interventions in low-carbon energy and development, like the green charcoal projects in Madagascar described by Walsh (this volume).

The conference's opening film reiterated these ethical credentials and, in doing so, also neutralized any moral ambiguities or critiques about money making in contexts of chronic global poverty. The film screening was followed by a keynote address by the Nobel peace prize winner and microfinance champion Muhammad Yunus.

'How can solar technology flow to where it didn't flow before?', Yunus asked the audience in a recorded video statement. 'I invite you, the off-the-grid movement, to think about doing it as a social business, without making any money out of it', he said.

His speech received warm applause. Yet far from presenting the assembled entrepreneurs with a moral quandary – 'how to do good without doing well' – Yunus's invitation was politely ignored. After his speech, many people in the audience muttered about the irony of his words, given how much money he was reputed to have been paid to deliver them. Instead, the words of Bill Gates appeared to provide a stronger inspiration and intellectual scaffold for action. If there was an implicit moral message to the conference, it was that it was acceptable, appropriate, and necessary to do good by doing well.

In the plenaries that followed, speaker after speaker from international financial institutions, governments, and oil companies gave the gathered solar entrepreneurs a 'green light' to do business. Some made the moral case with facts and figures, detailing the numbers of people living at different tiers of access to modern forms of energy.

A director of the GOGLA, for example, gestured to the industry's grand ambitions. 'Markets for solar energy in the Global South are not just confined to people who live off the grid', he told the assembled guests. 'We're not just talking about the 1.2 billion people with no access to electricity. We're also talking about the 1 billion people with only partial access to electricity'.

Some outlined the moral imperative in personal terms, with stories of their own experience of worlds without electricity. A senior executive from the French oil company Total, for example, described his grandfather's life without electric light in the Netherlands during the 1930s. A senior head of marketing for the multinational lighting company Philips described his father's life as a 'country boy', growing up without electric power in the Midwestern United States. And a senior representative from the World Bank, a high-caste Indian woman, described her childhood in Mumbai. 'The best sound of my childhood was the sound of the fan coming back on after a power cut', she said. 'When the electricity was off, we had to study by the headlights of our car, and we were the rich ones. We could only imagine what life was like for the poor'.

Other speakers made the moral case for market action a response to broken public infrastructures. 'Where infrastructure is failing or insufficient or non-existent, we need to encourage innovative alternatives, rooted in commercial models, rooted in the scalability and viability of the private sector and private sector capital', the vice-president of the World Bank's International Finance Corporation told the audience'. The UK Minister for International Development told the gathering that it was 'unimaginable to speak of development without energy'. 'But accelerating sustainable access to energy in the developing world needs competition', he said. 'That is the future: a race, village to village, as commercial companies compete to supply energy to people'.

On the main stage and in off-stage discussions, conference delegates largely cleaved to this ordering narrative in which market actors and solutions were unquestionably successful. Occasionally, however, there was whispered ambivalence at this collective social and technical imaginary from the sidelines.

During one coffee break, I was buttonholed by a smartly dressed, middle-aged Indian man, the senior manager for a major global social investment fund. My interlocutor had flown into the conference from Mumbai for just one day.

'I'm here to keep my ear to the ground', he said. 'My first teacher was Mozi', referring to the Chinese philosopher who lived in the fourth century BCE. 'Just listen, Mo Tzu taught. I'm here to listen'. But he also had questions.

'Does more light really improve people's lives?', he asked me. 'Come on! You're the social anthropologist. Does a solar light really bring development? Does it really improve well-being? Does it really make people happy? Can we prove it?'

He paused. 'That's what we really need to know. Because that's how we can attract money!'

Like Bill Gates, the social entrepreneurs or humanitarian capitalists circulating around the solar industry make an ethic of care for distant others a core business proposition. They make market exchange the 'source and circumference' of what it means to do good. And they perform as moral actors through a commitment to market-driven systems of mass production and consumption.

If the proper and heroic job of the capitalist entrepreneur is to match supply to unmet wants and desires, the proper and heroic job of these social or humanitarian capitalists is to match supply to unmet needs. In the following section, I explore how the performance of these market moralities plays out on the floor of a solar distribution company in India.

## Selling in the dark

The rickshaw bounced over a collapsing road in a leafy Hyderabad suburb and dropped me at a nondescript three-storey building in a quiet lot. The young rickshaw driver asked me with a smile if I had come to see Mahesh Babu, a Telugu film star who lived in the area, but I was looking for a solar lighting company. The driver looked up at the shoddy façade.

'Brother, are you sure this is the place?', he asked.

I was not sure. There were no signs on the gate and the courtyard was deserted. A guard, hanging about in the forecourt, pointed me towards the stairwell. I walked up the stairs behind a fruit salesman, laden with papaya. On the first floor, a Brahmin woman, *tilak* on her forehead, opened her front door to the fruit salesman. When I asked her, in my politest Telugu, where the solar energy company was, she told me to go away with a flick of her hand.

On the top floor, I rang an unmarked buzzer on an unmarked wooden door and hoped for the best. The door was opened by a beaming young European man. He ushered me over the threshold, bouncing across the marble floor in shorts and bare feet, his t-shirt the colour of iridescent sunlight. I had come to the right place. This was the Hyderabad office of a company I will call Radiate Energy, an international social enterprise that was making a name for itself by selling solar lanterns to India's urban poor.

In the 2010s, small solar lighting devices had become market leaders for a new kind of company in India, one whose core business was the sale of small, durable consumer goods to rural and urban consumers under the rubric of development. Selling solar in India involves new kinds of practices, strategies, and organizational collaborations. The sale of solar lighting systems has allowed distributors and salespeople to acquire new knowledge about the aspirations of consumers, to test new sales strategies, and to develop new market strategies. As one of the directors of Radiate Energy put it, 'We're good at solar lights. We know how to sell them'.

On the third floor of the suburban apartment, an open-plan living area had been converted into a makeshift distribution centre. Cardboard boxes full of solar lanterns ordered direct from the manufacturer were stacked against doorframes. Bright yellow motivational posters were taped onto white walls. 'Stop being afraid of what could go wrong, think of what could go right', they read. Or, 'It always seems impossible until it's done – Nelson Mandela'. On a desk lay a stack of corporate brochures, newsletters, a calendar, and a profile piece published in a regional newspaper, 'Lighting the urban slums'.

Radiate Energy's operations in Hyderabad were set up by two young European men whom I will call Guy and Logan. Guy and Logan share much with a generation of global social entrepreneurs. Aged in their late twenties, with graduate degrees in business and law from internationally recognized universities, they were driven by a desire to do good in the world while navigating through a graduate labour market characterized by its precariousness and a post-neoliberal transformation in the arena of international development. 'We just hit sales of 10,000 solar lanterns in India', Guy told me.

> We could have given away those lights. But we sold them. And if I can sell one, I can sell another. We could sell another 10k here. In the long term, selling solar lights is more sustainable than charity. And our generation are looking for ways that you can do that and make money on the side. Everyone is talking about social entrepreneurship. It's become sexy. It's become cool.

*Journal of the Royal Anthropological Institute (N.S.), 47-66*
© Royal Anthropological Institute 2019

Radiate Energy had been operating a successful venture in another South Indian city for two years. Guy and Logan had flown into Hyderabad with the aim of opening a new office and creating a new market for solar lanterns amongst the city's urban poor. Their target customers were people living in the city's informal and irregular housing settlements. But they arrived with a very limited knowledge of the city's geography or demographics. Neither of them had visited Hyderabad before, neither of them spoke Telugu, and they had few if any local contacts.

The company's business model was simple: recruit a network of young local people and train them to become sales agents, selling door-to-door in poor urban communities. The move to Hyderabad was the company's first attempt to scale up its business model in India and, when I first visited, it had been there for eight months. Logan explained how he and Guy began.

> From the beginning, we knew that just because our strategy had worked in one Indian city, that didn't mean it was going to work here too. We knew that we had to be flexible. We knew we had to adapt locally. We knew that every Indian city was different, that populations are different, that the labour markets are different. Basically, we were creating the process from scratch.

On the day Guy and Logan flew into Hyderabad for the first time, they began fixing up meetings with companies, NGOs, and other social enterprises in the city, introducing themselves and the company, and mapping the institutional landscape. Within two weeks they had rented and furnished an apartment, which doubled up as their home and their office space. Over the next fortnight, they turned themselves to the challenge of mapping potential markets onto the city's social and economic geography. One of their early moves was to approach Hyderabad's municipal corporation, the urban planning authorities, and ask for access to detailed maps of the city. This proved unsuccessful, an outcome that they blamed on the corruption of Indian officials. Instead, they found a novel work-around solution.

The company does not just sell solar light to the poor. It also packages and sells a social impact experience to a market of students, young professionals, and budding entrepreneurs in the United Kingdom and Europe, North America and Australia, as well as in India. These market internships offer a social impact experience or intensive training programme that provides a hands-on experience. Within a month of their arrival in Hyderabad, Guy and Logan hosted the first month-long impact experience programme. Their first intake included ten people whom they categorized simply as 'internationals', with differential fee rates depending on their country of origin, and six Indians.

This team helped to set up the office, painting walls and varnishing tables, and also helped to establish Radiate Energy's city strategy. Charged with mapping the city's solar markets, the first group of interns came up with an alternative strategy. Opening up laptops, they pored over Google's satellite imagery of Hyderabad, scrolling over the city, identifying potential bottom-of-the-pyramid urban markets based on a typology of roofing material. They were looking for blue tarpaulins, which the organization's managers associated with the presence of un-electrified informal settlements; what some civil planners and activists in India call 'slums', but what this organization called 'tents'. 'Yes! Just on the basis of what a roof looks like we can identify our target bottom-of-the-pyramid solar market', Guy told me with pride.

Identifying the communities on the ground was, of course, a much more complicated operation. Once a location had been identified from Google's satellite imagery, Radiate

Energy sent a team on what it called 'verification' trips. These teams comprised both Indian and non-Indian team members. The international composition was deemed particularly important. 'Having a white face is a simple weapon for entrepreneurs entering communities', Logan told me. The two managers wrestled with the implications of this strategy, at one point introducing all-Telugu teams, but they eventually made the mobilization of 'internationals' into a key part of their work.

Before heading off into the city by bus or on foot, the team downloaded a set of co-ordinates from Google Maps and uploaded them onto a smartphone mapping application that could be used off-line and without mobile reception. These preliminary visits were intended as 'baseline surveys' that would give a broad-brush picture of market demographics and income. Each team had a form to complete, again using their smartphone, in which they would 'name the community', give the 'number of tents', and provide details of community 'access to water and electricity'. As Guy and Logan acknowledged, this was an imperfect and, at times, wholly subjective method. There was a time delay between the acquisition of the satellite imagery and the field trips. Sometimes people discovered that there was no tented community at all or that blue tarpaulins had been erected over open spaces for public functions, ceremonies, or festivals rather than above informal settlements. Meanwhile, the organization discovered the limits to its data collection capacities. 'If the community is very big, with more than 200 people, then it is very difficult and our database is not very clean. We ask our teams to keep updating the numbers. It's not a precise science', Logan admitted.

With little or no information about these locations from the civic authorities or from the communities themselves, the teams assigned their own names. When they looked over the map on a laptop in the company's office, the cartography of Hyderabad's squatter settlements that they produced read more like a work of psycho-geography than an exercise in participatory mapping. I traced my finger across the new chart of the Telugu capital, tracing the experiences of the map makers: 'The Descent', 'The Valley', 'Pellets', 'Train Junction', 'Smelly Stream', 'Pride Rock', 'Shepherd'.

By the end of February 2015, Radiate Energy had mapped and validated 400 communities across Hyderabad. Over eight months, this combination of remote mapping exercises and first-person visits had allowed the company to build up its own grid of communities or markets across Hyderabad, dividing the city's temporary migrant communities and longer-term squatter settlements on the basis of whether or not they had access to mains electricity and the number of 'tents'. 'Somewhere between 600 and 800 tents feels like the right market to start with, but we might cut the community differently', Logan said.

When a team made it into one of these communities, the moment of sale involved a slow set-up. In pre-visit briefings, team members were taught not to introduce themselves as salespeople or even to mention solar lanterns on their initial entry. 'A good salesperson does not even show the solar light on the first visit', people were taught. Instead, the sales representatives were coached to introduce themselves as 'working for an organization that wants to help people' and use this to initiate conversations about people's living conditions. These early visits were described as a 'way of getting a feel for the market'. As Guy and Logan put it, during training sessions for new salespeople, knowing when the moment of sale had arrived was a skill acquired through practice and patience. 'For that first sale you have to use your gut feeling. You have to think, is this person going to be a reliable customer?'

*Journal of the Royal Anthropological Institute (N.S.), 47-66*
© Royal Anthropological Institute 2019

On the streets of Hyderabad's squatter settlements, the unique qualities or affordances of the solar lantern allowed it to be sold in particular ways. As one of Radiate Energy's sales team put it:

> You can sell a solar light at night, you call sell it in the darkness. At night, people can actually see what it does. You can see it immediately. Kerosene lanterns are smoky and dirty. But if you come in with a solar light, people can see there is something in it. People can see that solar light fixes the problem immediately. They can see the change in front of their eyes as soon as the light is turned on. You can't see that with any other products. In fact I don't know any other product where you can see the change. Try selling a water filter. You put water in the filter, four hours later it comes out and it looks more or less the same. The water might have been filtered but you can't see it!

In such everyday interactions, as solar entrepreneurs work to create markets for their goods in places of global poverty, the pursuit of 'solar goods' subtly reproduces modes of relational power and differential authority. On the ground, the distribution of solar goods involves a moment of encounter between people who occupy radically different positions of wealth and poverty, caste and class. Salespeople reassert and entrench these socioeconomic differences by asserting their superior, expert knowledge of technology, and by drawing on local idioms of language, style, and dress to make a sale. As they do so, selling solar re-inscribes forms of class inequality and vernacular caste prejudice into the market economy (Cross 2019).

### Solar utopias and beyond

Just as life with climate change is creating new anxieties and compulsions, so, too, it is creating new ethical elisions, horizons, and commitments. Across both the locations presented above – an investment forum for the solar industry and the offices of a solar enterprise – we can discern a kind of collective refusal of 'structural pessimism' about climate change. To listen to the chief executives, chief technical officers, sales executives, and regional managers of solar companies is to hear the outlines of a politics of hope, founded in the promise of solar energy. 'The solar light is a means of communication', the founder of one solar lantern company told me.

> It is a means of communication through something that actually contributes to the solution. It helps people to imagine that solutions are possible, because they just have it in their hands and because it is very simple ... It's communicating, conveying a message, that renewable energy is available and can help right away, that by just pushing a button you can tap into the power of the sun. It makes people feel that they are, albeit on a small scale, actually and effectively co-operating to make change happen. And people really like that.

Such visions of the solar good are both pre-figurative and pastoral. They grant small-scale solar energy technologies a decisive role in materializing a low-carbon future. And they suggest the possibility of a pure, unmediated relationship to sunlight. In these visions, the technology that converts sunlight into electricity fades into the background, doing invisible work, and the mass production and consumption of solar power take place without contradictions.

How are we to engage with attempts to do well by doing good at the intersection of climate change and chronic energy poverty? How do people come to see the marketing and distribution of small-scale solar technology as, simultaneously, an engine of corporate value, a means of alleviating suffering, and a solution to ecological crisis? As Didier Fassin might put it, the only way to 'grasp the logics and the assumptions, the ambiguities and the contradictions, the principles of justice and the practices of judgment' (2012: 13) that come together in the solar industry is to explore them head-on: examining the pursuit of solar goods in relation to capitalist political economy. This essay has outlined the beginnings of such a task, following ethical projects, logics, assumptions, principles, and practices that are articulated by entrepreneurs and executives in the off-grid solar industry.

Doing so reveals how ecological-economic utopias hinge upon what Fredric Jameson has called a 'dialectic of identity and difference' (2005: 170). Solar entrepreneurs promise a world that is radically different from this one, but not so radically different as to be unimaginable. Utopian visions of a global solar future present a world that is liberated from twentieth-century commitments to fossil fuels, a world without kerosene or energy poverty. But it is a future that remains tethered to the systems of production and exchange, ownership and property, and relations of power and exchange that are defining features of the contemporary capitalist economy. In this sense, the utopian conditions of possibility are premised upon an identity with the present.

Such commitments are not universally shared, even by solar advocates. Anti-capitalist social and environmental activists who promote bottom-up or community-based solar development projects, for example, map other pathways to environmental justice and social equity. These pathways are defined by notions of a 'solar commons' and of collectively owned and managed resources. Yet such projects are no less utopian. The contours of these alternative solar futures are also rooted in a 'dialectic of identity and difference', tethered by actually existing and idealized forms of community, non-hierarchical exchange, and horizontal organization.

As people seek to bring about rapid social and economic transitions to a low-carbon or post-carbon economy, they make pragmatic decisions and choices, evaluating the trade-offs between outcomes. As one of the original reviewers of this essay wrote,

> The need to transition to lower-carbon fuels is in fact critical for many different reasons, climate change and human health among them, and being somewhat flip about market efforts doesn't change that – while it would be nice to see more non-profit effort, I think that we need as many different kinds of efforts toward energy transition as possible.

Many readers may agree. Yet the question is not whether markets are good or bad but rather what it means for our energy ethics when it is almost impossible to imagine a future without them. In the off-grid solar industry, for example, markets provide a total moral scaffold for action: the source and circumference of what it means to do good. Such an insight offers grounds for an anthropological understanding of ethics in practice. But the production of anthropological knowledge need not be our only endpoint. Understanding the grounds upon which interlocutors in the solar industry seek to act ethically can also be the starting point for an ethnographically informed ethics of engagement with solar corporations, solar entrepreneurship, solar supply chains, and solar goods that seeks to foster a more just solar economy through critical analysis, design, and advocacy. After all, what hope is there if – for all the stellar talk – the ethical trajectories of solar power in the twenty-first century fail to escape the orbit of the Capitalocene?

ACKNOWLEDGEMENTS

Sections from this essay have been variously presented at the University of Copenhagen, the University of Witwatersrand, and the University of Edinburgh. Thanks to Mette High, Jessica Smith, Alice Street, Peter Redfield, Sharad Chari, Toby Kelly, and Tom Neumark and the anonymous reviewers for comments on previous versions of the text. The fieldwork on which this essay is based has been funded by the Leverhulme Trust, the Economic and Social Research Council, and the Engineering and Physical Sciences Research Council.

## REFERENCES

AKRICH, M. 1994. The de-scription of technical objects. In *Shaping technology/building society: studies in sociotechnical change* (eds) W.W. Bijmer & J. Law, 205-24. Cambridge, Mass.: MIT Press.

APPEL, H., A. MASON & M. WATTS (eds) 2015. *Subterranean estates: life worlds of oil and gas.* Ithaca, N.Y.: Cornell University Press.

ARGENTI, N. & D.M. KNIGHT 2015. Sun, wind, and the rebirth of extractive economies: renewable energy investment and metanarratives of crisis in Greece. *Journal of the Royal Anthropological Institute* (N.S.) **21**, 781-802.

BAZILIAN, M.D. 2018. The mineral foundation of the energy transition. *The Extractive Industries and Society* **5**, 93-7.

BENIOFF, M. & K. SOUTHWICK 2004. *Compassionate capitalism: how corporations can make doing good an integral part of doing well.* Franklin Lakes, N.J.: The Career Press.

BENSON, P. & S. KIRSCH 2010. Corporate oxymorons. *Dialectical Anthropology* **34**, 45-8.

BISHOP, M. & M. GREEN 2008. *Philanthrocapitalism: how giving can save the world.* New York: Bloomsbury.

BORNSTEIN, E. & P. REDFIELD (eds) 2011. *Forces of compassion: humanitarianism between ethics and politics.* Santa Fe, N.M.: School for Advanced Research Press.

BOYER, D. 2011. Energopolitics and the anthropology of energy. *Anthropology News* **52: 5**, 5-7.

BUCK-MORSS, S. 2002. *Dreamworld and catastrophe: the passing of mass utopia in East and West.* Cambridge, Mass.: MIT Press.

CALLON, M. 2007. An essay on the growing contribution of economic markets to the proliferation of the social. *Theory, Culture & Society* **24**, 139-63.

———, C. MEADEL & V. RABEHARISOA 2002. The economy of qualities. *Economy and Society* **31**, 194-217.

———, Y. MILLO & F. MUNIESA 2007. An introduction to market devices. *The Sociological Review* **55**, 1-12.

COLEMAN, L. 2017. *A moral technology: electrification as political ritual in New Delhi.* Ithaca, N.Y.: Cornell University Press.

COLLIER, S., J. CROSS, P. REDFIELD & A. STREET 2018. Preface: Little development devices/humanitarian goods. *Limn* **9** (available on-line: *https://limn.it/articles/precis-little-development-devices-humanitarian-goods/*, accessed 9 January 2019).

CROSS, J. 2013. The 100th object: solar lighting technology and humanitarian goods. *Journal of Material Culture* **18**, 367-87.

——— 2014. *Dream zones: anticipating capitalism and development in India.* London: Pluto.

——— 2016a. Current. *South Asia: Journal of South Asian Studies* **40**, 291-3.

——— 2016b. Off the grid: infrastructure and energy beyond the mains. *Infrastructures and social complexity: a companion* (eds) P. Harvey, C.B. Jensen & A. Morita, 186-96. London: Routledge.

——— 2018. Solar basics. *Limn* **9** (available on-line: *https://limn.it/articles/solar-basics/*, accessed 9 January 2019).

——— 2019. Selling with prejudice: social enterprise and caste at the bottom of the pyramid in India. *Ethnos* **84: 2**, 78-96.

———, M. DOUGLAS, C. MARTIN, C. RAY & A. VERHOEVEN 2018. *Energy and forced displacement in eight objects: stories from sub-Saharan Africa.* London: Chatham House.

——— & D. MURRAY 2018. The afterlives of solar power: waste and repair off the grid in Kenya. *Energy Research & Social Science* **44**, 100-9.

——— & A. STREET 2009. Anthropology at the bottom of the pyramid. *Anthropology Today* **25: 4**, 4-9.

DELBOURGO, J. 2006. *A most amazing scene of wonders: electricity and enlightenment in early America.* Cambridge, Mass.: Harvard University Press.

DWORSCHAK, A. & S. KLEIMAN 2016. 'With light there is more life': energy access for safety, health and well being in emergencies. *Boiling Point* **68**, 2-5 (available on-line: *https://www.mercycorps.org.uk/sites/default/files/Mercy_Corps_HEDON_Nepal_Earthquake_Response_and_Energy_Access.pdf*, accessed 9 January 2019).

ELYACHAR, J. 2012. Next practices: knowledge, infrastructure, and public goods at the bottom of the pyramid. *Public Culture* **24**, 109-30.

ESCOBAR, A. 2011. *Encountering development: the making and unmaking of the Third World*. Princeton: University Press.

FASSIN, D. 2012. *Humanitarian reason: A moral history of the present*. Berkeley: University of California Press.

FERGUSON, J. 1990. *The anti-politics machine: 'development', depoliticization and bureaucratic power in Lesotho*. Cambridge: University Press.

FOSTER, R.J. 2007. The work of the new economy: consumers, brands, and value creation. *Cultural Anthropology* **22**, 707-31.

GATES, B. 2008. How to fix capitalism. *Time*, 11 August, 26-31.

GRAEBER, D. 2013. *The democracy project: a history, a crisis, a movement*. London: Penguin.

GUPTA, A. 2015. An anthropology of electricity from the Global South. *Cultural Anthropology* **30**, 555-68.

HARAWAY, D. 2015. Anthropocene, Capitalocene, Plantationocene, Chthulucene: making kin. *Environmental Humanities* **6**, 159-65.

HOWE, C. 2014. Anthropocenic ecoauthority: the winds of Oaxaca. *Anthropological Quarterly* **87**, 381-404.

——— & D. BOYER 2016. Aeolian extractivism and community wind in southern Mexico. *Public Culture* **28**, 215-35.

JACOBSON, A. 2007. Connective power: solar electrification and social change in Kenya. *World Development* **35**, 144-62.

JAMESON, F. 2005. *Archaeologies of the future: the desire called utopia and other science fictions*. London: Verso.

KIRSCH, S. 2018. *Engaged anthropology: politics beyond the text*. Berkeley: University of California Press.

LAIDLAW, J. 2002. For an anthropology of ethics and freedom. *Journal of the Royal Anthropological Institute* (N.S.) **8**, 311-32.

——— 2013. *The subject of virtue: an anthropology of ethics and freedom*. Cambridge: University Press.

LAMBEK, M. (ed.) 2010. *Ordinary ethics: anthropology, language, and action*. New York: Fordham University Press.

LEPAWSKY, J. 2018. *Reassembling rubbish: worlding electronic waste*. Cambridge, Mass.: MIT Press.

LI, T.M. 2007. *The will to improve: governmentality, development, and the practice of politics*. Durham, N.C.: Duke University Press.

MACKENZIE, D.A. 2007. *An engine, not a camera: how financial models shape markets*. Cambridge, Mass.: MIT Press.

MILLER, D. 2012. *Selling solar: the diffusion of renewable energy in emerging markets*. London: Routledge.

MIYAZAKI, H. 2006. Economy of dreams: hope in global capitalism and its critiques. *Cultural Anthropology* **21**, 147-72.

MOORE, J.W. 2015. *Capitalism in the web of life: ecology and the accumulation of capital*. London: Verso.

MORTON, T. 2018. *Being ecological*. London: Penguin.

NEWELL, P. & D. MULVANEY 2013. The political economy of the 'just transition'. *The Geographical Journal* **179**, 132-40.

NGAI, P. 2005. *Made in China: women factory workers in a global workplace*. Durham, N.C.: Duke University Press.

NYE, D.E. 1990. *Electrifying America: social meanings of a new technology, 1880-1940*. Cambridge, Mass.: MIT Press.

PERLIN, J. 1999. *From space to earth: the story of solar electricity*. London: Earthscan.

REDFIELD, P. 2012. Bioexpectations: life technologies as humanitarian goods. *Public Culture* **24**, 157-84.

REVETTE, A.C. 2017. This time it's different: lithium extraction, cultural politics and development in Bolivia. *Third World Quarterly* **38**, 149-68.

ROBBINS, J. 2012. On becoming ethical subjects: freedom, constraint, and the anthropology of morality. *Anthropology of This Century* **5** (available on-line: *http://aotcpress.com/articles/ethical-subjects-freedom-constraint-anthropology-morality/*, accessed 9 January 2019).

——— 2013. Beyond the suffering subject: toward an anthropology of the good. *Journal of the Royal Anthropological Institute* (N.S.) **19**, 447-62.

SCHWITTAY, A. 2011. The marketization of poverty. *Current Anthropology* **52**, S71-82.

SINGH, B. 2015. *Poverty and the quest for life: spiritual and material striving in rural India*. Chicago: University Press.

SIVARAM, V. 2018. *Taming the sun: innovations to harness solar energy and power the planet*. Cambridge, Mass.: MIT Press.

SMITH, J. & M.M. HIGH 2017. Exploring the anthropology of energy: ethnography, energy and ethics. *Energy Research & Social Science* **30**, 1-6.

SZEMAN, I. 2014. Conclusion: On energopolitics. *Anthropological Quarterly* **87**, 453-64.

WORLD BANK/DALBERG 2018. Off-grid solar market trends report 2018 (available on-line: *https://sun-connect-news.org/fileadmin/DATEIEN/Dateien/New/2018_Off_Grid_Solar_Market_Trends_Report_Full.pdf*, accessed 9 January 2019).

ZEHNER, O. 2012. *Green illusions: the dirty secrets of clean energy and the future of environmentalism.* Lincoln: University of Nebraska Press.

## Le bien solaire : éthique énergétique dans les marchés des pays défavorisés

*Résumé*

Quels sont les engagements éthiques de ceux qui conçoivent, construisent et vendent des installations photovoltaïques aux habitants des régions d'Afrique subsaharienne et d'Asie du Sud-Est mal desservies en énergies ? Avec la baisse spectaculaire du coût de l'énergie solaire au cours des dix dernières années, notre capacité accrue de convertir la lumière du soleil en électricité s'est vue intégrée dans des projets de gouvernance, de réforme sociale ou morale, et dans l'expression de notre souci pour les autres qui vivent au loin. En suivant la piste de ces projets dans les stands d'un salon international à Dubaï et au sein d'une entreprise sociale en Inde, l'auteur montre que la poursuite du bien solaire s'articule sur la base connaissable qu'est le capitalisme actuel.

# 3

# Orphaned wells, oil assets, and debt: the competing ethics of value creation and care within petrocapitalist projects of return

C A U R A  W O O D *Independent Scholar*

This essay explores the phenomenon known as 'orphaned wells', meaning unprofitable oil and gas wells ('legacy wells') that have become disentangled from their corporate owners owing to insolvency, or owing to a failure to comply with local regulations. Drawing from an ethnographic example of a near-insolvent oil and gas corporation in Alberta, Canada, and its strategies of refinancing, the essay explores how value creation and the moral force of the obligation to create a financial return give rise to a 'durational ethics' that shapes corporate and financial performativities and prolongs the 'life' of legacy oil and gas assets. Legacy assets, understood as potential orphans, are thus caught up in a lively corporate practice of asset circulation and recombination often deployed by producers for the moral work of 'cleaning balance sheets'. This essay calls for 'thinking with orphans' to recognize the competing ethical registers which produce them in addition to the growing need for responsibility and corporate care for legacy oil and gas assets.

'Why is this even allowed?', I thought, after reading a news story about a bankrupt company named Redwater Energy Corp. The small private company had eighty-four licensed wells in its inventory of Alberta oil and gas assets when its primary lender, ATB, called in its secured loan and put the company into receivership (i.e. bankruptcy) in May 2015, appointing Grant Thornton Limited as Redwater's receiver and trustee.[1] To maximize recoveries to creditors, Grant Thornton Limited then made novel use of the Bankruptcy and Insolvency Act, which it found to be in conflict with Alberta's Oil and Gas Conservation Act, and renounced Redwater's uneconomic wells and pipelines (often called end-of-life assets or legacy assets), while taking possession of only those with economic value (i.e. the 'good' assets).[2] Through this manoeuvre, the receiver intentionally made orphans (i.e. ownerless assets) out of Redwater's uneconomic assets, while also disclaiming the high costs of future asset retirement and environmental clean-up obligations associated with them.[3] Since the receiver's tactics of disclaiming some assets and keeping others broke the rules that normally govern how oil and gas property can transfer, the Alberta Energy Regulator accused the receiver of attempting to avoid the required 'care, custody and abandonment obligations over Redwater's properties', and took the matter to court.[4] The court's decision in 2016 favoured the receiver and was upheld by the Court of Appeal of Alberta in April 2017. Redwater's orphaned assets and their future costs thus became wards of the Orphan Well Association (OWA), an over-burdened non-profit organization funded by industry and charged with the work of decommissioning orphaned wells.[5] The case is now before the Supreme Court of Canada, but unless ruled otherwise, Redwater sets a precedent in Alberta giving the rights and claims of secured lenders priority over the unsecured claims of other creditors and the environmental and asset retirement obligations to the regulator.[6]

While government, industry, and public eyes were following this case for the important and alarming precedent it would set, it also raised a number of anthropological points of interest for me on the intersection of ethics, assets, liabilities, and the everyday practices that my interlocutors refer to as 'value creation' (see Muniesa 2017). As the Redwater case was unfolding, I was working for and doing fieldwork within a small corporation called Challenge Energy that could have been a case just like Redwater.[7] Challenge was on the verge of bankruptcy. The management team were proud of their 'clean' asset base – clean because it comprised mostly new oil and gas wells drilled since 2008 with relatively few end-of-life assets and therefore few associated liabilities for reclamation and environmental clean-up. Yet, to fend off bankruptcy, they elected to 'dirty' the balance sheet. Quite contrary to Redwater, Challenge avoided bankruptcy by adopting legacy assets along with productive assets as an unusual form of 'crisis capital'. By this I mean to say that such an adoption would only make sense in a crisis case where no other form of capital was available (i.e. normative equity finance capital or bank debt financing), and the very use of which, building from Roitman's definition of crisis, 'secures a world' (2013: 39) for capital. In the ethnographic case that I untangle below, Challenge's executives and advisers decided that taking on this form of capital, which they liken to eating excrement, was 'good' because it provided a viable answer to the problem of looming bankruptcy.

In this essay, I propose thinking with orphaned wells as a means to consider the contested ethical constitution of oil and gas resources through the asset form and the care they require. More specifically, I will illustrate that both orphans and assets are outcomes of uncertain processes of petrocapitalist value creation that are situated within projects of return (commonly referred to as the 'shareholder value paradigm' [Ho 2009]). I argue that 'value creation' – the term my interlocutors use to describe what they are doing – is approached by corporate actors as a moral and temporal 'puzzle' (Mattingly 2014: 479) concerning the best courses of action or the best uses of capital to churn out the most value for shareholders.

Muniesa (2017: 445-6) examines the concept of value creation, showing it to be a 'semantic hub' that interrelates the liberal concepts of finance, innovation, and democracy through a justificatory frame that often leads to investor 'disinhibition'. The concept offers a 'shared moral horizon' between investors and entrepreneurs that situates 'value' as generated through the pairing of capital investment with the corporate form. Alignment of vision to these shared purposes is accomplished through the affective stance of an 'investor gaze' (Muniesa et al. 2017: 92-5) that adheres the ideal of a 'free and rational investor' intending to maximize 'the productivity of money' (Muniesa 2017: 448; Ortiz 2014: 39) to the work of attracting and deploying capital expressly to make assets that will produce future returns (Muniesa et al. 2017: 11). Using a broader scan of the moral horizon of a resource scape, Weszkalnys (2016: 127) theorizes a 'resource affect', or the mix of anticipation, transformation, hope, and friction that variously shape the 'affective horizons generated by hydrocarbon exploration', which also includes the state and citizens and not strictly the capital investors. These affective stances are also anticipatory and restless, characterized by seeking to produce particular imagined futures that may result from potential investment (Muniesa 2017; Weszkalnys 2016; Zaloom 2009).

While the moral horizons of resource value creation can be observed as a powerful and legitimating force in the 'ethical worlds' (Appel, this volume) of Alberta's junior oil and gas companies, I argue that more attention needs to be given to the moral temporalities shaped through debt and indebtedness that also shape industry valuations and performativities.[8]

Unlike investors, energy producers – and, indeed, their assets – confront a much longer development time span that is also characterized by responsibility and commitment to providing energy commodities and to cultivating a financial return over time (see also High, Smith, and Cross, this volume). Once a decision is made by a CEO and management team to accept investor capital, they must also commit to the temporality of labouring for that capital (Wood 2015).[9] Over that uncertain duration, management teams carry the moral (but not the contractual) obligation to return the invested capital to shareholders. While shareholders are warned in the prospectus that accompanies such opportunities that they could 'lose all their money', this only protects management teams from legal repercussions. As I will show below, the 'moral hook' of this obligation to capital continues through the weighty local stakes of market reputation that cement successful return to staying in business and obtaining future capital. Further, management teams also carry the stakes that come from having 'skin in the game',[10] meaning personal investment (a point I elaborate on later, but which often also means 'kin in the game'), which ties passionate interests, ethics, and neoliberal ideology quite tightly together.[11] The commitment to labour for others' and one's own capital is a commitment to a moral temporality: to 'stay with it', to persevere, to responsibly steward that capital, and to care about ensuring capital's return. These characteristics are central to what Guyer (2014) refers to as *durational ethics*. I apply her concept here to describe the *affective and productive meantime* between the investment and its return or failed return, which is shaped as much by hope as it is by enduring commitment and responsibility (see Miyazaki 2006; 2013).[12] This is not to suggest that all corporate actors make such commitments evenly. They certainly do not.[13] Rather, it is to include the evaluative work so central to recent definitions of ethics (High & Smith, this volume; Keane 2014; 2016; Laidlaw 2014; Lambek 2011; Muniesa 2017; Ortiz 2013), along with the durational ethics of responsibility and commitment (Guyer 2014) to the constellation of distributed agencies and contingencies (including the technical, the calculative, the regulatory, for example) that perform value creation and produce an uneven landscape of resource development and entitlement to its returns through the materiality of the asset form (Guyer 2014; Richardson & Weszkalnys 2014). With this lens, it also becomes easier to see the importance of debt and relations of indebtedness to oil and gas industry practices, financial arrangements, materialities, and temporalities (Graeber 2011; High 2012; Mitchell 2009; Peebles 2010; Roitman 2003).[14]

As the Challenge case will illustrate, durational ethics make an appearance through the moral and temporal work of cleaning balance sheets. Yet the investor gaze, shaped through the durational ethics of value creation and indebtedness, often results in the perpetual circulation of legacy assets, which, under conditions of bankruptcy, could produce more orphans in need of care. Thus orphans refract our gaze, reminding us

*Journal of the Royal Anthropological Institute (N.S.), 67-90*
© Royal Anthropological Institute 2019

that the ethics of value creation often collide with those of asset care, and so both are also political (Barry 2013; Fassin 2015; Guyer 2014; Muniesa 2017; Muniesa *et al.* 2017).

### Thinking with orphans

Before turning to the ethnographic case of Challenge Energy, I will briefly elaborate on the ethical framing of orphans, those alleged by the Redwater plaintiffs to be 'legitimate' and 'illegitimate', and which cast in relief the normative world of assets that are mobilized by Alberta's junior oil and gas corporations and their balance sheets.

First, the term 'orphan' refers to displacement and, typically, loss of parental kin. According to *Merriam-Webster*, an orphan is defined as 'a child deprived by death of one or usually both parents'; 'a young animal that has lost its mother'; or 'one deprived of some protection or advantage'.[15] The term invokes abandonment – possibly even rejection – vulnerability, and the need for care and placement. While assets are not kin per se, the definitional and relational link between a responsible party and one needing care and the legal status of corporations as persons points us and the plaintiffs to the Redwater case (see below) to stretch the analogy to a corporation's assets. The OWA defines an upstream oil and gas industry orphan as a 'well, pipeline, facility or associated site which has been investigated [by the regulator] and confirmed as not having any legally responsible and/or financially able party to deal with its abandonment and reclamation responsibilities'.[16] Orphans, as ownerless assets of now defunct or insolvent corporations, thus point us to how things *should* be, in the normative sense. Orphans were once productive assets: that is, sites of corporate value or that came into being through the pairing of investor capital and corporate performativities to convert expert knowledge and geological reservoirs into sites of extraction (called 'locations', 'properties', or 'wellsites' by industry) that return hydrocarbons and cash flow over time (Mason, this volume; Muniesa *et al.* 2017: 1-20; Wood 2016).[17] In other words, productive assets are like a child who is dependent on a parent who is responsible for his or her maintenance and care.

A point often overlooked in anthropology is that corporate assets are quite different from commodities and normally entangled in longer-term relations of obligatory care and responsibility. Corporate assets are also bound to corporate lives and livelihoods, values and futures (Appel *et al.* 2015; Rajan 2012). Unlike the commodity form (in this case oil and natural gas, for example), which is more readily alienable (but see Walsh, this volume), the corporate asset requires a shift in gaze. Ideally, it is the archetypal 'golden goose' that is found or made, kept and tended; it is the object of investment valued for its work, in this case, of generating hydrocarbon commodities and returning the cash flow that builds corporate worlds (and often radically exceeds them).[18] Entrepreneurs are expected to tend their assets as a critical part of minding a business. For my interlocutors, 'doing good with oil' (High, this volume) means creating returns on investment from them. In local industry, this often means privileging capital spending on new wells, which helps to create returns, versus spending capital on decommissioning old wells, which does not. Asset care is not therefore left to business morality (see Barry 2013: 78-89). Regulatory rules dictate the minimum standards and 'best practices' for asset care, even if these same rules have been complicit with the practice of deferring the decommissioning of end-of-life wells.

More than just property, assets occupy a moral space for corporate actors. They are 'good' on the balance sheet because they 'add value' to it. But as property, and as the plaintiffs to the Redwater case suggest, they cannot and *should* not be easily

**Figure 1.** Orphaned natural gas well. (Photo by the author.)

discarded. While assets can be alienable in that they can transfer from one set of owners to another, such transfers are mediated, regulated, and governed by law. In normative oil and gas asset transfers by means of sale or swap, the duty and cost of care, the everyday responsibility for the asset and for its location in leased space, transfers along with it. 'Legitimate orphans' are thus made in exceptional and often historical cases of misfortune (i.e. bankruptcy), such as wells drilled a generation ago and for which no owners or responsible parties can be found. Additionally, the regulator can seize and designate as orphans any corporate properties found to be in poor repair or otherwise in violation of regulatory standards. These orphans are accounted for by the Alberta Energy Regulator and taken in by the OWA for care. Funding of the OWA is provided by an annual tariff to corporations that are licensed by Alberta's regulator. The OWA reports, as a point of pride, that the industry has predominately funded this care to date and has not required public funds to do so. Yet the Redwater precedent of asset disclaiming is cause for public concern.

Asset disclaiming is the bank's means of making 'illegitimate' orphans. This new class of orphan does not allegedly qualify for OWA care. Indeed, a representative of the Canadian Association for Petroleum Producers (CAPP) made this explicit in an affidavit to the courts over Redwater, stating that: 'The orphan fund is designed to deal with orphans not the children that the parent wishes to disown'.[19] Here, 'legitimate orphans' are only those that have lost the corporate parent owing to insolvency and when no other responsible or accountable party (such as a solvent working interest partner, for example) can be found. In the view of the regulator, the CAPP, and the OWA, receivers must take *all* the assets of an indebted corporation that pledged them and should not be allowed to 'pick and choose' from the debtor's remains. Illegitimate orphans are seen by the regulator and the OWA to be made by these immoral means. In their 2017 Annual Report, the OWA describes the recent and unusual 'surge' of orphaned wells growing from 74 in 2012 to over 1,778 in 2017 (up by 650 from the prior year alone, not including leases and pipeline segments), which they attribute largely to insolvencies or states of asset disrepair that followed the commodity price downturn.[20]

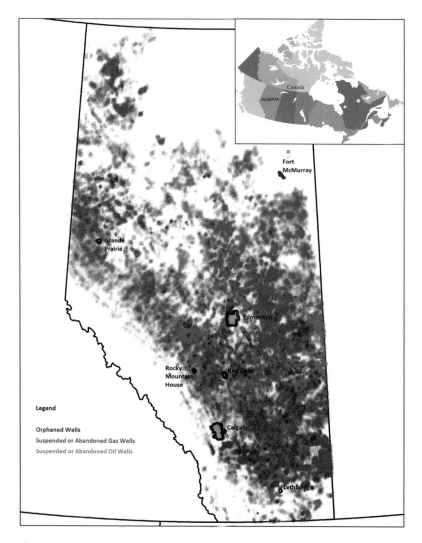

**Figure 2.** Map of suspended, abandoned, and orphaned wells in Alberta. (By permission of Challenge Energy. Inset map from *https://www.graphic-flash-sources.com/canada-vector-map/*, made available by mediakitchen.fr.)

The Redwater case is bringing this emerging class of 'illegitimate' orphan into view, as 'overflow' (Çalışkan & Callon 2009; 2010), resulting from having crossed moral and juridical boundaries. Orphans also index a larger petrocapitalist system failure in Alberta.

If accelerated capital investment, drilling frenzy, and asset circulation characterized Alberta's most recent fourteen-year-long oil boom, indebted corporations, end-of-life assets, and 'unexpected orphans' now characterize its post-2014 bust (see also High, this volume). In aggregate, at the time of writing, there are approximately 180,000 active wells in Alberta, but there are also a nearly equal number of legacy wells comprised of 83,000 suspended wells and 69,000 abandoned wells (see Fig. 2). In aggregate, the

*Journal of the Royal Anthropological Institute (N.S.), 67-90*
© Royal Anthropological Institute 2019

estimated liability of these industry ruins is a staggering $58.7 billion.[21] Under normal circumstances, owners are to pay for their end-of-life care. Yet, given the startling number of legacy wells and the number of companies on the verge of bankruptcy owing to the commodity price downturn since 2014, the question of who will pay, and, indeed, how and when they can pay, becomes rather urgent, especially if significant numbers of these wells are to unexpectedly become orphans.[22] During the boom, there was plenty of 'value creation' to afford the work of end-of-life care, yet it is typical in Alberta's industry to instead defer this work through the circulation of legacy assets.

To illustrate, during the boom economy of the early to mid-2000s, as much as 30 per cent of the Western Canadian Sedimentary basin's production changed hands in a single year (Wood 2015). Every well may have multiple owners during its lifespan. Often legacy wells, even though they are not producing and even though nobody wants them, transfer as part of a larger acquisition package. This is often the case during corporate takeovers, but also with smaller property acquisitions. Energy corporations are masterful at tying their unwanted assets with their good ones to help compel them into circulation. In other words, to get the assets they want, acquiring parties must also agree to take whole batches of *extra* assets, often as many undesired as desired ones, to get the parcels of land and production assets that they want. In turn, the acquirer may repeat the same process, tying unwanted assets to something 'good' in their portfolio that can be sacrificed to rid their balance sheet of the unwanted assets and associated liabilities. The result is a convoluted 'biography of things', to borrow Kopytoff's (1986) phrasing, where legacy wells circulate, like a game of 'hot potato', among different corporations and their balance sheets until no further deferrals or circulations are possible. The result is that most corporations, especially larger ones, end up with a mixture of assets that are at various stages of productive life and end-of-life, which compete for capital within corporate budgets. Owing to the post-2014 industry consolidation, there are now fewer companies that must provide more of the care. Here the balance between these ethical domains of value creation, on the one hand, and end-of-life asset care, on the other, is directly tied to the performance of the balance sheet where there are enough 'good' assets to offset end-of-life liabilities (referred to on balance sheets as 'Asset Retirement Obligations'). Orphans, by contrast, are severed from the logics of balance sheets and are reconstituted as a group of actors that work primarily to cost the OWA. The unexpected and 'illegitimate orphans', mobilized in the Redwater case as ethico-political 'matters of concern' (Latour 2004), signal the potential for a growing group of new orphans that may exceed the capacity of the OWA. Taken together, legitimate and illegitimate orphans offer cultural critique of both asset disclaiming and the economies of circulation and deferral that shape Alberta's 'oil patch' (see High & Smith, this volume).

## Challenge Energy, debt, and the duration of value creation

I now turn to the story of Challenge Energy and its struggle against insolvency, which began in early 2015 after the sudden drop of oil prices by roughly half in the fall of 2014. Like Redwater, Challenge had become a debt story. The corporation had maxed out its lines of credit in the years leading up to 2014 as a source of financing because new equity investors were in short supply. The latter are typically preferred by small oil and gas companies because equity investors become shareholders and do not have to be paid back but instead receive their share of the gains or losses once crystallized through a liquidity event, such as a sale of all assets or a merger. When debt financing is used, lenders must be paid back each month, which uses up critical cash flows, and the total corporate asset value must adequately 'secure' the loan. After the halving of commodity prices, Challenge became overwhelmed by debt obligations. The company's thirty or so employees had by now given up their long-held anticipatory dream of extreme return, built up by the fourteen-year-long perpetual boom, and they were instead focused on minimizing losses.

Working in the field of corporate governance – at times as a consultant and at times as an employee – had become my own solution for over a decade to the problems of access that I faced while 'studying up' (Nader 1972) in junior oil and gas companies. In this instance, work-as-method afforded me a chance to observe and participate in this unfolding story.[23] I began taking this approach years ago because many aspects of petrocapitalism, particularly the corporate performativities associated with value creation that were of interest to me, were difficult to observe from the outside and were less transparent than they are now. They were also difficult to access even from the inside. Working as an executive in governance opened to me the world of oil executives in action. It also limited other research paths, such as detailed ethnographic attention to the lived experience of oil and forms of dispossession confronted by those living in proximity to energy assets, which is often the case for Indigenous peoples, rural landholders, and other nonhumans, such as cattle, migrating elk, bears, crops, birds, and the invasions by odours, weeds, and toxins that these groups variously endure (for an overview of this literature, see High & Smith this volume; Rogers 2015; for an example concerning wind energy, see Howe, this volume).[24] Rather, I looked to how these spaces were produced, managed, or externalized through the boardrooms and meeting rooms that were opened through my approach. Gaining access to these worlds and the levers they pull was especially important to me as a researcher because I am an Albertan and these corporate worlds (and 'oilmen' as a category) directly and disproportionately shape the conditions of life here.

Intermittently, for just over a year, I was asked to attend routine meetings and to write reports summarizing Challenge's strategies for restructuring and recapitalization. I was to note the advice given by lawyers and other experts for the board of directors, as well as to note market trends and valuations given to 'peer producers' in mergers and acquisitions that might offer exemplars of value for Challenge. During this time, I observed my co-workers put their working days to the problem-solving task of how to 'salvage value', how to make their roster of wells 'return' something *more*; how to best describe the situation to investors; and how to forge a path that did not result in market death and loss. At first 'recapitalization' meant cost cutting and asset optimization. Challenge employees were given pay cuts and offered shorter work weeks. Supply-chain contracts were renegotiated to reduce the rates paid to supply-chain service labour. Spare equipment that had piled up in 'bone yards' was sold off, as were any undrilled and 'unproven' lands. Smaller amounts were spent on wellbore and reservoir optimization measures that were often overlooked when capital was plentiful (i.e. workovers, pump changes, experimenting with pressures and flow rates, valve changes, 'refracks', or perforating and commingling additional subsurface zones). For example, to save cost and increase cash flow, Challenge was negotiating with a fracking company to 'refrack' a few wells in exchange for a profit share of any improvements to well production. At the same time, Challenge continued, without any luck, to seek new investor capital, or to find a buyer for the corporation, or a compatible corporation to merge with. As the example below will illustrate, recapitalization would later come to mean a highly complex deal that severed ties with some actors while enlisting new ones in an effort to preserve a world for the original capital invested.

Yet what caught my attention during this time was the reappearing sense of duty and obligation – the moral force of the binding obligation to return capital (Guyer 2012; Mauss 2016 [1925]). In this sense, as Appadurai (2011) has observed, there is an affinity between the force of return that Marcel Mauss (2016 [1925]) ascribes to the gift and those ascribed to processes of capitalization that are meant to return investment (see also Muniesa *et al.* 2017; Smith, this volume).[25] Appel (2012) has similarly pointed to this affinity in her discussions of the work of disentanglement of offshore oil and profit from local onshore social and political life in Equatorial Guinea. She points us to Mauss's descriptions of Maori gifting, where the spirit of the gift propels its return, which can be seen as another possible source of the 'how of capitalism'. As she writes: 'By extension, the hau of capitalism – that which propels it to continue – is, arguably profit' (2012: 698). Often struck by the tenacious hold that oil and gas projects have on their participants, I suggest that the connection between ethics and processes of return (as opposed to the calculation of profit or rate of return) needs a closer look.

Over the course of my research in Alberta's oil patch, I have observed that profits, while circulated to shareholders, also tend to remain attached to the reputations of particular corporate actors and their assets, working as a critical source of differentiation of CEOs and management teams within and by the capital markets. It rings familiar as something of the giver remaining in the gift in the Maori gifting practices described by Mauss (2016 [1925]). Only here, as Appel (2012) suggests, it is a profit returned that compels these relations to continue. While the calculation of profits that CEOs and their teams have made for the market over time is an important method of making them commensurable to the market, it is also what affords them local fame and recognition as 'oilmen' (see Mason 2015). Shareholders rarely forget who it was who made them money, just as they rarely forget those who lost their money. Those who create a return are more highly prized and tend to get repeat business.

For Challenge's management team, concern with the stakes and socialities of capital filled the daily meantime of value creation with a durational ethics, where responsibility, perseverance, and obligation both facilitated and often overcame the very fraught ideals of the 'investor gaze' (Muniesa *et al.* 2017: 92-6), and which, following Guyer's definition (2014: 399), were critical to and inhabited their 'near futures'.

### Calling in debt: monitoring (a)moral disentanglements

I arrived at the office a few minutes before the bankers, who were scheduled to meet with the management team of Challenge that morning. The management team of Challenge, comprised of the CEO (William), a geologist (Pat), an engineer (Rick), an accountant (Barb), and a landman (Jacob) – the usual cast of organizational actors in small oil and gas companies – were already assembled in the boardroom to greet the bankers. The management team, though worried, still mustered some humour and were busy renaming the yet-to-be-met bankers as 'the undertakers'. The bankers had previously given formal notice that things would now change because the new reduced commodity price environment had led Challenge's debt value to exceed the value of the assets it pledged to securitize the loan. The common stock owned by Challenge's investors was now worthless and the value of the assets, if immediately sold, would cover only half the debt.

*Journal of the Royal Anthropological Institute (N.S.), 67-90*
© Royal Anthropological Institute 2019

> *William* [Challenge's CEO]: Welcome to our office. We've put together a presentation today to show you our plan to create value and continue to pay our debt.
>
> *Banker* [A representative from ACME Bank]: Thank you. My name is Carmen McKay. I'm actually just here to notify you that your file has been moved to Special Loans and to provide you with some information regarding process. A presentation isn't necessary at this point. We have assigned an independent third party at your expense to assess your plan and the value of all Challenge's assets, so your presentation should be directed to them.
>
> *William*: I think it's important to stress that our company has not defaulted – we have never failed to make our monthly payment. This plan that we have will bring our asset value back up and we should be good.
>
> *Banker*: We realize that you have been able to make your payments so far. However, your asset value has fallen to below 50 per cent of your outstanding debt. That is a problem and we notified you about it six months ago. Under these circumstances [i.e. when assets no longer securitize debt], it is our policy to work with you to recover our loan value. If it appears that a suitable plan to recapitalize cannot be accomplished, the corporation will be put into receivership.
>
> *William*: But that's what I'm saying to you. We have a plan and we haven't defaulted. Let's just go through this plan while you're here. At least then you will know what we are thinking, and you can take it back to your office.
>
> *Banker*: Sir, with all due respect, we have frozen your bank line. You have no money to spend. We cannot allow you to spend any of what is now *our* cash flow on anything other than debt reduction. We cannot allow you to spend on this refracking plan that you have and therefore take risk with our security [i.e. collateral]. Your only option is to recapitalize. We are willing to work with you to that end.

In this exchange, the immediate temporality of repayment is in stark contrast to the investment in and entanglement with assets in everyday life and the uncertainty of returns over time (Guyer 2012). As Graeber (2011: 21) has pointed out, unlike 'mere obligation' or the forms of indebtedness that keep relationships going, debt can be precisely quantified, and its repayment cancels the debt contract. While the deadline for recapitalization was not fixed during this meeting, the temporal urgency was clear, as was the consequence: in short order the bank would seize remaining assets and sell them to the highest bidder. Amoral and, indeed, impersonal.

Yet, for William, having the bank call in Challenge's loan was far from amoral. Debt was tied to a multiplicity of other shareholder relationships which the bank's cancellation, if it came to that, would also undo. Those relationships were characterized by the moral obligation of indebtedness. The company's shareholders included friends and family of management as well as most of Challenge's employees. Management and employees were invited to purchase common stock when they were hired in addition to being granted stock options, which never came to be 'in the money'. With the bank's proposition, shareholders would get no returns, employees would lose their options and would have to line up with other creditors to petition for the severance pay owed to them. Hedge fund investors had already made it clear that they would not 'bail out' William by refinancing the corporation but would unhappily take their losses instead – their portfolios were designed to absorb some loss as part of their strategy of capital management even though this loss would be greater than they had anticipated. Finding fresh capital at this juncture had already proven unlikely. Owing to the reputational damage already caused by insolvency, William found the capital markets as chilly as his own meeting room. As Challenge's Chairman (an oil patch veteran and head of a drilling company) often put it: 'Nobody wants to snuggle up to a tragedy. You have to have a good story, the kind that shows you can make money'. Challenge's current story did not have the sizzle of 'money making' and was more likely to repel investors than attract them. Any new investments would get applied to old debts and

*Journal of the Royal Anthropological Institute (N.S.), 67-90*
© Royal Anthropological Institute 2019

the project of return would be in the hands of those who had already failed to 'make good' on prior capital invested.

By freezing the line of credit, the bank had also put a stop to the choreography of practice so familiar to William and indeed to most small and intermediate-sized corporate oil and gas producers in Canada's upstream sector. The normative choreography goes more or less like this:

- *Raise big capital* from institutions (i.e. hedge funds) often identified through investment banks;
- *Deploy big spending* on focused inventories of subterranean prospects for selective exploration and extraction, and by using the Big Capital Raised to pit actors in the supply chain against one another in a competition to win contracts that will be awarded for drilling, completions (i.e. multi-stage hydraulic fracturing), lease preparation, modular housing, tank rentals, water hauling, and so forth;
- *Build infrastructure* to separate emulsion (i.e. undifferentiated hydrocarbon fluid) into purified commodities of crude oil, natural gas, and natural gas liquids, transportable to market by truck, pipeline, or rail, that convert to near-term predictable flows of cash;
- *Liquidate the corporation* by having left enough 'upside' in the ground to attract a buyer at a competitive valuation;
- *Return bigger capital to shareholders*, which most often includes themselves as managers, their circle of close business associates and friends and family – something recognizable as what Tsing (2005: 55) refers to as the cronyism typical of frontier zones.

From William's perspective, the bank had also undermined its own and the industry's practices of qualification that made Challenge's wells investable in the first place. William insisted that Challenge's wells were as 'good' today as they were when the bank accepted them as loan collateral in 2012. He and his team had performed the geological and technical work of qualification considered to be critical to value creation (i.e. use of core analysis, open-hole well logs, cross-sections, and pay maps that make the subterranean legible, mappable, comparable).[26] They had ranked their prospects and assigned capital for drilling only the worthiest targets across their lands. They had also made use of the multiple metrologies, forecasts, and calculations that are standard practice for anticipating potential economics (i.e. reservoir volumetrics, type curves, net present value and discounted cash-flow forecasts, netback and rate of return estimates) (Wood 2016).

Indeed, after Challenge had spent all the original equity finance capital, the bank approved the company's expanding line of credit to drill more wells based on these same 'investable' formulaic results. These forms of modelling and evaluation used to both generate and qualify prospective drilling locations are critical to sustaining the anticipatory affect that fuels economies of speculation and capital attraction (Bear, Birla & Puri 2015; Li 2012; Tsing 2005; Weszkalnys 2015; Wood 2016; see also Kneas 2016 for mining context). It seems they are also critical to generating economies of demise and contraction. Price, a critical variable in these formulas and the calculation of value, struck William as quite arbitrary and as something that would eventually recover if the bank would continue to be patient. His plea to the bank for patience was a plea to introduce morality into the space of an amoral contract. In his view, it was not enough that the bank may have been responding to obligations to its own shareholders. William wanted it to be held accountable for years cultivating his debt, and for offering him more debt each year that new wells drilled increased the value of Challenge's reservoirs when, all the while, said William, 'they knew the risks of price'.

Interestingly, success or failure of capital to return is often attributed by equity investors and lenders (banks) alike not to price strength, but to good management, especially with these formulaic methods of evaluation and qualification of prospective geological sites. Omitted from discussion are the other factors that ensure that Alberta's basin remains 'hyperpermeable' to capital. (This is the term I use to describe the fluidity enabled for capital investment through systems of rule and land tenure that make oil and gas production zones out of the property of [un]willing landholders, through colonial settler relations, and through pre-existing and ever-expanding networks of infrastructure).[27] Success with capital not only relies on these factors but is directly generated from them, and from matrices of gender, race, and class that also infuse industry processes (Bear *et al.* 2015; High & Smith, this volume). They are sources of what Tsing (2015*b*) calls 'salvage accumulation' or the generation of wealth by means of 'conversion of stuff with other histories of social relations (human and not human) into capitalist wealth'.

With no capacity to use the line of credit and no capacity to raise new equity (nobody wanted to invest in a story about loss), it looked like William and his shareholders would walk away empty-handed after nearly a decade of working to create financial returns. William's lament over Challenge's losses resembled discourses surrounding the subprime mortgage crisis of 2008, though in his version, oil losses were also tied to Canadian regional east vs west politics:

> The banks knew the risks. Prices have always been volatile. They know prices will rebound. This is just prices. We've been making our payments so why call the loan? They're just raiding us. These eastern banks are raiding us and selling off our assets to those vulture hedge funds![28]

And, summoning his moral sense of accountability,

> How am I going to look my shareholders in the face? These shareholders aren't just hedge funds. My friends and family are invested ... this is their retirement money and their kids' educations. Heck, it's my retirement, too.

William also worried about his employees. 'What will they do? There are no jobs out there right now. We have to try to do *something*'. A response that no doubt came from having 'skin in the game', his own and that of others.

'Skin in the game' refers to a sizeable personal investment in the corporation by management as a condition of hedge fund investment. While it is a key source of access to the distributions of oil wealth that link teams such as Challenge to social stratification (see Mason, this volume), it also quite forcefully ties them to their project. When hedge funds agree to invest in a management team, they are capitalizing the CEOs and team just like assets, or *as* assets. Various institutional investors have explained to me that decisions to invest are based equally on the desirability and credibility of the geological prospect – that is, 'the size of the prize' (a key ingredient of a 'good story') – and the confidence they have in the leadership team to accomplish the task (see High and also Cross, this volume). Practices of due diligence are applied to vet both the technical and financial validity of the prospect and the history of the leadership team.[29] Assuming potential candidates and prospects get past this vetting process, institutional hedge funds require management teams to make substantial personal investments. In the same way that management teams have indicated to me that they like employees to have 'big mortgages' because it means 'we will have them forever', hedge funds like to see management teams 'invest in themselves', which they also supplement with various market instruments such as stock options. Together, these 'management incentives' are intended to create 'alignment' between shareholders and managers. In this way, as Ho has argued, 'supermanager incomes actually blur the boundaries between capital and labour' (2015: 484). In addition to converting the act of work into a market spectacle where the daily act of value creation is simultaneously observed through the behaviour of a corporation's stock, such investments work to hold labour in place and hold hostage past savings that are invested in the hope of future profits to the rhythm of daily work for a pay cheque (Wood 2015).

'Skin in the game' also resembles a 'responsibility to kin' (Sykes 2015) or an investment for 'the good of kin' (Penfield, this volume) that are obligations beyond rates of return that tie corporate managers to their projects.[30] As a CEO explained to me,

> Skin in the game means that you're not going anywhere. Your world is stuck in this thing that you're building. And you've brought your people, your family and friends into it with you. If you fail; they fail. Your ass is totally on the line. The flip side of our hopes for profit is the fear of failure and loss. Most days it's the fear that keeps me going.

Management teams are expected to produce financial returns for equity investors and futures for CEOs and management teams: that is, their future employability/investability is contingent on whether they are deemed 'competent with capital' by the capital markets. In this context, the quarterly publication of financial statements serves as a market report card through which the oil and gas industry, constituted as a market arena by financial analysts, makes the various basins across North America symmetrical to one another and to their state-sanctioned subterranean formations of value (i.e. Marcellus, Eagle Ford, Permian, Duvernay, Montney, Bakken). Market research analysts stage the geological science of vertical zones as flattened spaces of competition for capital (Braun 2000). In this market space, where both geological zones and management teams are compared for their specific rate of return, an insolvency event does not just kill dreams of extreme return, it also kills market reputations and dampens the likelihood of obtaining future capital. Given the uncomfortable alliance between William's passionate interests and his obligations to shareholders, he elected to press on and seek recapitalization. As he put it, he simply could not 'quit on his people' who had stayed with him for so long. Here, labouring for capital meant labouring for shareholders, those he personally knew and those he did not, and where the latter directly benefit from his relations with the former. William then enlisted the help of a friend and fellow CEO named Reynold who was willing to advise for a contingency fee. Whereas William and his team were known for their 'growth by the drill-bit' methodology of value creation, meaning they grew their business strictly by buying land and drilling wells, Reynold was known for his debt management expertise and for value creation by means of financial (re)structuring.

### Petro-deals: how to clean up a balance sheet (by eating a shit sandwich)
Very shortly after accepting the job, Reynold laid out his strategic plan initially to William and his team, and then to Challenge's board of directors. His first order of business was to 'clean up' the balance sheet. That meant dealing with debt. As he saw it, two things had to happen for Challenge to avoid immediate receivership:

1. Propose that Challenge buy out its debt from the bank at market value, terminating Challenge's obligations to it. In order to buy out the debt, Challenge would need to qualify for a new loan from a new lender.
2. As it currently stood, there were not enough assets to securitize a new loan, meaning that, new equity was needed to qualify for new debt. New equity investments would not be in the typical form of money capital, which was scarcely available in industry, but instead in the form of assets from another corporation in exchange for Challenge's common stock. I will return to this matter below.

However, in an interesting role reversal, debtors (i.e. banks as lenders) had begun to behave like equity investors and vice versa. Normally, lenders only require securitization of assets based on a percentage of market value as the basis for providing debt. Yet in response to the number of insolvencies that were hitting the banks from corporations having become 'over-leveraged', lenders had begun to vet management teams. The banks argued that management competence in these volatile commodity markets were now as important a criterion to loan security as the security itself. Where lenders were now vetting management team credibility, equity investors had begun to behave like lenders. For hedge funds, it was no longer enough to be lured by confidence in a team and a target asset. Imagining Redwater scenarios, investors had begun to scrutinize existing compositions of assets, screening for legacy assets, asset retirement obligations (AROs), and other liabilities that might subtract from value, just as a lender would do.

Taking these new criteria among lenders into account, Reynold argued that in order to inspire renewed market confidence, Challenge would need to be rebranded with a new name – he proposed Phoenix Oil – that had new faces attached, meaning that William and members of his team would be replaced. This was a blow to William. While he was willing to concede his own chair for the greater good, asking some of his team to resign was a 'hard pill to swallow'. He had for several years now fought to keep his team in place even when the dictates of the neoliberal market suggested that declines in the company's production warranted lay-offs and substantial cost reductions. 'This isn't "management entrenchment"', he once explained to me. 'Management entrenchment' had become the new buzzword for *bad* management behaviour in the shareholder value paradigm. It meant that people were too comfortable, subtracting value from corporations in the form of paycheques when no value was being created. It meant people kept their jobs at the shareholders' expense:

> We need these people for when prices turn around. I cannot cut the receptionist, she's the lowest-paid person here … I cannot cut my geologists … how will we find new opportunity? I cannot cut anyone. We are working to turn this company around and to an exit. We simply cannot do that without people.

As for the needed new assets that would secure the outstanding loan, they would be new to Phoenix Oil but they were hardly 'new' in the definitional sense. The assets Reynold proposed that Phoenix accept as an 'investment' came in the form of over 1,000 wellbores, over half of which were legacy assets that were 'shut-in', suspended or in need of abandonment, and many with 'environmental liabilities'. Some of us looked more than a little confused by the notion that this 'crap' would somehow equal 'cleaning up the balance sheet'. Reynold summed it up thus: 'Sometimes, to stay alive, you have to eat a shit sandwich'.

*Journal of the Royal Anthropological Institute (N.S.)*, 67-90
© Royal Anthropological Institute 2019

As a 'deal type', Reynold's proposal was a 'balance sheet deal', sometimes called a 'liability deal'. Phoenix would take more liabilities on to the balance sheet, including legacy wells of the kind Redwater's lender had intentionally orphaned, and which might become orphan candidates for Phoenix's new lender if Reynold were to fail. While far from the ideal form of capital investment, balance sheet deals are strategies that work in the absence of other forms of equity. Reynold was in touch with the local investment bankers who brokered investment capital to the network of local private equity. He was therefore in touch with 'deal flow' and 'accretive ideas', meaning value-creating ideas, such as forms of 'asset recombination' that such networks are known to generate (Ho 2009). From those networks, he conjured possible combinations of those that might be willing to push assets (a few good ones that produce monthly cash flow and a whole bunch of bad ones that do not) off their books in exchange for shares, and those that might be willing to buy out the former debt by accepting these 'new' wells as collateral. Phoenix had the capacity to 'eat' this 'sandwich' because its current assets were 'new' and therefore without any meaningful liabilities. It had been a point of pride for William and his team that their asset base was 'clean' in this regard, which now afforded Reynold the 'balance sheet flexibility' that he needed to save Challenge.[31] At the same time, it was now possible for the seller of these assets to move them around on its own balance sheet from the status of a 'bad' liability to that of a 'good' investment in the form of new common shares of Phoenix Oil, of which it would now be a major shareholder. This feat is one that underscores the constitutive force of accounting classification to make and shape worlds.

The process of exchange was also decidedly messy. In these kinds of corporate transactions, rarely is there a straight exchange of properties for money. That only appears to be the case after the fact. While in the making, deals are made through complex negotiations, often on-the-spot calculation, tit for tat and cash for things. Rogers' notion of 'petrobarter', meaning 'a class of transactions in which goods are exchanged for goods without the direct intervention of monetary currency' (2014: 132), is usefully applied to Alberta's oil patch deal making, especially with regard 'to transforming existing local configurations and thereby empowering new elites and certain factions of old elites' (2014: 150). As Rogers notes, valuation practices can encompass more than one form of exchange (see also Maurer 2006). For Reynold, to reach a final settlement to be formulated as a cash sum for which shares could be exchanged, a number of items needed to be 'thrown in' and then 'taken out' of the mix of things that would count in the deal to be exchanged for common shares. Barter enters the transaction here as these specific throw-ins, take-outs, and swaps that occur alongside specific measures of 'fundamental' and 'market' value of the assets, when combined, make closing possible. Deal fairness, however, often favours those less weakened by failed value and by pressing obligations.[32]

Once a deal was reached, Phoenix 'ate' the combination of assets that comprised the 'shit sandwich'. Here the adoption of legacy assets with good ones did not carry the same ethic of care as displayed by the OWA. Instead, 'eating' these assets appeared a little cannibalistic. Old assets and good assets were the source of continued life rather than new equity investment. It was an act that William very reluctantly agreed to and which gave him indigestion. After closing, the team had to rework how best to generate value (or minimize loss) given their new responsibility for over 2,000 legacy assets along with the fewer than 500 good ones that would need to pay for all operations. To reduce their financial burdens, the new team (which no longer included William at this point) immediately began looking for groupings of assets – some good with some bad – that they could divest to another corporation with problems similar to their own. Even the outright gifting of high-liability assets to other parties was contemplated to move them off the balance sheet (i.e. expressly to render them alienable), but they were not actually given away owing to a change in regulatory rules which significantly restricted the eligibility rules for those on the receiving end of such a gift.[33]

In these discussions, the motive for this form of *petrogifting* was 'accretion' – the balance sheet looked better without those assets 'holding it back'. Offering up these assets as a gift looked like less to me like gifting in the anthropological sense and a lot more like another form of asset disclaiming. While the gift of assets would no doubt produce a later return in the economy of debts and favours among industry executives that I describe below, the gift in this context was an act of disentanglement, meant to sever corporate ownership of a mature asset with high liabilities even if it meant sacrificing an additional cash-flowing property (i.e. a 'good' asset) to compel its acceptance. That there were willing parties on the receiving end of this potential gift indexes the absence of conventional investor capital in Alberta. This was not the 'spectacular accumulation' (Tsing 2005) that raged through Alberta a decade ago, but something far more precarious. Easy 'prizes' and easy capital had fallen out of the picture, replaced by what Tsing refers to as 'patchy' capitalism (2015a: 4). That is, value creation had become increasingly creative, squeezed out of the unplanned and the ad hoc. It was what Alberta petrocapitalism had begun to look like now that many oil and gas wells and companies were reaching the near end of profit.

While Reynold's particular brand of 'liability deal' was out of the ordinary, deal making is well known to be at the heart of Alberta's oil patch. For Reynold, access to deals was generated through an economy of debts and favours that took shape as tit-for-tat exchange. It was the method of inclusion in a network that mattered both by association and by participation in its (re)making. To obtain the debt financing that Challenge urgently needed, Reynold pressed the bank to reduce its claim to market share by leveraging its capital markets arm, which had been trying to attract his business on another project. (He was also a CEO with 'chips in other games'.) Then, to find new sources of debt to buy out the former bank, he called every financer and brokerage house that had ever substantially profited from any of his prior corporations, and he called every brokerage house that may have wanted a stake in his current corporation. In Reynold's words, he had called on those with money who owed him one or who wanted to owe him one. As he noted, 'Lots of guys out there are good for a favour or two'.

Reynold also called people who he thought would be amused by his call. One such call was made to someone he called 'Johnny the Kneecapper', who specialized in providing mezzanine-level debt (a category of debt that will provide debt financing at astonishing interest rates as high as 18 per cent after service charges and usage fees are factored). Having already called in any prior debts from the Kneecapper, Reynold positioned the call as a favour, offering a 'near risk-free opportunity' and 'first charge on the assets' (meaning that if the company tanked, the Kneecapper would be first in line at an insolvency sale). Smelling the odour of a misrecognized moment, the Kneecapper then suggested that he might do the deal if, in turn, Reynold took a problem property off his hands as part of it. Reynold quickly agreed, seeing it merely as 'one more shit sandwich'. Returns on credit/debt for the Kneecapper were a given requirement, but what made those returns possible was the reaffirmation of a relationship, the dispelling of an old debt, and the attachment of a new favour (i.e. a 'contract behind the contract') (see Peebles 2010). As Reynold explained it, sounding much like Bohannan's (1964) description of Tiv women who build community through reciprocal debts (cited in Graeber 2011: 104-5): 'I don't want to be free of my debts to others [i.e. indebtedness]. Without debts, I have nobody to call and nobody to call me. Without debts, you're alone; it's hard to do business'.[34] Here, quite unlike the amorality of bank debt, deals rely on social debt, so CEOs seek it for the reciprocal relations of obligation they compel (see Ferguson 2013; Golub & Rhee 2013; James 2012).

Debt and legacy assets are mobilized in these spaces of corporate precarity. Both appear in this story simultaneously as dirty forms of excrement and moral disorder *and* as a source of life and potential renewal. Reynold would hardly be the first to claim that one person's excrement was another's gold (see Parry & Bloch 1989; High and also Penfield, this volume). In this deal, Reynold and William would accept dilution (i.e. many more owners of the same corporation at a much-reduced share value), but the company would not be dead. Jobs were protected, shareholders could recover some of their losses, and directors and officers did not have to admit to being associated with an insolvency. In the end, Challenge was able to liquidate by in turn investing those same mature assets along with its few remaining good ones into a company also fighting off the special loans department of a bank about to call in the balance of its outstanding loan. In other words, Challenge-cum-Pheonix ended by an odd form of 'rescuing' another indebted corporation, and by doing so recovered only 0.15 cents on each original dollar invested in Challenge. As a result, it did not produce any unexpected orphans. The future of these legacy wells worried William but it was not something he could solve. He may have damaged his reputation as an oilman competent with capital, yet it was more important to him to protect his shareholders, employees, and kin, to the best of his ability, with the help of Reynold. It is important to note that in these deals the care of employees and shareholders (both skin and kin) was possible because Reynold and also the board of directors prioritized it as good management.

## Conclusion: Returns on ethics

In the above account of Challenge Energy, the ethics and practice of value creation make assets, people, and futures out of hydrocarbons. The case offers important theoretical and methodological insights: the importance of durational ethics and petrocapitalist dependence on obligation and social debt; the im/mobility of assets; and thinking with orphans as a mode of critique.

With regard to the first of these insights, as this essay has illustrated, oil at the end or near end of profit looks different than it does from the perspective of the boom. In cases of failure (not by insolvency but by returning a loss to shareholders), corporate value creation is shaped less by the promise-filled moral horizons of a beginning than they are by the commitment, responsibility, and perseverance required to reach an ending under conditions of financial and temporal uncertainty. In this context, social debts and indebtedness made pressing by both 'skin' and 'kin' also carry these projects forward and are thus an important part of the social, material, and political arrangements through which oil is produced in Alberta.

Second, it is worth making the obvious point that these assets do not actually move. Asset circulation deployed to churn value or to morally clean up balance sheets appears to be a lively practice within the financial worlds of corporations. But the assets themselves are long-term residents on landholder fields and Indigenous lands,

**Figure 3.** Orphaned natural gas header. (Photo by the author.)

for example, where they are well known to come into being through friction (de Rijke, Munro & de Lourdes Melo Zurita 2016; Nikiforuk 2001; 2015) and through the collision of ethical worlds (Appel, this volume). Thus, these groups are called to participate in value creation projects through (un)consenting surface lease arrangements and the receipt of compensation in return, even while they are externalized from them. (Owing to split land titles, they do not, in most cases, share in the gains or royalty payments derived from 'value creation'.)

Finally, I return to the orphans and thinking with them as a mode of critique, with which I opened this essay. Orphans as displaced ownerless assets severed from balance sheet logics become strictly liabilities that cost and that create burdens and potential hazards to their host landholders until they can receive proper care by the OWA. Yet in this new landscape where oil has often reached the end of profit, the group of wells that have run dry or which have become uneconomic owing to price have become a legacy all their own. Legacy assets used by Challenge and by other corporations as a form of crisis capital are not just objects requiring end-of-life care that has been perpetually deferred. They are also potential orphans in the making. These new value creation arrangements that increasingly pair corporations with both legacy assets and high bank debt set up the conditions for orphan making. Indeed, the company that Challenge eventually sold its assets to has since gone insolvent owing to a bank calling in its secured loan. The legacy assets transferred to it may yet turn up as orphans. Thinking with orphans therefore pushes us beyond value creation and durational ethics of oil patch corporations to the duration of the asset itself. Specifically, responsibility for cost and care of an asset's end of life can be assigned to the beginning of an asset's life when it is productive, rather than at the end when it becomes a 'shit sandwich' to be bartered and brokered as an object of petrocapitalist crisis.

## NOTES

My sincerest thanks to the Editors, Mette High and Jessica Smith, and to the *JRAI*'s anonymous reviewers, for their careful readings and commentary, which helped me to shape this essay into its current form. Thank you also to Karl Schmidt, Mary-Lee Mulholland, and Jens Kjaerulff for important feedback on earlier drafts and ongoing energy dialogue. I remain deeply indebted to my former Challenge co-workers, colleagues, and interlocutors in Alberta who so graciously spared the time to talk orphans, oil, and debt with me. The essay and any errors are of course my own responsibility.

[1] For the Receivership Order, 12 May 2015, briefs, court orders, and all Creditor Updates relating to the Redwater Energy Corp. case, see *http:// www.grantthornton.ca/en/service/advisory/creditor-updates/ #Redwater-Energy-Corp* (accessed 17 January 2019).

[2] The Bankruptcy and Insolvency Act (BIA), Sec. 14.06(4), was also in conflict with the Pipeline Act. Under the former, non-producing wells and pipeline segments can be disclaimed, but under the latter act, they cannot. The Alberta courts privileged the BIA.

[3] In financial terms, ATB (through the receiver) stood to recover approximately $6 million from twenty 'economic' assets while orphaning uneconomic wellbores and pipelines that the Alberta Energy Regulator valued at $664,000 but with associated costs of approximately $4.6 million, meaning a potential net loss to the Orphaned Well Association (OWA) of $3.94 million. See Affidavit of Patricia Johnston, 18 August, p. 3 (item 19), at *https://www.grantthornton.ca/en/service/advisory/creditor-updates/#Redwater-Energy-Corp* (accessed 21 January 2019). See also *http://www.aer.ca/documents/news-releases/AERPS2016-01-Backgrounder.pdf* (27 May 2016; accessed 21 January 2019).

[4] See Affidavit of Patricia Johnston, 18 August 2015, to be found along with all other court filings for the Redwater case at *http://www.grantthornton.ca/en/service/advisory/creditor-updates/#Redwater-Energy-Corp* (accessed 21 January 2019).

[5] See *https://www.aer.ca/protecting-what-matters/protecting-the-environment/orphan-energy sites and also http://www.orphanwell.ca* for the AER & OWA criteria for taking orphans (i.e. 'legitimate' orphans), including recovering end-of-life costs from working interest partners.

[6] The case was heard on 15 February 2018. At the time of writing, no decision has been announced. See Case #37627, Orphan Well Association, *et al.* v. Grant Thornton Limited, *et al.*: *https://www.scc-csc.ca/case-dossier/info/parties-eng.aspx?cas=37627* (accessed 21 January 2019). While the case names the receiver, Grant Thornton Limited, it is popularly known as the 'Redwater case'. Whatever the ruling, the legacy well problem in Alberta remains to be addressed.

[7] All names and corporate names in this essay are pseudonyms, other than Sequoia and those relating to the public case of Redwater.

[8] My use of performativities is shaped by both social studies of finance (e.g. Callon 2006) and feminist philosophy and anthropology (e.g. Dear, Ho, Tsing & Yanagisako 2015; Butler 2010). For other discussions of oil performativities, see Appel, Mason & Watts (2015) and High & Smith (this volume).

[9] Labouring for capital has much in common with Neff's excellent term 'venture labour' (2012). By 'labouring for capital', I mean to point to more than 'upside' potential from options. 'Skin in the game' is direct investment intended to create alignment between management and hedge funds, and the different entitlements that come from those privileged positions. In industry, option holders are not considered by management teams to have 'real' stakes because they do not carry any 'downside' risk. As a result, some executives have been known to disparagingly refer to the 'wins' from options alone as 'lucky money', even while they simultaneously present options to employees as an important component of compensation that justifies reduced salaries despite the fact that reward from options may never be realized.

[10] See previous note. 'Skin in the game', first coined by Warren Buffett, is an oft-used phrase in business vernacular. Insiders often mention the phrase to indicate that they have a 'material' (i.e. meaningful) stake in a venture. For additional discussions on 'skin in the game', see Taleb (2018).

[11] If these value creation projects succeed, the personal investments of CEOs and management teams can convert to an extremely good life where energy becomes luxury (see Mason, this volume). Many of my interlocutors describe small oil and gas companies as affording them a 'chance at a big score'. I argue

elsewhere that, while minor in the global picture of oil producers, these small companies are directly tied to local stratifications of wealth and power through their ability to capture not just oil but also global sources of capital from which they sequester some for themselves through the dilutive means of option securities and discounted stock purchase.

[12] After her initial reading of the new virtue ethics literature, Guyer 'wonder[ed] how [it] configured this component of moral regimes, where accepting a domain, then holding steady, hanging on, keeping going and enduring through thick and thin would be individually ethically crucial' (2014: 399). She continues: 'Because of duration and contingency, which require recurrent, nested temporal-ethical imaginations, the narrow cause and effect interpretation of the durational aspects of responsibility and perseverance does not seem reducible to simply submitting to obligations that have been specified and imposed from outside, or even committed to explicitly at the outset' (2014: 399). Guyer draws her analysis from Fouconnet, a student of Durkheim and a colleague of Mauss, who paid careful attention to the concept of responsibility.

[13] For example, a company called Sequoia recently notified that it was cutting losses and departing from its Canadian operations. It notified the regulator of its intention to abandon its assets and leave the country. See note 22 below.

[14] While there is no space here to address it, the productivity of capitalization, assets, and financial accounting to produce both lifeworlds and things we differently live with links to questions taken up more broadly by infrastructure scholars (see Anand, Gupta & Appel 2018; Appel 2012; Larkin 2013).

[15] *http://www.merriam-webster.com/dictionary/orphan?src=search-dict-hed* (accessed 10 January 2019).

[16] *http://www.orphanwell.ca/?page_id=13* (accessed 10 January 2019).

[17] In some cases, orphaned wells are still productive, as in the recent case of Lexin assets that were seized by the regulator for being in substandard condition. These orphans created a surge in OWA intake but many of them are productive assets with economic value and can be sold by the regulator. They are therefore unlikely to remain orphans for long.

[18] Tsing (2015a: 122-7) 'sorts out commodities', noting how they differ from gifts in that alienation is required. However, I argue that the asset form is much closer to the gift in this regard in that things and persons are formed through them.

[19] See Affidavit of Nikol Schultz, 25 September 2015: *http://www.grantthornton.ca/en/service/advisory/creditor-updates/#Redwater-Energy-Corp* (accessed 11 January 2019).

[20] See *http://www.orphanwell.ca/wp-content/uploads/2018/10/OWA-2017-18-Ann-Rpt-Final.pdf*. An additional 283 ophaned wells have since been added to the OWA inventory, bringing the total as at September 2018 to 2,061. For current totals or lists of orphaned wells, pipeline segments, and facilities, see *http://www.orphanwell.ca/?page_id=160* and *https://fuzeium.com/alberta-inactive-orphan-wells/* (accessed 25 February 2019).

[21] For active and inactive well counts, see *http://www.energy.alberta.ca/oil/Pages/AUWI.aspx* (accessed 21 January 2019). For recent estimated liabilities of abandoned infrastructure, see Bellefontaine (2018).

[22] According to the OWA 2017 Annual Report (*http://www.orphanwell.ca/wp-content/uploads/2018/10/OWA-2017-18-Ann-Rpt-Final.pdf*, accessed 11 January 2019), there are approximately thirty bankrupt companies that hold licences with the Alberta Energy Regulator that may produce orphans in the manner of Redwater. The Sequoia assets alone are expected to raise the number of orphans by a further 2,300, in addition to a vast number of facilities and pipeline segments (see McIntosh 2018).

[23] I clearly disclosed my research intentions to the CEOs and team members described in this work. I was permitted to do research while working provided that I changed company names and deal terms enough to ensure the anonymity of my interlocutors, as promised. The consent I received in this context was due to relations of trust that were developed over many years of my own awkward and often uncomfortable entanglement of work and fieldwork in the industry.

[24] For an excellent example regarding the bitumen sands, dispossession, berry contamination, and orphaned man camps in Northern Alberta, see Baker (2016).

[25] Here, the socialities of capitalization track the morality surrounding the credit/debt nexus so well described by Peebles (2010) and other debt scholars (e.g. Graeber 2011; High 2012; James 2012; Roitman 2003).

[26] Open-hole logs are routinely performed in industry. Typically, a wireline company is contracted to drop a logging tool down the open wellbore. Three types of logs are usually generated: gamma ray, resistivity, and porosity. Taken together they detect the presence of permeable rock vs impermeable shale and clay, degree of water saturation, and degree of porosity. Details on logging instruments used in industry can be found at *http://petrowiki.org/Resistivity_and_spontaneous_(SP)_logging* (accessed 11 January 2019).

[27] Alberta has 'split title' rights, meaning that landholders own the surface rights while mineral rights are owned by the Crown in approximately 80 per cent of the cases. Unless there has been a violation of AER rules, landholders with split title cannot refuse a well but can negotiate its location. They receive annual rentals for

loss of use and other forms of consideration but do not share in corporate or well proceeds. The remaining 20 per cent of land titles are freehold rights. First Nations own mineral rights underlying treaty lands and have the right to be consulted for proposed petroleum and natural gas projects on land under claim. The federal government also manages First Nation oil and gas affairs, a colonial arrangement that is being contested by First Nations.

[28] Western alienation and the long-held resentment of western Canadians to 'eastern' Canada has shaped the nation's history and regional identities in important ways. Eastern Canada is host to the nation's political capital as well as its financial headquarters, and its links to Alberta's provincially owned resources have been contentious in this regard (see, e.g., Henry 2000).

[29] The effectiveness of these vetting practices, by which a sense of rational calculation and verification is expected to offset excitable passions, is called into question by the many market bubbles, stock market fevers, and outright acts of fraud that characterize the history of capitalism (see Graeber 2011; Tsing 2005).

[30] For examples of kin relations that sustain oil projects in Argentina through neoliberal labour arrangements, see Shever (2012).

[31] The Alberta Energy Regulator manages the transfer of licences through its Long-Term Liability Rating (LLR), which required, at the time, a Liability Management Ratio (LMR) of at least one times assets over liabilities before the transfer of a well licence would be approved. See AER Directive 006 and Directive 011: *https://www.aer.ca* (accessed 11 January 2019).

[32] In his comments to Rogers (2014), Maurer anticipates this kind of exchange entanglement. Drawing from Strathern, he notes that barter exchanges are precise: 'This pig for that sow' (Maurer in Rogers 2014: 146). Also, the weakened position of a trading partner in these exchanges is consistent with Guyer's exploration of barter's etymology that links the concept to cheating (Guyer in Rogers 2014: 144).

[33] In response to Redwater, the regulator changed the LMR rules to require that corporation purchasing (or in this case, being gifted) an asset must have at least *two* times the assets over liabilities on their balance sheet, thus prohibiting the transfer of property to corporations with high liabilities. Also note that those that do not comply must pay a bond.

[34] Such networks are only open to those who can who can pull the levers of those prized 'fictitious commodities' (Polanyi 2001 [1944] in Guyer 2009: 207-10) in oil-based accumulation: land, labour, and capital – along with, as in Tsing's (2015a) analysis, all that goes unmentioned but must be subsumed, collapsed, colonized, and converted into capitalist value generation to keep these fictions alive (see also Graeber 2011: 346-8).

REFERENCES

ANAND, N., A. GUPTA & H. APPEL (eds) 2018. *The promise of infrastructure.* Durham, N.C.: Duke University Press.

APPADURAI, A. 2011. The ghost in the financial machine. *Public Culture* **23**, 517-39.

APPEL, H. 2012. Offshore work: oil, modularity, and the how of capitalism in Equatorial Guinea. *American Ethnologist* **39**, 692-709.

——, A. MASON & M. WATTS (eds) 2015. *Subterranean estates: life worlds of oil and gas.* Ithaca, N.Y.: Cornell University Press.

BAKER, J.M. 2016. Harvesting ruins: the im/permanence of work camps and reclaiming colonized landscapes in the Northern Alberta oil sands. Anthropology and Environment Society. Engagement, 23 October (available on-line: *https://aesengagement.wordpress.com/2016/10/23/harvesting-ruins-the-impermanence-of-work-camps-and-reclaiming-colonized-landscapes-in-the-northern-alberta-oil-sands/*, accessed 11 January 2019).

BARRY, A. 2013. *Material politics: disputes along the pipeline.* Chichester: Wiley.

BEAR, L., R. BIRLA & S. PURI 2015. Speculation. *Comparative Studies of South Asia, Africa and the Middle East* **35**, 387-91.

——, K. HO, A. TSING & S. YANAGISAKO 2015. 'Generating capitalism.' Theorizing the Contemporary. *Cultural Anthropology* website (available on-line: *https://culanth.org/fieldsights/650-generating-capitalism*, accessed 11 January 2019).

BELLEFONTAINE, M. 2018. $260B liability figure for abandoned energy infrastructure an 'error in judgment': AER. Current liability figure is actually $58.7B, energy regulator says. CBC News, 1 November (available on-line: *https://www.cbc.ca/news/canada/edmonton/alberta-energy-regulator-liability-figure-error-1.4888532*, accessed 21 January 2019).

BOHANNAN, L. [as E. SMITH BOWEN] 1964. *Return to laughter: an anthropological novel.* New York: Praeger.

BRAUN, B. 2000. Producing vertical territory: geology and governmentality in late Victorian Canada. *Cultural Geographies* **7**, 7-46.

BUTLER, J. 2010. Performative agency. *Journal of Cultural Economy* **3**, 147-61.

ÇALIŞKAN, K. & M. CALLON 2009. Economization, part 1: Shifting attention from the economy towards processes of economization. *Economy and Society* **38**, 369-98.

———— & ———— 2010. Economization, part 2: A research programme for the study of markets. *Economy and Society* **39**, 1-32.

CALLON, M. 2006. What does it mean to say that economics is performative? CSI Working Paper Series 005.2006 (available on-line: *https://halshs.archives-ouvertes.fr/halshs-00091596/document*, accessed 11 January 2019).

DE RIJKE, K., P. MUNRO & M. DE LOURDES MELO ZURITA 2016. The Great Artesian Basin: a contested resource environment of subterranean water and coal seam gas in Australia. *Society and Natural Resources* **29**, 696-710.

FASSIN, D. 2015. Troubled waters: at the confluence of ethics and politics. In *Four lectures on ethics: anthropological perspectives*, M. Lambek, V. Das, D. Fassin & W. Keane, 175-210. Chicago: HAU Books.

FERGUSON, J. 2013. Declarations of dependence: labour, personhood, and welfare in southern Africa. *Journal of the Royal Anthropological Institute* (N.S.) **19**, 223-42.

GOLUB, A. & M. RHEE 2013. Traction: the role of executives in localizing global mining and petroleum industries in Papua New Guinea. *Paideuma* **59**, 215-36.

GRAEBER, D. 2011. *Debt: the first 5000 years*. Brooklyn, N.Y.: Melville House.

GUYER, J. 2009. Composites, fictions, and risk: toward an ethnography of price. In *Market and society: the great transformation today* (eds) C. Hann & K. Hart, 203-39. Cambridge: University Press.

———— 2012. Obligation, binding, debt and responsibility: provocations about temporality from two new sources. *Social Anthropology* **20**, 491-501.

———— 2014. Durational ethics: search, finding and translation of Fauconnet's 'Essay on responsibility and liberty'. HAU: *Journal of Ethnographic Theory* **4**, 397-409.

HENRY, S. 2000. Revisiting western alienation: towards a better understanding of political alienation and political behaviour in western Canada. Ph.D. dissertation, University of Calgary.

HIGH, H. 2012. Re-reading the potlatch in a time of crisis: debt and the distinctions that matter. *Social Anthropology* **20**, 363-79.

HO, K. 2009. *Liquidated: an ethnography of Wall Street*. Durham, N.C.: Duke University Press.

———— 2015. Supermanagers, inequality, and finance. HAU: *Journal of Ethnographic Theory* **5**, 481-8.

JAMES, D. 2012. Money-go-round: personal economies of wealth, aspiration and indebtedness. *Africa* **82**, 20-40.

KEANE, W. 2014. Affordances and reflexivity in ethical life: an ethnographic stance. *Anthropological Theory* **14**, 3-26.

———— 2016. *Ethical life: its natural and social histories*. Princeton: University Press.

KNEAS, D. 2016. Subsoil abundance and surface absence: a junior mining company and its performance of prognosis in northwestern Ecudaor. *Journal of the Royal Anthropological Institute* **22**: SI, 67-86.

KOPYTOFF, I. 1986. The cultural biography of things: commoditization as process. In *The social life of things* (ed.) A. Appadurai, 64-94. Cambridge: University Press.

LAIDLAW, J. 2014. *The subject of virtue*. Cambridge: University Press.

LAMBEK, M. 2011. *Ordinary ethics*. New York: Fordham University Press.

LARKIN, B. 2013. The politics and poetics of infrastructure. *Annual Review of Anthropology* **42**, 327-43.

LATOUR, B. 2004. Why has critique run out of steam? From matters of fact to matters of concern. *Critical Inquiry* **30**, 225-48.

LI, T. 2012. What is land? Anthropological perspectives on the global land rush. Paper presented at the Second International Conference on Global Land Grabbing, Cornell University, 17-19 October.

MCINTOSH, J. 2018. Sequoia Resources to orphan thousands of wells after ceasing operations. *Huffington Post*, 3 August (available on-line: *https://www.huffingtonpost.ca/2018/03/08/sequoia-resources-to-orphan-thousands-of-wells-after-ceasing-operations_a_23381107/*, accessed 11 January 2019).

MASON, A. 2015. Events collectives: the social life of a promise-disappointment cycle. In *Subterranean estates: life worlds of oil and gas* (eds) H. Appel, A. Mason & M. Watts, 325-39. Ithaca, N.Y.: Cornell University Press.

MATTINGLY, C. 2014. Moral deliberation and the agentive self in Laidlaw's ethics. *Hau: Journal of Ethnographic Theory* **4**, 473-86.

MAURER, B. 2006. The anthropology of money. *Annual Review of Anthropology* **35**, 5-36.

MAUSS, M. 2016 [1925]. *The gift* (Expanded edition, trans. J. Guyer). Chicago: HAU Books.

MITCHELL, T. 2009. Carbon democracy. *Economy and Society* **38**, 399-432.

MIYAZAKI, H. 2006. Economy of dreams: hope in global capitalism and its critiques. *Cultural Anthropology* **21**, 147-72.

——— 2013. *Arbitraging Japan: dreams of capitalism at the end of finance*. Berkeley: University of California Press.

MUNIESA, F. 2017. On the political vernaculars of value creation. *Science as Culture* **26**, 445-54.

———, L. DOGANOVA, H. ORTIZ, *et al.* 2017. *Capitalization: a cultural guide*. Paris: Presses des Mines.

NADER, L. 1972. Up the anthropologist: perspectives gained from studying up. In *Reinventing anthropology* (ed.) D. Hymes, 284-311. New York: Vintage.

NEFF, G. 2012. *Venture labour: work and the burden of risk in innovative industries*. Cambridge, Mass.: MIT Press.

NIKIFORUK, A. 2001. *Saboteurs: Wiebo Ludwig's war against big oil*. Toronto: Macfarlane Walter & Ross.

——— 2015. *Slickwater: fracking and one insider's stand against the world's most powerful industry*. Vancouver: Greystone Books.

ORTIZ, H. 2013. Financial value. HAU: *Journal of Ethnographic Theory* **3**, 64-79.

——— 2014. The limits of financial imagination: free investors, efficient markets, and crisis. *American Anthropologist* **116**, 38-50.

PARRY, J. & M. BLOCH 1989. Introduction: Money and the morality of exchange. In *Money and the morality of exchange* (eds) J. Parry & M. Bloch, 1-32. Cambridge: University Press.

PEEBLES, G. 2010. The anthropology of credit and debt. *Annual Review of Anthropology* **39**, 225-40.

POLANYI, K. 2001 [1944]. *The great transformation*. Boston: Beacon.

RAJAN, S.K. (ed.) 2012. *Lively capital: biotechnologies, ethics, and governance in global markets*. Durham, N.C.: Duke University Press.

RICHARDSON, T. & G. WESZKALNYS 2014. Introduction: Resource materialities. *Anthropological Quarterly* **87**, 5-30.

ROITMAN, J. L. 2003. Unsanctioned wealth; or, the productivity of debt in northern Cameroon. *Public Culture* **15**, 211-37.

——— 2013. *Anti-crisis*. Durham, N.C.: Duke University Press.

ROGERS, D. 2014. Petrobarter. *Current Anthropology* **55**, 131-53.

——— 2015. Oil and anthropology. *Annual Review of Anthropology* **44**, 365-80.

SHEVER, E. 2012. *Resources for reform: oil and neoliberalism in Argentina*. Stanford: University Press.

SYKES, K. 2015. Priceless value: from no money on our skins to a moral economy of investment. In *Knowledge and ethics in anthropology* (ed.) L. Josephides, 123-42. New York: Bloomsbury Academic.

TALEB, N. 2018. *Skin in the game: hidden asymmetries in daily life*. New York: Random House.

TSING, A. 2005. *Friction: an ethnography of global connection*. Princeton: University Press.

——— 2015*a*. *The mushroom at the end of the world: on the possibility of life in capitalist ruins*. Princeton: University Press.

——— 2015*b*. Salvage accumulation, or the structural effects of capitalist generativity. Theorizing the Contemporary. *Cultural Anthropology* website (available on-line: https://culanth.org/fieldsights/656-salvage-accumulation-or-the-structural-effects-of-capitalist-generativity, accessed 11 January 2019).

WESZKALNYS, G. 2015. Geology, potentiality, speculation: on the indeterminacy of first oil. *Cultural Anthropology* **30**, 611-39.

——— 2016. A doubtful hope: resource affect in a future oil economy. *Journal of the Royal Anthropological Institute* **22**: SI, 127-46.

WOOD, C. 2015. Taking over the gift. In *Flexible capitalism: exchange and ambiguity at work* (ed.) J. Kjaerulff, 116-45. Oxford: Berghahn Books.

——— 2016. Inside the halo zone: geology, finance, and the corporate performance of profit in a deep tight oil formation. *Economic Anthropology* **3**, 43-56.

ZALOOM, C. 2009. How to read the future: the yield curve, affect and financial prediction. *Public Culture* **21**, 245-68.

## Puits orphelins, actifs pétroliers et endettement : les éthiques concurrentes de la création de valeur et du *care* dans les projets de retour sur investissement du capitalisme pétrolier

*Résumé*

Cet essai explore le phénomène des puits dits « orphelins », les puits de pétrole et de gaz (« hérités ») non rentables qui ont été dissociés des entreprises qui en étaient propriétaires pour cause d'insolvabilité ou de non-respect de la réglementation locale. À partir de l'exemple ethnographique d'une société pétrolière et gazière au bord de l'insolvabilité dans l'Alberta, au Canada, et de ses stratégies de refinancement, il examine la façon dont la création de valeur et la force morale de l'obligation de rentabilité donnent naissance à une « éthique de la persistance » qui modèle la performativité entrepreneuriale et financière et prolonge la « durée de vie » des actifs pétroliers et gaziers hérités. Les actifs hérités, perçus comme des orphelins en puissance, sont donc récupérés dans une pratique d'entreprise vivace de circulation et de recombinaison des actifs, que les producteurs déploient souvent en vue de la tâche morale « d'apurer leur bilan ». Cet essai appelle à « penser avec les orphelins » afin de reconnaître les registres éthiques concurrents qui les produisent, en plus du besoin croissant de responsabilité et de soin des entreprises envers les actifs pétroliers et gaziers hérités.

# 4

# Boom to bust, ashes to (coal) dust: the contested ethics of energy exchanges in a declining US coal market

JESSICA M. SMITH *Colorado School of Mines*

This essay explores how rank-and-file producers of energy evaluate the ethics of energy exchanges, which sheds light on some of the unexamined assumptions animating anthropological studies of energy and ethics. Exploring how coal miners experience a massive downturn in Wyoming, the centre of US coal production, reveals differing logics of exchange between the producers and consumers of electricity. Most Americans engage with electricity as consumers through a commodity framework, paying utility companies a fee to purchase kilowatt hours that are abstracted from their productive origins. In contrast, the miners experience energy as more of a gift exchange, keeping in view the network of the ultimate consumers of the coal they produce. These differing logics of exchange entail different ethical obligations in the face of the termination of those relationships as the country moves away from coal-fired electricity, helping to explain the outrage that was felt in 'coal country' – an outrage that Donald Trump exploited for political purposes during the 2016 US presidential election.

In March 2016, more than 500 full-time coal miners were laid off in one day in Wyoming's Powder River Basin, a region that has been the United States' largest coal producer since the mid-1990s. That number represented about 10 per cent of the region's workforce and did not include the hundreds of temporary workers who had lost their jobs in smaller batches over the course of the previous year. The layoffs sent shockwaves throughout the state, even though the declining fortunes of the coal industry were well known by most. Natural gas started displacing coal in US electric markets in 2008, making headlines out of closing mines and dwindling communities in Appalachia. The Wyoming miners hoped they would be shielded from the worst losses in production. In contrast with their Appalachian counterparts, the coal they mined was low in sulphur and therefore appealing to power plants held to stricter emissions standards. Their mines were also some of the most efficient in the world, producing 45 per cent of the country's coal while employing only 10 per cent of the country's coal miners (Berkowitz & Meko 2017). The Powder River Basin mines are surface operations, where seams that stretch upwards of 100 feet tall allow for quick extraction by miners operating gargantuan heavy equipment, including two-storey haul trucks and draglines the size of suburban homes (Rolston 2013a; 2014). Whereas coal production had weathered booms and busts

*Journal of the Royal Anthropological Institute (N.S.), 91-107*
© Royal Anthropological Institute 2019

in other parts of the country, Wyoming coal employment had increased steadily from the mines' opening in the 1970s until 2008, fuelling miners' hopes that they would once again be immune from a national downturn. The massive layoffs, delivered by company personnel flanked by security guards, shattered that fantasy.

Coal downturns are not new to anthropology. In the United States and the United Kingdom in particular, anthropologists have theorized these downturns largely in terms of how workers and mining communities try to remake a sense of place in the midst of de-industrialization (e.g. Charlesworth 2000; Degnen 2012; Kideckel 2008; Stewart 1996; Thorleifsson 2016). Coal has been 'good to think with' for understanding labour politics, so much so that the 'image of the militant, class conscious coal miner has played a powerful role in constituting knowledges of "the working class" and "working-class struggle"' (Gibson-Graham 2006: 208; see also Rolston 2014).

Yet nuanced ethnographic understanding of how downturns are lived and understood by the people directly affected by them have remained analytically distinct from anthropological theorizing about energy and its mutual imbrication with other forms of political, sociocultural, and economic power. This essay seeks to bring together these two literatures by exploring how coal's energy-based properties come to matter as miners in Wyoming reimagine their work and its place in the shifting US economy. For the miners I came to know, the significance of their work was not 'labour' or 'mining' in a general sense but *providing electricity* to a wide network of consumers around the nation. This framing stretches back to the 1970s, when the region's mines were first opened in the shadow of that decade's oil crisis. Transitions away from coal-based electricity, felt most viscerally in the post-2008 coal market downturn, thus threatened the grounds on which they staked their sense of national belonging.

This essay draws attention to labour as an overlooked but crucial dimension of anthropological theorizing about energy. Anthropologists have studied the social movements that criticize coal production (McNeil 2011) and coal-fired electricity generation (Powell 2018). The existing literature also memorably tracks the impacts of energy production on nearby communities, from indigenous communities who grapple with the social and environmental dilemmas of oil production (Cepek 2012; Sawyer 2004) or ostensibly 'green' wind parks (Howe 2014), to a substantial literature on the dislocations occasioned by hydraulic fracturing (e.g. Grubert & Skinner 2017; Mercer, de Rijke & Dressler 2014; Willow & Wylie 2014). Inspired by Laura Nader's (1981) critiques of nuclear scientists and policy-making on the US Committee on Nuclear and Alternative Energy Systems, anthropologists have also examined the professionals and experts who are central to energy infrastructures, such as engineers who make electricity markets (Özden-Schilling 2015; 2016), biofuel scientists who enact 'responsible' research innovation (McLeod & Nerlich 2017), and the executives and consultants who lead companies and shape national energy policies (High, this volume; Hughes 2017; Mason 2013; this volume; Wood, this volume).

Few scholars working in the anthropology of energy study rank-and-file workers (for an exception, see Smith & Tidwell 2016), despite the central role that Timothy Mitchell (2011) grants to labour in his foundational account of the transition from coal- to oil-based energy economies. The strength of coal miners' labour politics, Mitchell suggests, came from the centrality of workers to the mining process and their ability to shut down the supply of coal by targeting chokepoints on the railroads that transported it. In contrast, oil was pumped to the surface and then transported by pipeline or ship, making it less susceptible to strikes (see Atabaki, Bini & Ehsani 2018 for more nuanced histories of oil labour activism). A few anthropologists have engaged oil workers to illuminate key transformations in the organization of oil industries: Diane Austin and Tom McGuire (2017) analyse the insecurities of work in offshore oil in the Gulf Coast region, for example, and Elana Shever (2012) poignantly argues that the kinship practices of oil workers accompanied and facilitated the privatization of the Argentine oil sector. With these exceptions, workers have largely been 'disappeared' (Ehsani 2018) from the anthropology of energy.

This essay thus carves out a space for labour in the anthropology of energy by exploring how rank-and-file producers of energy evaluate the ethics of energy exchanges. The Wyoming miners share a sense of under-appreciated provisioning in common with other energy producers, such as the Colorado oil executives and managers described by Mette High (this volume). Exploring this ethical stance-taking in depth, I argue that attention to the Wyoming miners' experience of the coal downturn reveals a disconnect between the expectations of exchange held by the miners and those generated by the US electricity market and its infrastructure. With few exceptions, such as those who generate their own power, most Americans primarily engage with electricity through a commodity framework, paying utilities a fee to purchase kilowatt hours (see also Walsh, this volume). The source of that energy is almost always opaque: while some utilities publish the sector mix of their energy sources, documenting which percentages come from coal, natural gas, nuclear energy, and renewables, and others offer consumers the option of buying electricity from renewable sources, it is notoriously difficult to trace the origin of that electricity back to particular places of production. In contrast, the Wyoming miners experience energy as more of a gift exchange, keeping in view the network of the ultimate consumers of the coal-fired electricity they produce. These differing logics of exchange entail different ethical obligations in the face of the termination of those relationships, helping to explain the outrage that was felt in 'coal country' – an outrage that Donald Trump exploited for political purposes during the 2016 presidential election.

The essay draws on research I have conducted in the Powder River Basin since 2004, including participant observation at four of the region's twelve active mines. For twenty-two months of formal research, I lived and worked in Gillette, the region's largest town with about 30,000 residents, including 5,000 directly employed by the coal industry. As detailed elsewhere (Rolston 2014), that research continues to be informed by my own experiences growing up in Gillette as the daughter of a mine mechanic. During summer breaks from college I worked in two additional mines myself for ten months as a haul truck driver and plant technician. Those experiences and close workplace relationships inspired my later fieldwork and my desire to pursue research questions that were not only theoretically valuable but also vital for my interlocutors. Their perpetual critique of the industry differed from the concerns that animated most anthropological scholarship and popular culture on coal mining: coal consumers, the Wyoming miners lamented, could not see beyond the light switch to appreciate the everyday lives of the people who made that consumption of electricity possible.

## Energy exchanges

Energy is a fundamental resource that flows through and between groups of people on scales both large and small. Entire disciplines chart the geopolitics of energy as it crosses and confounds national borders, affording particular kinds of political regimes and labour movements (Mitchell 2011). Anthropologists show that these flows of energy are intertwined with political power, with energy production, distribution, and consumption serving as a form of governance akin to Foucault's biopower – what Dominic Boyer (2014) terms 'energopower'. On a smaller scale, anthropologists also trace exchanges of energy among households. Stephen Gudeman (2012) memorably shows that the concept of 'vital energy' infuses the everyday thoughts and practices of agricultural groups in rural Panama and Colombia. As the 'current of life', *fuerza* does not just shape activities that analysts would view as economic, but also permeates kinship and religion (2012: 57). Humans replenish their stores of this energy through consuming the crops they have put energy into cultivating, building up the strength of households (2012: 64). Vital energy 'connects house members within the dwelling, making them shared persons, one to another, while also connecting a house to the past and to other houses in a community' (2012: 69). Households exchange this energy through reciprocal work, festive labour, and hospitality. This exchange of labour is neither barter nor market trade, but mutual and delayed assistance, evocatively expressed in the language describing the exchange of 'strength for strength': 'arm for arm, rib for rib, back for back, loaned arm, loaned hand, returned hand, or returned arm' (2012: 69). Houses that do not assist others are deprived of connections with others. This ethnography forms one piece of Gudeman's overall theorization of mutual (distinguished from market) exchanges as those in which sharing makes and maintains community (see also 2001: 86).

The analytic framework of mutual exchange also sheds light on contemporary practices of energy exchange. Whereas most social science research on 'energy trading' among households with access to off-grid renewable energy assumes that these energy exchanges are motivated by rational choice theory, anthropologists show that they are informed by complex logics of exchange. In rural India, for example, Abhigyan Singh and colleagues argue that villagers with access to off-grid solar electricity engage in both mutual and market exchanges as they provide electricity access to those who lack it (Singh, Strating, Romero Herrera, van Dijk & Keysen 2017). Motivated by culturally specific moral obligations of kinship, energy providers engage in mutual exchanges with people in their kin network, emphasizing 'morality, sociability and sociality', but engage in market exchanges with non-kin, prioritizing 'calculations, strategizing for material benefits, profit, economistic and rational thinking' (Singh *et al.* 2017: 112). Energy exchanges, in this case, form one arena through which people make, remake, and evaluate the moral obligations of kin and non-kin.

A division of academic labour has thus emerged concerning the scale at which energy exchange takes place: while accounts of individuals and households that generate their own energy illuminate the lived worlds of the people engaging in these exchanges, energy exchange at larger scales is made to appear as occurring among national-level actors such as politicians, policy-makers, utilities, and major corporations. It is telling that the analytic language of how energy at this large scale moves from production to consumption utilizes the language of 'flows' (e.g. Boyer 2014; Strauss, Rupp & Love 2013). The term makes a clever play on an everyday description used to describe energy, layering it with social theory (see especially Appadurai 1986). The focus on flow can, however, obscure the human agents whose labour enables those flows. Coal does not 'flow' from pit to plant to railroad to utility without people at each step of the way.[1]

## Coal miners as energy providers

Since the coal market collapse began in 2008, the Wyoming miners and their families have felt cast off by a country that previously depended upon their everyday labour for their energy-dependent lives. The coal mine jobs appealed to the people who became miners because they pay well enough to comfortably raise a family: depending on overtime, miners could make $100,000 or more a year. But for the miners I came to know, the meaning of that labour was greater than a paycheque as it was infused with their status as providers of energy for the rest of the country. The mines that currently make the Powder River Basin the largest producer of coal in the country first opened in the 1970s and early 1980s in the wake of the national energy crisis prompted by the OPEC oil embargoes. More than a dozen mines opened over the course of just a few years, animated by a feverish rhetoric about the need for affordable, abundant, and American sources of energy to wean the country from its dependence on unreliable oil from the Middle East. For example, in 1975, as Exxon was planning two coal mines, the company ran a series of full-page ads in *The Gillette News Record* to garner local support. Under the headline of 'Coal can get America fired up again', the text reads:

> US coal contains twice as much energy as all the oil in the Middle East … although supplies of domestic oil and natural gas are dwindling, the US has about half of the coal reserves in the free world … If more of this energy can be developed, it can help replace some foreign oil, stimulate the economy and help fight unemployment … It will take time and the best efforts of all of us before America's huge coal reserves can come to the rescue. But work must begin now. At Exxon, we're doing our best to get on with the job.

The men and women who went to work in the mines thus found themselves enrolled in an undertaking of great national significance: they were not simply taking a job, but also providing a patriotic duty for their country.[2] Industry proponents and local government began referring to the Powder River Basin as the 'Saudi Arabia of coal', simultaneously evoking the enormity of the basin's coal reserves and domesticating the industry, its intentions, and its personnel. Casting coal extraction as a patriotic duty would continue throughout the following four decades, as companies encouraged Americans to 'imagine a world where our country runs on energy from Middle America instead of the Middle East', as the CEO of Peabody Energy charged in 2007. Foundation Coal titled its 2005 Annual Report *Reliable American energy*, which appeared on the cover in red, white, and blue font above a photo of a bald eagle superimposed on a coal seam, making its body appear to be made of coal. In an ad with a photo of a young boy running with an American flag and the tagline 'Keep the lights on, America', the Federation for American Coal, Energy, and Security group warned that Americans would lose electricity, jobs, and economic growth without coal (Schneider, Schwarze, Bsumek & Peeples 2016: 68). The coal advocacy group AmericasPower.org developed a widely circulated image of an orange extension cord plugged into a piece of coal, as well as an image of the US lit up at night behind the words 'Coal-based electricity: Our past. Our present. Our future'. These images sought to make the country's dependence on coal visible through public relations campaigns directly tying consumers' familiar uses of electricity back to coal, otherwise maligned as a key contributor to global climate change.

As they made sense of the post-2008 coal downturn, miners and their families continued to share the major features of this framing, positioning themselves as providing a needed service to the rest of the country and explaining that the privileged lives of people living in cities would grind to a halt if the miners did not go to work. On tours and in conversations, they explained the scale and significance of their labour by translating the coal tonnage into hours of electricity use for others. Truck drivers who spent their shifts hauling 300- to 400-ton loads of coal from the pit shovels to

**Figure 1.** A train leaves the Powder River Basin, bringing coal to power plants outside Wyoming. (Photo courtesy of David Brossard under a Creative Commons license and available at *https://tinyurl.com/yayquhdq.*)

the processing plant and back again, for example, quantified each load as providing a certain number of hours of electricity that would enable people around the country to keep their lights on, to run their computers, and to charge their cell phones. One truck driver boasted, 'The bed of one 320-ton haul truck carries enough coal to supply one American home for forty years'. A lifelong equipment operator explained, 'What we do is important because the nation depends on coal to turn their lights on … Coal is affordable, it's very efficient. It powers this nation and we take a lot of pride in that'. Another drew attention to the everyday activities that coal facilitated, saying, 'It's nice to be able to help millions of people out, you know, in their daily life. So they can see at night, alarm clocks go off in the morning, they can fix their breakfast'. These statements call attention to the intimacy of energy dependence, as did Mette High's interlocutors in the oil industry (this volume).

While statements such as these appear to construct a somewhat abstract American consumer of coal-fired electricity, miners and managers alike traced the specific network of people who consumed the electricity generated from the coal they mine. The primary way they did this was by keeping track of the power plants from around the country, in about thirty states, that purchase their coal. Beyond reading the news and keeping track of their companies' sales, experienced miners could determine the destination of the mile-long trains that move Powder River Basin coal around the country by reading the series of letters emblazoned on the side of the rail cars (Fig. 1). Even though the distance between coal producers and consumers is more dispersed than the network of charcoal producers, consumers, and prosumers analysed by Andrew Walsh (this volume), they share in common that neither the coal nor charcoal was 'fully alienated'.

While anthropologists argue that electricity *consumption* from the grid connects households not just with electricity, but also with a sense of national belonging (e.g. Boyer 2014), *production* played a major role in how miners imagined their sense of belonging to the United States. Miners imagined themselves and their labour as directly linked to the people who consume their coal, even if those relationships stretched hundreds of miles away and were mediated by vast sociotechnical networks, starting with railroads that led to utilities, where it joins electricity produced from other energy sources and travels along power lines to outlets and ultimately to electrically powered devices. That infrastructural distance creates a 'mystery' not unique to coal. As Sidney Mintz first wrote about sugar, 'The mystery was not simply one of technical transformation, impressive as that is, but also the mystery of people unknown to one another being linked through space and time – and not just by politics and economics, but along a particular chain of connection maintained by their production' (1985: xxiv). The 'misrecognitions' (Foster 2008) that happen along that chain give rise to differing understandings of those relationships and the ethics enjoined by the exchanges that form them.

## Coal as gift

When considering the relationships among coal producers and coal consumers, the Wyoming miners regarded themselves as embedded in what anthropologists might call gift exchanges. That notion might seem strange to readers more accustomed to coal symbolizing a type of anti-gift – after all, in the United States and other parts of the world, children are threatened that Santa Claus will bring them coal instead of presents if they misbehave. But the miners' organic critiques of their invisibility in electricity networks have much in common with anthropological theories of gift exchange.

Anthropologists distinguish gift and commodity exchanges in order to highlight the differing logics and ethics underlining them, all the while recognizing that these distinctions are 'convenient and controlled fictions' like other analytical tools (Strathern 1988: 6). Gift exchange emphasizes 'a qualitative relationship between the *transactors*' in a 'state of reciprocal independence', in contrast with commodity exchange, which emphasizes 'a quantitative relationship between the *objects* exchanged' among people in a 'state of reciprocal independence' (Gregory 1982: 100-1, emphasis added). While this neat dichotomy has been rightly critiqued and reworked many times over, it remains a useful heuristic to draw out different logics of exchange that are nonetheless materialized and experienced with the messy complexity of social life.

Returning to coal, the Wyoming miners certainly experienced it as a commodity. They were paid (they would say handsomely) for their labour, and as a product of their labour, the coal was alienated from them as it travelled from the truck bed through the processing plant and into railcars to be transported to power plants. Taking a cue from Andrew Walsh's treatment of charcoal (this volume), a case could be made for coal being an excellent commodity – perhaps one of the origins of the Santa Claus coal as anti-gift myth. A quick glance at coal gives the untrained eye the impression that all coal everywhere looks the same, making Wyoming coal as offensive to put into a Christmas stocking as its counterpart from a different part of the world.[3] Producing coal-fired electricity requires breaking down the coal hauled by many different workers in one mine, mixing it together to be transferred and sold to utilities, which, in turn, burn it and transfer electricity to the grid. Rather than engaging with coal directly, consumers engage with electrically powered devices.[4]

Yet when considering the relationships engendered by coal production and consumption, the miners viewed them more as gift rather than commodity exchanges. As elaborated by Marilyn Strathern, things and persons assume the social form of things in commodity economies and persons in gift economies (1988: 134). While the consumers dependent on coal-fired electricity were central to how miners understood their labour, the miners lamented that coal consumers did not see and could not appreciate the miners as the source of their electricity.

*Journal of the Royal Anthropological Institute (N.S.), 91-107*
© Royal Anthropological Institute 2019

One source of this misrecognition, miners said, was the inability of electricity consumers to see that they were dependent on coal, even if they opposed coal-fired electricity for contributing to climate change. The second was that even those consumers who recognized that a portion of their electricity comes from coal most likely believed it originated in Appalachia, the symbolic heartland of the industry, rather than Wyoming. Every miner I knew had a story in which they explained their work to someone, only for that person to make a joke about pickaxes (required for historical underground mining) or express disbelief that more coal was mined in Wyoming than Appalachia. The lament of one miner who had just reached her thirty-year work anniversary was typical: 'I don't think people understand what it looks like to be a Wyoming coal miner. Someone thousands of miles of here could switch their light switch on and have no idea it's because we work in the coal mines in Wyoming'. This widespread sentiment was also succinctly captured by Rob Godby, the director of the Center for Energy, Economics, and Public Policy at the University of Wyoming: 'I think most Americans do think that coal still comes from Appalachia. They have that traditional idea of the underground coal miner with the dirty face and the pickaxe. Coal really hasn't been mined like that in almost fifty years'.

The miners wished that the consumers of coal-fired electricity would recognize that their own energy consumption cannot exist separately from the miners' energy production. As one long-time equipment operator imagined herself saying to one of those consumers, 'When you wake up in the morning and you put your slippers on and you stumble to the door and you flip that switch on the wall, it's what I do out here in the morning that makes that light come on'. Note how she contrasted the morning routines of electricity consumers and coal miners: the electricity consumer enjoyed a cushy life, sleepily putting on comfortable slippers on her way to the light switch, while she spent her mornings mining coal. The miners were virtuosos of good jokes, including those poking fun at 'yuppies' who drove hybrid cars, unaware that the electricity used to charge them may come from coal. During a commute, I once encountered a black electric Chevy Volt emblazoned with a personalized Colorado licence plate that simply said COALCAR, mischievously connecting the 'green' car with an energy source its proponents normally disparaged.

For the Wyoming miners, their labour was intricately embedded in a kind of gift exchange with far distant consumers: the miners hoped that Americans would see an outlet and also see them, since when the miners saw a piece of coal, they saw consumers and their electronic goods. They wished for electricity consumers to see a charged cell phone, a lit home, or an outlet and look beyond it to see Wyoming miners and their labour. Thinking in a particularly Melanesian way (e.g. Strathern 1988), I would even propose that the miners saw their labour expressed not just in their own activities, but also in the activities of the people who used the electricity generated by the coal. Recall the miner's appeal to connect the light switch on the wall with her work in the mine. For miners, their labour was expressed by teenagers playing video games, by yuppies driving hybrid cars, and by lights that shone in the dark across the country. Their labour provided the 'conditions of possibility' (Appel, this volume) for the lives of millions of energy consumers.

In their critique of the invisibilities produced by the vast electricity infrastructure, the miners fundamentally desired to be seen, to be recognized as the source of the electricity that powers the everyday lives of people around the United States. This connection was obscured by the infrastructural networks that make energy exchange possible, distancing electricity producers and consumers or, from the perspective of the miners, gift givers and receivers. The dilemma evokes Mintz's observation that 'the chemical and mechanical transformations by which substances are bent to human use and become unrecognizable to those who know them in nature have marked our relationship to nature ... but the division of labour by which such transformations are realized can impart additional mystery to the technical processes' (1985: xxiii). Dispelling the 'mystery' of electricity was an especially desirable and urgent task for the miners as appropriate compensation for their labour in the ongoing energy transition away from coal-fired electricity was dependent on recognition by electricity consumers of their gifts to the country.

### Ending exchange

What happens when gifts given are no longer desired by the receiver? When a country, expressed through a network of power plants, no longer accepts them? When the miners' labour has no outlet to be expressed in the activities of others? In an otherwise vast literature, 'the focus on the performative aspects of exchange has diverted ethnographic attention from the implications of unsuccessful transactions' (Kirsch 2006: 79). With the exception of work on exchanges near or at the end of life – frequently theorized as a strategy for reconstituting the self or the kin group (e.g. Conklin 2001; Marcoux 2001) – anthropologists have had precious little to say about ending exchanges beyond the observation that the cessation of the exchange ends the relationship. Filling this gap, Stuart Kirsch offers the term 'unrequited reciprocity' to refer to a 'failure to fulfil exchange obligations, whether by design or default, [that] is experienced as a negative assessment by the person who does not receive his or her due' (2006: 80). The term captures the miners' predicament as they reimagined themselves and their labour as public sentiment in the United States turned against coal and towards less carbon-intensive sources of energy, chiefly natural gas.

As the coal market started deteriorating, miners felt spurned by a disparate network of consumers who seemed to no longer desire or require their labour. 'We've been out here working for the past twenty, thirty years so that these people in the cities can have their lights and electronics and all of the other things they need', said one mechanic on the cusp of retirement. 'They were happy to burn our coal and we arranged our whole lives around these mines. But now they're putting us out of business and don't even care about what happens to us here'. This broad sentiment was captured in the headline of the August/September 2015 *Wyoming Energy Journal*: 'A little help from your friends? How decisions in other states are shaping Wyoming's energy future'. The title evokes the famous Beatles song, in which the chorus refrain 'I get by with a little help from my friends' wards off loneliness.

Miners used to receive some indirect symbolic acknowledgement, on top of their monetary compensation, for their work. From films and books to music and news media, popular culture celebrated coal miners as stalwarts of American pride in hard work. Even though these portrayals almost exclusively covered miners in Appalachia, with whom the Wyoming miners otherwise feel little occupational kinship (Rolston 2014: 54-7), the Wyoming miners took a degree of pride of belonging to a venerated occupation. It felt, however, as though that public appreciation for their work had evaporated. A long-time equipment operator began her explanation of why she switched from voting for Obama in 2008 to voting for Trump in 2016 by saying that previously 'coal miners were seen as the heroes of energy production', but they now feel personally attacked by advocates for clean energy, such as when Hillary Clinton infamously announced during the 2016 election that she was going to 'put a lot of coal miners and coal companies out of business'.

Prominent calls-to-arms for cleaner energy futures also placed blame for climate change squarely on the Wyoming miners. Journalist Jeff Goodell opens his book *Big Coal* with the following vignette set in Gillette:

> At a coffee shop in town, I met a woman who told me that when she runs on the treadmill in her living room, she likes to turn all the lights on in the house, as well as the stereo, the TV and every electronic appliance. 'I like to feel the energy,' she told me. 'It keeps me going.' At Energy Dodge, one of the several national park-size car dealerships in Gillette, you'll find row after row of 4 × 4s with big, thirsty Magnum V-8 engines. 'You mean "high-birds"?' A salesman joked when I stopped in to ask if any customers were asking for more fuel-efficient vehicles. 'We shoot them out here' (2008: 1).

Naomi Klein's description of the Gillette miners in her influential book on climate change, *This changes everything*, is even more blunt in assigning blame to them:

> There is a real sadness to many of these choices [of working in the fossil fuel industry]: beneath the bravado of the bar scene are sky-high divorce rates due to prolonged separations and intense work stress, soaring levels of addiction, and a great many people wishing to be anywhere but where they are. This kind of disassociation is part of what makes it possible for decent people to inflict the scale of damage to the land that extreme energy demands (2014: 343-4).

These portrayals of Gillette residents are cut in the vein of a much longer scholarly literature on boomtowns, in which the term 'Gillette Syndrome' was coined to refer to a suite of social ills that a social psychologist argued accompanied boomtown development there: drugs, divorce, drinking, depression, and delinquency. Despite the fact that the statistical analysis that formed the basis of the original argument would later be debunked and that the community would go on to craft enduring social relationships and senses of belonging (Rolston 2013*b*), the syndrome became a resilient matter of 'local, regional, and national folklore' (Limerick, Puska, Hildner & Skovsted 2003: 18). In fact, the Gillette Syndrome has been referenced in relation to everything from current oil boomtowns in North Dakota to oil development in Nigeria (Kashi & Watts 2010: 37), from meatpacking in Canada and Kansas (Broadway 2007) to planning for the 1994 Winter Olympic Games in Lillehammer (Leonardsen 2007). The editors of a recent cutting-edge, interdisciplinary social science volume on oil also reference it in the introduction to provide a cautionary tale of development gone awry (Appel, Mason & Watts 2015: 3, 13).

These passages and the wider literature they reference interlace their descriptions of miners and Gillette residents with judgements of the moral character of the actors, as people willing to commit massive ecological damage for their own gain. Implicit in this formulation is that labour in fossil energy is immoral in character, both in terms of its environmental effects and in its political economic complicity with neoliberal forms of governance (Tidwell & Smith 2015). This view is made explicit in David Hughes' (2017) recent indictment of fossil fuels as 'energy without conscience'. After conducting research with a range of people from petroleum geologists who work directly for the oil industry to environmental activists who 'fail' to protest it, he writes, 'My informants, I concluded, are mostly wrong – either mistaken on ecological grounds or conducting environmental malfeasance' (2017: 63). For Hughes, the immense scale of climate change means that there is only one acceptable moral stance: halting the 'great evil of dumping carbon dioxide into the skies' (2017: 14).

*Journal of the Royal Anthropological Institute (N.S.), 91-107*
© Royal Anthropological Institute 2019

Many of the coal miners I came to know, especially those who grew up on ranches or were outdoor enthusiasts, were convinced that climate change was happening and that burning coal exacerbated it; others were sceptics. Yet universally, they were quick to point to consumers as sharing culpability: according to this logic, without people using electricity, there would be no need to mine coal. This organic critique distributes responsibility for coal's contribution to climate change throughout a dispersed network of coal producers as well as the unwitting coal consumers who remain at the top of miners' minds as they think about their labour. This is more than 'implicatory denial . . . accepting the fact of carbon emissions but avoiding the moral consequences' (Hughes 2017: 129). It is an ethical standpoint in itself, grounded in the miners' gift-like view of the energy exchanges they make possible. Because they had poured their souls into the coal they produced, they sought recognition and appreciation for that work rather than demonization by the people who depended upon it for so long. After all, 'to make a gift of something to someone is to make a present of some part of oneself' (Mauss 1954 [1925]: 12). With the gift not simply unacknowledged but rejected and the long-term relationship of dependence spurned, the miners experienced unrequited reciprocity. Ethical sensibility is 'part of the human condition' (Lambek 2010: 1), embedded in categories of speech and modes of everyday practice, rather than solely the purview of anthropologists who judge the rightness and wrongness of energy systems and their consequences. Understanding these other ethical sensibilities may help to avoid surprise when one's vision of a progressive expansion of one's own ethical stance (Hughes 2017: 152) fails to materialize as expected.

## Unpaid debts

Gift exchange is powerful in forming relationships precisely because the delay in reciprocating places the recipient in debt. Relationships of credit and debt contribute to defining 'who stands inside and outside of community borders or who stands above or below' (Peebles 2010: 228), with these distinctions and positionings inflected with moral judgements about the exchanges and the people who participate in them (see also Gudeman 2001). Anthropological research with middle-class Americans struggling with debt suggests that the dislocations and debt engendered by larger, impersonal forces are typically understood in terms of the moral culpability of individuals who did not manage their financial decisions properly (Dudley 2000; Jefferson 2013). Indeed, this line of reasoning animates many of the national-level apologias for the sacrifice of coal mining jobs in clean energy transitions, as exemplified by the passages from Goodell and Klein: coal miners themselves are at fault because they are irresponsible people.

For their part, the miners and Gillette residents reject attributions of self-guilt for the current predicament in which they find themselves. 'When you see people leave your community because there's no jobs here', said a long-time resident, 'it puts a heavy burden on your shoulders. It makes you feel like, what did we do to deserve this?' The answer for most was that the actual person to blame was President Obama, at the helm of an administration that enacted policies to reduce coal production. As one lifelong miner said:

> When the clean power policies started rolling out, that was really difficult for us because we're still doing the same job. We're still shipping out the same coal and we're still powering the same power plants. But it felt different and it felt very personal. It was personal for all of us because it was not only an attack on what is our livelihood but on who we are and what we do.

Signs calling for an end to Obama's 'War on Coal' decorated the lawns of houses that were bought and paid for with coal mining salaries.

Some miners began pointing blame at corporate executives who collected generous bonuses at the same time as they announced layoffs among the rank and file. 'I personally have a problem with the extremely high-paid upper, upper management of all the companies', said a plant technician. 'They seem to come out quite well'.[5] Miners in the most precarious employment situations – those who work at the smallest mines that produce coal with lower heat indexes and will therefore be the first to close – critiqued their employers by making a play on the workplace kinship terminology that otherwise creates a sense of solidarity among the crews. A crew at one of the smaller mines pointed to the company's differential treatment of them and their larger counterpart by referring to their mine as the 'ugly stepsister of the family'. The kin term is salient because miners refer to their co-workers as a crew family, and managers encourage the rank and file to identify with a larger corporate family (Rolston 2014). Describing themselves as step-children was a way to signal distance from or hypocrisy in corporate care. Companies are now shifting contracts (in other words, tons produced) and employees to the large mines, a process that one mechanic and his co-workers called 'feeding the beast' – the 'beast' being the significantly larger, more well-known mine. Management wanted to 'pay the bills' at the large one, but also 'keep it looking good . . . it's the shining star of the company. They want to keep its reputation'. A plant technician at the mine that had lost many of its contracts described it as being 'eerie, like a ghost mine' since production had slowed almost to a standstill. With fewer contracts to fill, less coal needed to be mined, so the loud heavy machinery that miners normally drove in circles from the coal face to the plant and back again was silent and parked. Whereas they used to fill up multiple mile-long trains of coal every day, they started feeling lucky to see even a solitary one parked on the tracks outside the silos.

Miners thus felt that coal consumers owed them an unpaid debt for the gifts of coal produced through their labour. Electricity consumers, according to the miners, seemed to feel no such debt, believing that they satisfied their obligations for the energy they used by paying their utility bill. Until the Trump campaign, that debt was similarly not acknowledged by much national-level policy or popular media on the coal downturn, which instead blamed miners for their own predicament. For the miners, this denied a long history of mutual dependence and insulted a long history of exchange in which they provided energy for a society that demanded it, at no small peril to themselves: they risked their lives and strained their relationships with their own spouses and children to keep those jobs, which rewarded them with paycheques as well as pride in providing a service to the rest of the country.

## Conclusion

Coal itself is 'not intrinsically wicked or profane' (Powell 2018: 147) but takes on ethical valences in particular ethnographic contexts. The Wyoming miners I came to know experienced coal as a gift in addition to its usual status as a commodity. This insight is obscured by the sociotechnical infrastructures that actually make the coal useable by others in the first place: the intended recipients of their gifts – electricity consumers – do not receive coal, but what miners suspect to be decontextualized and depersonalized electricity that they engage with as a commodity. Indeed, the miners' critiques invite us to consider whether most US residents experience alienation from energy production, as these activities are concentrated in particular places, done by small groups of people

**Figure 2.** Trump imitating coal miners during a 2016 rally in West Virginia. (Photo courtesy ABC.)

who maintain sensuous, embodied experiences of it. The miners thus interpreted their relationship with electricity consumers as one of unrequited reciprocity, in which they received little acknowledgement for their service to the nation. While they distributed responsibility for coal's contribution to climate change among a network of producers and (even unwitting) consumers, popular calls for clean energy transitions placed the blame squarely on miners' shoulders.

As natural gas continues to displace coal in electricity markets, despite Trump's support for coal, the impending end of energy exchange relationships threatens not just the miners' job security, but also the basis for their personhood and vocation. This provides a novel twist on anthropologies of other declining industries. As Kathryn Dudley (1994; 2000) powerfully demonstrates in her research with displaced Wisconsin autoworkers and Minnesota farmers, losing one's way of making a living is 'also the loss of a sense of community and one's place in the world' (2000: 164). The loss not just of jobs but entire industries alters 'the way people feel about the cultural meaning of their work and the value of their contribution to society' (2000: 152). In the Wyoming case, the 'value of their contribution to society' was tied up in the exchange of energy and their status as energy providers. The coal market collapse shook the ground on which miners had staked their claims to national belonging and their own personhood as workers whose labour was valuable because they performed a needed service for country.

The ways in which this sense of displacement played out in the 2016 US presidential election raises greater questions about ethnography, empathy, and political difference. In the election and its aftermath, Trump capitalized on this sense of displacement. His boisterous performances supporting coal (Fig. 2) were certainly meant to appeal to miners and other unemployed blue-collar workers in swing states, but they also accomplished much more. By aligning himself with an iconic group of people left behind by progressive politics, their livelihood and sense of national belonging in danger, Trump appealed to a wider swathe of Americans who felt like 'strangers in their own land' (Hochschild 2016; Smith 2017).

But we should pause when considering recommendations to overcome these political divides by leaping over 'empathy walls', as Arlie Hochschild (2016) influentially recommends. Instead, we should recognize empathy 'as always necessarily involving a self-other relation, in which neither self nor other can be taken as entirely given

*Journal of the Royal Anthropological Institute (N.S.), 91-107*
© Royal Anthropological Institute 2019

– as existing prior to the relationship' (Rumsey 2011: 220). Senses of Us and Them are *produced by* our relationships and our encounters, including anthropological ones, rather than existing prior to them. Ethnographic accounts of miners and other working people do not just describe already existing difference, but create it, raising the question of the ethics and politics of our own work and its representations of political others.

In the midst of the uncertainties and dislocations of the coal market downturn, the Wyoming miners mourn the unravelling of the relationships that used to tie them as energy producers to energy consumers. But they also asked that the people who – unwittingly or not – called their labour into being and relied on it to power their energy-based lives recognize that long history of mutual dependence in a socially thick commodity chain (see also Walsh, this volume). Recognition is the prerequisite of responsibility, Susanna Trnka and Catherine Trundle argue, allowing 'one to take up the duty of care and shoulder the responsibilities of not only oneself but of another' (2017: 14). This requires recognizing 'one's self, one's place and one's time vis-à-vis others' (2017: 14, quoting McCarthy 2007: 4). What the miners ask is that we move away from persistent stereotypes of them as cultural Others (Smith 2017), to chart a path forward starting from the recognition of a history of mutual dependence and its ethical implications for managing the ongoing transition away from coal-fired electricity. They ask that as we consider the contribution of coal to climate change, we not ignore the contribution of their labour to our energy-based lives.

## NOTES

I am indebted to my long-time interlocutors in Wyoming who make this work possible and rewarding. This research has been generously supported by the US National Science Foundation (Awards 1540298 and 0612829), a fellowship from the US National Endowment for the Humanities, and a fellowship from the British Academy (VF1101988). The essay benefited from discussion at the Energy Ethics conference held at University of St Andrews in March 2016 and the Energy Ethics retreat held at The Burn in October 2016, as well as generative feedback from the anonymous *JRAI* reviewers and Mette High. All shortcomings of this essay are my own.

[1] See Rolston (2014) for a more complete description of surface mining processes. Even the more 'socially thin' industries like oil (Ferguson 2006) still require workers.

[2] This linking of coal and patriotism is not historically unprecedented. In 1918, the US Fuel Administration published a poster of a miner and First World War soldier back to back with the headline 'Stand by the boys in the trenches – Mine more coal'.

[3] Experienced miners, in contrast, recognize the unique qualities and chemical properties of different kinds of coal based on their appearance and touch (Rolston 2013*a*).

[4] The distancing between the coal and its consumers is common to electricity in general, standing in stark contrast to the intimacy of other uses of energy, such as the Venezuelan Sanema's relationship with gasoline (Penfield, this volume) or Malagasy engagements with charcoal (Walsh, this volume).

[5] While this behaviour may be unsurprising to those well steeped in the rich history of US labour activism among coal miners, it is remarkable for the Powder River Basin, the stronghold of non-union mining in the United States, where miners defeated the only major union drive in the basin in the late 1980s by arguing that it was the 'duty' of companies to 'make money' (Rolston 2014: 43-8).

## REFERENCES

APPADURAI, A. 1986. Disjuncture and difference in the global culture economy. *Theory, Culture & Society* 7, 295-310.

APPEL, H., A. MASON & M. WATTS 2015. Introduction: Oil talk. In *Subterranean estates: life worlds of oil and gas* (eds) H. Appel, A. Mason & M. Watts, 1-26. Ithaca, N.Y.: Cornell University Press.

ATABAKI, T., E. BINI & K. EHSANI (eds) 2018. *Working for oil: comparative social histories of labor in the global oil industry.* Basingstoke: Palgrave Macmillan.

AUSTIN, D.E. & T.R. McGUIRE 2017. The great crew change? Structuring work in the oilfield. In *ExtrACTION: impacts, engagements, and alternative futures* (eds) K. Jalbert, A. Willow, D. Casagrande & S. Paladino, 17-30. Abingdon, Oxon: Routledge.

BERKOWITZ, B. & T. MEKO 2017. Appalachia comes up small in era of giant coal mines. *Washington Post*, 5 May (available on-line: *https://www.washingtonpost.com/graphics/national/coal-jobs-in-appalachia/*, accessed 15 January 2019).

BOYER, D. 2014. Energopower: an introduction. *Anthropological Quarterly* **87**, 309-33.

BROADWAY, M. 2007. Meatpacking and the transformation of rural communities: a comparison of Brooks, Alberta and Garden City, Kansas. *Rural Sociology* **72**, 560-82.

CEPEK, M. 2012. The loss of oil: constituting disaster in Amazonian Ecuador. *Journal of Latin American and Caribbean Anthropology* **17**, 393-412.

CHARLESWORTH, S.J. 2000. *A phenomenology of working-class experience*. Cambridge: University Press.

CONKLIN, B.A. 2001. *Consuming grief: compassionate cannibalism in an Amazonian society*. Austin: University of Texas Press.

DEGNEN, C. 2012. *Ageing selves and everyday life in the North of England: years in the making*. Manchester: University Press.

DUDLEY, K. 1994. *The end of the line: lost jobs, new lives in postindustrial America*. Chicago: University Press.
——— 2000. *Debt and dispossession: farm loss in America's heartland*. Chicago: University Press.

EHSANI, K. 2018. Disappearing the workers: how labor in the oil complex has been made invisible. In *Working for oil: comparative social histories of labor in the global oil industry* (eds) T. Atabaki, E. Bini & K. Ehsani, 11-34. Basingstoke: Palgrave Macmillan.

FERGUSON, J. 2006. *Global shadows: Africa in the neoliberal world order*. Durham, N.C.: Duke University Press.

FOSTER, R. 2008. *Coca-Globalization: following soft drinks from New York to New Guinea*. New York: Palgrave.

GIBSON-GRAHAM, J.K. 2006. *The end of capitalism (as we knew it): a feminist critique of political economy*. Minneapolis: University of Minnesota Press.

GOODELL, J. 2006. *Big Coal: the dirty secret behind America's energy future*. Boston: Houghton Mifflin.

GREGORY, C. 1982. *Gifts and commodities*. London: Academic Press.

GRUBERT, E. & W. SKINNER 2017. A town divided: community values and attitudes towards coal seam gas development in Gloucester, Australia. *Energy Research & Social Science* **30**, 43-52.

GUDEMAN, S. 2001. *The anthropology of economy: community, market, and culture*. New York: Wiley-Blackwell.
——— 2012. Vital energy: the current of relations. *Social Analysis* **56**, 57-73.

HOCHSCHILD, A.R. 2016. *Strangers in their own land: anger and mourning on the American right*. New York: The New Press.

HOWE, C. 2014. Anthropocenic ecoauthority: the winds of Oaxaca. *Anthropological Quarterly* **87**, 381-404.

HUGHES, D.M. 2017. *Energy without conscience: oil, climate change, and complicity*. Durham, N.C.: Duke University Press.

JEFFERSON, A. 2013. Narratives of moral order in Michigan's foreclosure crisis. *City & Society* **25**, 92-112.

KASHI, E. & M. WATTS 2010. *Curse of the black gold: 50 years of oil in the Niger delta*. New York: PowerHouse Books.

KIDECKEL, D.A. 2008. *Getting by in postsocialist Romania: labor, the body and working-class culture*. Bloomington: Indiana University Press.

KIRSCH, S. 2006. *Reverse anthropology: indigenous analysis of social and environmental relations in New Guinea*. Stanford: University Press.

KLEIN, N. 2014. *This changes everything: capitalism vs the climate*. New York: Simon & Schuster.

LAMBEK, M. 2010. Introduction. In *Ordinary ethics: anthropology, language, and action* (ed.) M. Lambek, 1-36. New York: Fordham University Press.

LEONARDSEN, D. 2007. Planning of mega events: experiences and lessons. *Planning Theory & Practice* **8**, 11-30.

LIMERICK, P.N., C. PUSKA, A. HILDNER & E. SKOVSTED 2003. *What every Westerner should know about energy*. Boulder: Center of the American West, University of Colorado at Boulder.

McCARTHY, E. 2007. Land of saints and tigers: the transformation of responsibility in Ireland? *Journal of the Society for the Anthropology of Europe* **7**, 3-7.

McLEOD, C. & B. NERLICH 2017. Putting bacteria to work: the social constructions of ethical energy within synthetic biology. *Energy Research & Social Science* **30**, 35-42.

McNEIL, B.T. 2011. *Combating mountaintop removal: new directions in the fight against Big Coal*. Urbana: University of Illinois Press.

MARCOUX, J.S. 2001. The 'casser maison' ritual: constructing the self by emptying the home. *Journal of Material Culture* **6**, 213-35.

MASON, A. 2013. Cartel consciousness and horizontal integration in the energy industry. In *Cultures of energy: power, practices, technologies* (eds) S. Strauss, S. Rupp & T. Love, 126-38. Walnut Creek, Calif.: Left Coast Press.

MAUSS, M. 1954 [1925]. *The gift: forms and functions of exchange in archaic societies* (trans. I. Cunnison). New York: Norton.

MERCER, A., K. DE RIJKE & W. DRESSLER 2014. Silences in the boom: coal seam gas, neoliberalizing discourse, and the future of regional Australia. *Journal of Political Ecology* **21**, 279-302.

MINTZ, S. 1985. *Sweetness and power: the place of sugar in modern history*. London: Penguin.

MITCHELL, T. 2011. *Carbon democracy: political power in the age of oil*. New York: Verso.

NADER, L. 1981. Barriers to thinking new about energy. *Physics Today* **34**: **9**, 99-104.

ÖZDEN-SCHILLING, C. 2015. Economy electric. *Cultural Anthropology* **30**, 578-88.

——— 2016. The infrastructure of markets: from electric power to electronic data: infrastructure of markets. *Economic Anthropology* **3**, 68-80.

PEEBLES, G. 2010. The anthropology of credit and debt. *Annual Review of Anthropology* **39**, 225-40.

POWELL, D.E. 2018. *Landscapes of power: politics of energy in the Navajo Nation*. Durham, N.C.: Duke University Press.

ROLSTON, J.S. 2013*a*. The politics of pits and the materiality of mine labor: making natural resources in the American West. *American Anthropologist* **115**, 582-94.

——— 2013*b*. Specters of syndromes and the everyday lives of Wyoming energy workers. In *Cultures of energy: power, practices, technologies*. Walnut Creek, Calif.: Left Coast Press.

——— 2014. *Mining coal and undermining gender: rhythms of work and family in the American West*. New Brunswick, N.J.: Rutgers University Press.

RUMSEY, A. 2011. Empathy and anthropology: an afterword. In *The anthropology of empathy: experiencing the lives of others in Pacific societies* (eds) D.W. Hollan & C.J. Throop, 215-24. New York: Berghahn Books.

SAWYER, S. 2004. *Crude chronicles: indigenous politics, multinational oil, and neoliberalism in Ecuador*. Durham, N.C.: Duke University Press.

SCHNEIDER, J., S. SCHWARZE, P.K. BSUMEK & J. PEEPLES 2016. *Under pressure: coal industry rhetoric and neoliberalism*. New York: Palgrave Macmillan.

SHEVER, E. 2012. *Resources for reform: oil and neoliberalism in Argentina*. Stanford: University Press.

SINGH, A., A.T. STRATING, N.A. ROMERO HERRERA, H.W. VAN DIJK & D. KEYSEN 2017. Towards an ethnography of electrification in rural India: social relations and values in household energy exchanges. *Energy Research & Social Science* **30**, 103-15.

SMITH, J.M. 2017. Blind spots of liberal righteousness. *Cultural Anthropology* website (available on-line: https://culanth.org/fieldsights/1044-blind-spots-of-liberal-righteousness, accessed 15 January 2019).

——— & A.S. TIDWELL 2016. The everyday lives of energy transitions: contested sociotechnical imaginaries in the American West. *Social Studies of Science* **46**, 327-50.

STEWART, K. 1996. An occupied place. In *Senses of place* (eds) S. Feld & K. Basso, 137-66. Santa Fe, N.M.: School of American Research Press.

STRATHERN, M. 1988. *The gender of the gift: problems with women and problems with society in Melanesia*. Berkeley: University of California Press.

STRAUSS, S., S. RUPP & T. LOVE (eds) 2013. *Cultures of energy: power, practices, technologies*. Walnut Creek, Calif.: Left Coast Press.

THORLEIFSSON, C. 2016. From coal to Ukip: the struggle over identity in post-industrial Doncaster. *History and Anthropology* **27**, 555-68.

TIDWELL, A.S. & J.M. SMITH 2015. Morals, materials, and technoscience: the energy security imaginary in the United States. *Science, Technology, & Human Values* **40**, 687-711.

TRNKA, S. & C. TRUNDLE 2017. *Competing responsibilities: the ethics and politics of contemporary life*. Durham, N.C.: Duke University Press.

WILLOW, A. & S. WYLIE 2014. Politics, ecology, and the new anthropology of energy: exploring the emerging frontiers of hydraulic fracking. *Journal of Political Ecology* **21**, 222-36.

## Grandeur et décadence, cendres et poussière (de charbon) : l'éthique contestée des échanges énergétiques sur le marché du charbon déclinant des États-Unis

*Résumé*

Le présent article explore la manière dont les producteurs d'énergie « de la base » voient l'éthique des échanges d'énergie. Il met ainsi en lumière quelques idées reçues des études anthropologiques sur l'énergie et l'éthique. En étudiant la perception par les mineurs d'une baisse massive de production dans le Wyoming, cœur de l'exploitation du charbon aux États-Unis, il révèle des logiques de l'échange différentes entre les producteurs et les consommateurs d'électricité. La plupart des Américains consomment l'électricité comme une marchandise, payant à des compagnies productrices des kilowatts-heure qui sont déconnectés de leurs origines productives. En revanche, les mineurs voient davantage l'énergie comme un don/contre-don et gardent à l'esprit le réseau des consommateurs finaux du charbon qu'ils produisent. Ces logiques différentes impliquent des obligations éthiques différentes lorsque ces liens sont rompus par l'abandon des centrales au charbon. Elles contribuent à expliquer le ressentiment du « pays noir », que Donald Trump a su exploiter à des fins politiciennes lors des élections présidentielles de 2016.

# 5

# The ordinary ethics of charcoal in northern Madagascar

ANDREW WALSH *University of Western Ontario*

Charcoal producers are among the most frequently maligned entrepreneurs in Madagascar, often singled out in conservation reports and targeted in conservation measures as enemies of the island's threatened forests and ecosystems. And yet charcoal remains an important cooking fuel and thus a primary energy commodity for many people on the island. This essay addresses the ordinary ethics of charcoal production and consumption in northern Madagascar, focusing especially on how these processes are fundamental to an 'artisanal' energy system that involves people and engages them with one another in distinctive ways.

> How to light a Malagasy stove? Go outside. Fill with charcoal. Splash with diesel fuel. Flick a match. Douse with patience. Swing stove from side to side, like a pendulum, allowing the oxygen to permeate coals.

So writes Martha Weyandt (2013) in the travel journal *Nowhere*, giving instructions for a procedure familiar to anyone who has spent time in northern Madagascar. In Weyandt's description, cooking with charcoal is engaging, unfamiliar, and, thus, an especially memorable way of consuming energy. 'Many years' after leaving Madagascar, she remarks, 'you will catch a whiff of someone's backyard barbecue. The smoke and diesel fuel ignites that ancient part of the brain. There was something meditative, you think, about those months swinging the stove in tropical twilight, all the while longing for a microwave'. Not that such prospective nostalgia comes easy. Clearest of all in Weyandt's account is how difficult cooking with charcoal is. 'The first time', she writes, 'it took two hours to light. The second time? An hour and a half'.

Weyandt is not alone in experiencing charcoal as the distinctively engaging energy source that it is. A point she misses by self-deprecatingly comparing her own incompetence with the expertise of a 'six-year-old [Malagasy] neighbour' (who managed to prepare 'her family's stove in under five minutes') is that charcoal challenges *everyone* who tries to cook with it. Depending on the quality of the particular batch of charcoal at hand, and the conditions of the day, getting and keeping a Malagasy stove

*Journal of the Royal Anthropological Institute (N.S.)*, 108-123
© Royal Anthropological Institute 2019

going can be a problem for even the most experienced Malagasy cook. Where Malagasy cooks do differ from Weyandt, however, is in how using charcoal makes them *feel*. Weyandt ends her instructions with a warning:

> You will feel guilty. Many trees are felled for cooking fuel on the Big Red Island. This causes deforestation, which contributes to erosion. From the air, Madagascar seems to be disappearing into the ocean.

Here, Weyandt connects her sense of guilt to an image that has long figured in powerful, conservationist representations of Madagascar's ongoing 'environmental crisis' (Kaufmann 2006), implying that people who cook with charcoal are at least somewhat responsible for the fact that the island appears, from high above, to be slowly bleeding out into the Indian Ocean (Corson 2016: 66). In so doing, she reveals an ethical sensibility informed by what Keller terms the 'conservationist ethos' (2008: 651) underlying international concern over the future of Madagascar's biodiversity and, by extension, projects that aim to reform the country's existing charcoal energy systems. What is not apparent in this account and confession, however, is any sense of what Weyandt's Malagasy neighbours make of charcoal and the challenges of using it, let alone their perspectives on the ethics of this energy source.

In the more than three combined years I have spent in northern Madagascar since the early 1990s, I have never heard a Malagasy cook express anything like Weyandt's sentiments. Feeling guilty about one's choice of cooking fuel, like nostalgia for past travel to foreign locales, is simply not in the affective repertoire of the Malagasy people I know. This is not to suggest, however, that Malagasy people don't think and talk about charcoal in revealing ways. Charcoal and the known or imagined people who make and supply it *are* the focus of frequent deliberation and complaints, especially among those who handle and use it on a daily basis and, thus, know it best.

In this essay, I approach the ethical entanglements of charcoal in a way that highlights the significance of this energy source as a fundamental and engaging feature of the daily lives of the people who make, distribute, and use it in northern Madagascar. For such people, charcoal is not a matter of conservationist worry or an impetus for guilty reminiscence but a mundane concern that (1) engages them with the matter of the energy source on which they depend in the revealing manner of artisans and (2) entangles them in a profoundly social energy system comprised of familiar people and processes. To conclude, I introduce a project that has been encouraging 'greener' and more efficient methods for making, distributing, and using charcoal in the region, highlighting how the success of even the most modest attempt at effecting an energy transition in the name of sustainability depends not on the ethical sensibilities and orientations of planners but on the 'ordinary ethics' (Lambek 2010*b*) of people living day to day with energy systems and one another.

## Why charcoal?

Given the scale and scope of the crises (energy and otherwise) facing the world today, an essay on charcoal might seem trivial to some. Considered in the grand, global scheme of things, charcoal is neither a major player nor a major problem; nor does it promise much as an alternative to what is out there already. So why attend to this one energy source as carefully as I do here? It certainly matters that charcoal figures centrally in the lives of millions of people in Madagascar, and hundreds of millions of others in the world today (see, e.g., Gardner, Gabriel, John & Davies 2016; Mwampamba, Ghilardi, Sander & Chaix 2013). But there is more to it than that. What interests me most about charcoal is *how* it matters to the Malagasy people who make, trade, and use it. In engaging people in ways that other energy sources do not, charcoal offers opportunities for observing and reflecting on certain key processes that, although inherent in *any* energy system, are not always so obvious as they are in the commodity chain that links charcoal makers and users in Madagascar.

It is one thing to remark that the processes involved in fulfilling human needs for energy necessarily entangle people, as makers and users of energy, with one another and with environments in ways that are fundamentally human, fundamental to the political-ecological systems in which we operate, fundamental to capitalism, fundamental to the Anthropocene, and so on. But how are we to achieve a central goal of this volume: that is, to capture such processes ethnographically and in ways that might allow us to consider their 'ethical constitution'? The challenge is great, especially given how the entanglements entailed in these processes knot us all up, as individuals and as a species, in an ongoing story we would like to unravel. In introducing *Cultures of energy*, Strauss, Rupp, and Love draw attention to an oversight in the 'rapidly growing literature on energy' that is especially relevant to this challenge, noting how 'surprisingly little analysis has been brought to bear on what people think about energy, and how their beliefs and assumptions might shape their behavior' (2013: 22). What is more, they continue,

> there is a startling paucity of analysis of the everyday life of energy: how people view it, appropriate it, use it, conserve it – and why. If our current predicament of energy overconsumption has any chance of being nudged back in the direction of individual restraint and collective, society-wide conservation, changes will have to be made at the community, household, and individual levels. It would seem apparent that starting with baseline information about how people perceive energy in their everyday lives would be sensible (2013: 22-3).

Why hasn't 'the everyday life of energy' received more attention? It is not just unwilling or uncreative questioners who are to blame. That so little has been written about 'the everyday life of energy' seems at least partly a consequence of growing and spreading energy systems that simply do not engage people in the way that, for example, systems that supply charcoal to people in Madagascar do. One of the defining features of the world's most problematic, destructive, and far-reaching energy systems is that the 'better' (more efficient, more certain) they get, the less they offer their dependants opportunities to reflect on their dependence. For me and a growing number of others in the world today, the energy that powers daily life is drawn from a variety of sources, most of which have, as High and Smith note in this volume's introduction, an 'invisible quality' (see also Boyer 2015; Huber 2013; Hughes 2017). Energy enters and courses through many of our lives in ways we scarcely think about: cooking food, heating and cooling homes, powering electronics, lighting streets, fuelling transportation, and so on, to say nothing of the role it has already played in producing the food, consumer products, infrastructures, vehicles, and other stuff with which we share these experiences. Dependants of such energy systems fetishize commoditized energy in the way they do other commodities, experiencing its value as a fairly generic feature of what it enables in the moments it is needed and not as something with the distinct sources, properties, systems of processing, and trajectories we may know it to have. Not everyone is so oblivious, however.

When I ask Malagasy cooks about the single most important energy source and commodity in many of their lives – i.e. charcoal – their answers reveal a more engaged sort of dependence. Indeed, some respond more as connoisseurs than mere users of the stuff. They know, and many can talk at length, about charcoal's origins, its inherent properties, its advantages and disadvantages as a cooking fuel, the qualities that make one batch of it better than another, the techniques required to maximize its potential, the sorts of exchanges (and sometimes even the specific people) that have brought it into their lives, and so on. In fact, as I argue below, charcoal entangles these people with one another, with the region's landscapes and ecosystems, with markets, and with the very matter of a particular energy source in ways that have led me to imagine it as central to an 'artisanal' energy system.

As Antrosio and Colloredo-Mansfeld have recently noted, 'artisans are back!', cropping up as exemplary figures of our times in the work of a wide range of observers. While some have celebrated an 'artisanal' sensibility as key to how cutting-edge entrepreneurs and innovators navigate the uncertainties of twenty-first-century markets, others have portrayed artisans as embodying 'a precapitalist ethos' in which 'craft and cooperation' are taken as 'fundamental but threatened aspects of human nature' (Antrosio & Colloredo-Mansfeld 2015: 23). When we move past such broad renderings of artisans and the artisanal, however, and look more carefully at 'the more mundane realities of people crafting things, together . . . [w]e find [something more complicated] . . . neither blind adherence to tradition nor constant innovation, but people who must perpetually adjust and work skillfully with materials' (2015: 24) as obligated members of households and communities, and as players in risky and competitive industries. It is in this sense of the term that I have come to understand northern Madagascar's charcoal energy system as 'artisanal'. In the following section, I flesh out this vision by describing some of the processes at work in the everyday lives of northern Madagascar's charcoal makers, traders, and users, focusing ultimately on how these processes open up distinctive possibilities for those they involve to reflect on the social and ethical entanglements entailed by the energy system on which they depend.

### From kiln to stove: paths of artisanal energy in northern Madagascar

Making charcoal in northern Madagascar begins with living trees.[1] Although some species are widely regarded as making for better-quality charcoal than others, access to needed trees may be restricted by local land taboos, community forestry associations, 'forest guards' (gardes de forêt) associated with the Malagasy Ministry of Water and Forests, conservation workers employed in the national parks service, or some combination of these. Surveillance is limited, however, and in my experience neighbours tend not to report on one another, meaning that charcoal makers are generally able to access the raw materials they need.[2] Indeed, one of the most common criticisms of the country's charcoal industry is that it is so poorly governed. One report estimates that 60 to 80 per cent of the country's charcoal and wood production is illicit (Freudenberger 2010: 66).

Once trees have been selected, they are cut down, by men, by hand, with axes, and cut up into lengths of less than two metres. The wood must then be transported – by hand or cattle cart – to a processing site, often in an out-of-the-way place. Here it should be left to dry for at least a few weeks before further processing. When makers

**Figure 1.** Charcoal kiln. (Photo by the author.)

are after a quick turnaround, however, or are looking to minimize their exposure, they may move more quickly to the next step. The collected wood is stacked carefully in a shallow pit, ideally in a clearing that will serve as a firebreak. The pile is covered with leaves or straw, a layer of earth, and, sometimes, wood framing (Fig. 1), and the resulting kiln is ignited through a small opening. The ensuing burning should be closely monitored to ensure that the smouldering fire does not go out, burn too hot, or, most problematically, escape and spread. Surveillance is sometimes spotty, however, and poorly situated or unattended charcoal kilns are often blamed for bush fires. After four or five days of smouldering, the kiln is broken down, and the charcoal it contains is broken up. The yield of a single kiln depends on the quality and quantity of wood used, the quality of the kiln itself, and the maker's experience and skill. Using methods like those described here, getting 10 kilograms of charcoal out of 100 kilograms of wood would be a decent yield (Meyers, Ramamonjisoa, Sève, Rajafindramanga & Burren 2006: 20).

It is worth specifying that as a finished product, charcoal is a very inefficient way of accessing wood energy. Indeed, most of the rural charcoal makers I have met over the years do not use charcoal themselves. Rather, like rural dwellers generally, they rely on dry dead wood (*ajomaty*) to meet their daily needs for cooking fuel. What charcoal *is* good at is being a commodity – it is lightweight, easily transported, easily stored, and constantly in demand among Madagascar's growing urban population. The average inhabitant of a Malagasy urban centre is estimated to require over 110 kilograms of charcoal per year to meet his or her daily cooking needs (Meyers *et al.* 2006: 12).

Some specialists make charcoal all year round, starting work on preparing a new kiln as soon as another has been lit. Others, including most of those I have met and spoken with, produce charcoal only occasionally, most commonly as a supplement to agricultural work. These latter, occasional, makers tend not to bother with charcoal during the wet season (from November to May), when agricultural work is especially intensive and pit kilns are likely to need special attention – this despite the fact that this is the time of year in which charcoal can fetch the best price. These patterns can change in hard times, however. When a rice crop fails, for example, farmers commonly turn

**Figure 2.** Charcoal for sale by the side of the highway. (Photo by the author.)

to charcoal production for the sure, quick income it can offer (see also Bertrand 2001; Gardner *et al.* 2016).

Charcoal enables and sometimes maintains important connections between rural and urban people and livelihoods in northern Madagascar. Urban demand drives rural supply, and while charcoal generally moves from one context to the other as a commodity, it is never fully alienated. Makers know the uses to which charcoal will be put, and some may even know at least some of the users for whom their charcoal is destined, keeping part of what they produce for urban kin as they might do with the rice they harvest. Users, meanwhile, generally know charcoal's sources. They know not only that it comes from trees and that, in fact, its quality depends on what kinds of trees it comes from, but also that it comes from *people*, maybe even people they know, and certainly people they are familiar with – people who are, like them, 'looking for money' (*mitady vola*) in places of limited opportunity.

Charcoal is most commonly sold by makers in bulk by the measure of a rice sack (*gony*). Sometimes, as in cases discussed later in this essay, charcoal makers participate in co-operatives in which individuals compile what they make and market it collectively, but in the cases of the rural producers I know best, it is more common for makers to sell directly to collectors who take on the cost and trouble of transporting charcoal to the places where it will be bought and put to use. In these destination communities – urban centres, highway-side towns, artisanal mining settlements, and other contexts in which access to firewood is limited – charcoal is widely available in marketplaces, along roadsides (Fig. 2), and from mobile sellers. In some centres, alternative energy sources exist in the form of propane (sold in refillable tanks) and electricity, but these alternatives and the appliances necessary for harnessing them are beyond the reach of the majority of Malagasy people.

Making charcoal in Madagascar is unquestionably 'artisanal' in the most familiar sense of the term: it is undertaken by skilled practitioners using simple tools; it results in relatively small batches of varying quality; and it is commonly characterized by observers as 'traditional', 'small-scale', and poorly regulated. If, however, we adopt Tim Ingold's broader vision of artisans as people 'who [couple their] own movements and gestures – indeed, [their] very life – with the becoming of [their] materials, joining with and following the forces and flows that bring [their] work to fruition' (2012: 435), a case might also be made for charcoal *users* as artisans. Charcoal buyers tend to be discerning, inclined to carefully inspect what they are offered, and engage charcoal sellers in a conversation about its quality, before they commit. As noted previously, not all charcoal is the same, and more experienced buyers can (or at least attempt to) tell the better from the worse by assessing its properties: holding it in their hands, rubbing its surface, exerting a little pressure on it, and so on. The most common complaints I have heard about particular batches of charcoal are that it is too hard to light or that it goes out too easily if left unattended for a time – qualities that savvy cooks know to blame not just on the sort of wood used to make the batch, but on the makers, traders, and sellers who have passed it along the chain and into their stoves.

As should be clear by now, there is simply no avoiding charcoal in northern Madagascar. It is anything but invisible. You can see it being transported through villages by the wagon load, lining the single paved road that runs into the provincial capital in sacks, packed and stacked atop bush taxis ferrying it to markets, and for sale all over the place in the provincial capital of Antsiranana. You can also hear and smell it. The far-reaching sounds of trees being felled with a hand-axe or of mobile sellers announcing their arrival in the neighbourhood are as unmistakable as the smells of a smouldering kiln or a lit stove, and people attend to these sounds and smells as clear indications of what their neighbours are up to. It should also be clear that unlike the 'invisible' energy sources and systems on which so many in the world depend on a daily basis, charcoal is never fully alienated from the people who make it or fully fetishized by those who use it. As discussed in the next section, northern Madagascar's charcoal trade entangles people with one another in ways that lay bare the profoundly social foundations of the energy systems on which they depend, inviting consideration not just of how such systems power ordinary lives but also of how they are underlain and informed by 'ordinary ethics' (Lambek 2010*b*).

### The ordinary ethics of charcoal

As noted in the introduction to this volume, questions over ethics and energy commonly overlap in considerations and analyses of particular, often extraordinary, 'happenings [that] crystallize and accentuate the difficult energy dilemmas that confront us today' (High & Smith, this volume, pp. 9–10), in the wake of disasters like Fukushima, for example, or in the face of a new wind turbine in a neighbour's field, or, most broadly, amidst urgent concerns over the global climate crisis and the transformations it demands us to consider. As Latour (2014) notes with regard to the last of these extraordinary situations, humans have entered the Anthropocene as 'moral actors', meaning that we have a lot to answer for (regarding our reliance on energy in particular) and there is no question that our answers will, for better or worse, reflect situated visions of what we ought to be doing as right-thinking people working for the good of humanity and the planet. Ethical sensibilities do not kick in only under extraordinary circumstances, however. As Lambek notes, ethics are a fundamentally ordinary 'part of the human condition' (2010*a*: 1), 'intrinsic to speech and action', and apparent not only in explicit assertions of what is right and wrong or good and bad but also, and more commonly, in the 'everyday comportment and understanding' (2010*a*: 3) of people living alongside one another. Give the focus of this volume and the previously highlighted need for greater attention to 'the everyday life of energy' (Strauss, Rupp & Love 2013), there is good cause to consider how such 'ordinary ethics' help to shape the energy systems on which people depend.

Attending to the ordinary ethics of energy means recognizing how both ethics and energy are fundamental and intertwined features of lives lived with others, and, thus, that they interrelate not only at times of heightened concern over the right and wrong or good and bad of particular energy sources and their alternatives, but also, and more pervasively, in the mundane acts and relations of the day to day that keep us going, together, as the dependants of existing energy systems. Indeed, as Penfield notes in her contribution to this volume, in some contexts ethics might even be understood as a 'composite phenomenon' in which particular energy-based substances figure significantly. Here again, though, we must acknowledge that not all energetic substances or associated energy systems lend themselves to reckonings of their dependants' mutual dependence. Some do, however, and, as Penfield demonstrates so clearly, there is something to be gained by attending carefully to *how* they do. To reiterate a point made earlier, artisanal energy systems are not different from other energy systems in the *fact* that they engage people with energy sources and entangle them with fellow dependants. They differ in *how* they do so, and, as discussed further below, in how obviously they do so in ways shaped by ordinary ethics.

Ordinary ethics run through the lives of everyone implicated in northern Madagascar's charcoal energy system – not just makers, collectors, market sellers, and users, but also the neighbours and ancestors of makers, the girlfriends of collectors, the children of market sellers, and the parents of cooks. In fact, such ordinary ethics course through the sociality and networks these people share much as energy does when it is understood as 'an ingredient of practice' (Shove & Walker 2014: 56): both are essential to people's imaginings of good lives lived with others and to their efforts at achieving such ideals. This has become especially clear to me through research carried out in collaboration with an association of Malagasy students who have been working to establish a community-based conservation and ecotourism project in Bobaomby, a large expanse of land at the northernmost tip of Madagascar.

Bobaomby (translatable as 'many cattle') is best known to some in the region as the site at which cattle purportedly first came to Madagascar, walking ashore from out of the Indian Ocean hundreds of years ago. To others, however, it is more important as a source of cooking fuel. Sparsely populated and located just across the bay from the provincial capital of Antsiranana, it is ideally situated to serve the city's growing demand for charcoal.

Charcoal makers in both of the Bobaomby communities we surveyed shared key features with others I have met over the years: they had easy access to the required raw materials on common (untitled) land; were subject to little punitive surveillance by neighbours or public authorities; and cited poor crop yields as having forced them into charcoal making. Although not far from Antsiranana as the crow flies, the wagon, boat, and/or bush-taxi trips involved in getting charcoal to urban markets were discouragement enough to lead these makers to sell to mobile buyers in the manner described earlier. Although one of the appealing features of charcoal as an energy commodity is that it can be stored, possibly even in anticipation of a higher price, the part-time producers we interviewed in 2013 were more inclined to sell quickly. None had suitable buildings in which to keep the bulky stuff, and those who did not have permits for their work were concerned with the possibility of being discovered by authorities with the power to fine them or confiscate their charcoal.[3]

For their part, the collectors who travel to Bobaomby are generally not strangers to the charcoal makers from whom they buy. They return frequently, building up relationships with particular makers, sometimes even referring to them with kin terms like *zama* (mother's brother) or *baba* (father), and often bring them gifts of bread or other specialities from the city when they come (or are chastised if they don't). Where kin might be inclined to take advantage, however, collectors pay in cash, assuring the relationships necessary for a future supply of what for them is the stuff of a good living. Similar social entanglements follow as charcoal makes its way from these collectors to either end users or retailers in the city who divvy up sacks of charcoal into smaller quantities for sale on the street. As noted previously, while the price of charcoal is not generally negotiable, sellers and buyer do banter, most commonly about the quality of what is on offer, where it has come from, and, sometimes, what is likely to happen if it doesn't live up to expectations.

Even after it has been bought by prospective users, charcoal often continues along social pathways, shared with neighbours and kin who ask for it, for example, or contributed as a sign of one's participation in hometown association fundraisers, religious gatherings, or other collective events at which people will expect to be fed. More commonly, though, those who buy charcoal last will eventually use it themselves to cook with, affording them the earlier-described opportunity to consider the quality of what they have been sold and, for the cooks I know best, to assess the characters of those who have handled it previously. The most common scolding I have heard from such cooks is that makers and collectors who supply bad charcoal are people who 'love money' (*tia vola*), an insult that situates those to whom it is applied as fundamentally *un*ethical, outside of the norms of Malagasy *fomba* or 'custom'.

What I have described in the preceding paragraphs reflects my own experiences with, observations of, and research concerning northern Madagascar's charcoal trade. To propose that it represents anything more than that would miss one of its most important, and, to some, frustrating, features. As is the case with the rice it is most often used to cook, charcoal's essential supply is guaranteed not by a carefully planned, centrally managed, and impersonal infrastructure but by an uncertain, emergent, fluid, and profoundly social infrastructure that is enabled and maintained through relationships among people. The only constant in this system is the ordinary ethics of the people who depend on it: that is, the 'situating ethics' (Walsh 2006) of people who reckon themselves and others in relation to one another. This is not to suggest that Bobaomby's charcoal makers produce the best-quality charcoal they can for the good of cooks they likely don't know; that collectors strive only to deal fairly with those who sell to them; or that charcoal buyers ungrudgingly give charcoal to demanding neighbours and kin whenever asked. In fact, the complaints that the co-dependants of this energy system regularly voice about one another help to maintain the social infrastructure through which charcoal circulates. Like taboo transgressions (Walsh 2002) and unfulfilled obligations (Walsh 2009), bad charcoal and bad deals (and bad charcoal delivered through bad deals) are addressed not as products of systemic failure but as indications of the failings of particular people, whether known by name or not. Within such an energy system, seeking out better, alternative, energy sources does not involve plugging into different systems. It involves connecting (or threatening to connect) with different people.

However much they differ in their positions in northern Madagascar's charcoal trade, the makers, collectors, sellers, users, borrowers, and others who make up the energy system I have described thus far still share something important in common: as noted earlier, I have never heard any of them express feelings of guilt about charcoal making or use. Not that they are oblivious to others' disapproval, however. The people we interviewed in Bobaomby were certainly aware of the conservation-orientated goals of the young Malagasy researchers I was working with, and, like the dubious oil executives and mine workers with whom High and Smith began the introduction to this volume, they were understandably cautious when talking with us.[4] In answering general questions about *why* people in the region produce charcoal, however, they were always open and clear. One woman interviewed in 2015 made the predicament of her family and neighbours especially plain, noting with exasperation that 'in this life here [in Bobaomby], if you don't have cattle, [and you also] don't make charcoal, you'll finish nothing]'. She continued,

> Not all people have cattle you know! And [making charcoal] is hard work. It can take a month or more. You have to cut the wood, then you have to gather it up. If you don't have a wagon, you have to carry it on your shoulders. This is big work! But if you don't have anything, you've got to do it. You're certainly not going to go out and steal from someone else. You just have to do it.

Stealing from someone else is clearly wrong and an unquestionable violation of the ordinary ethics of people in this region. Doing what you have to do by working hard, making charcoal, and earning money so that you might 'finish something' in life is very different and, more importantly, completely ethical and in keeping with what Keller describes as a Malagasy 'ethos of life' based on 'the ideal of the fruitful continuation and growth of human life' (2008: 651). That this process involves cutting down trees does not present an ethical conundrum for this woman in the way that it does for others, including the foreign charcoal-using narrator with whom I began this essay.[5] And yet, as this same woman noted, there is nothing fundamentally good about making charcoal either. Like others we interviewed, she asserted that she would not be doing all of this hard work (or, at least, would be doing it less) if she had better crop yields or cattle she could sell. For her, and others we interviewed, in other words, charcoal making is not a traditional, inalienable component of a good life (in the way that not stealing is), but, rather, one among many means for achieving this end. The same can be said for charcoal collecting and use more broadly. Not surprisingly, then, people all along the region's charcoal commodity chain are not averse to alternatives inspired by the earlier-mentioned 'conservationist ethos' with which Keller contrasts the Malagasy 'ethos of life'. We would be wrong, however, to imagine interest and participation in such projects as signs of conversion. Whatever the ethical sensibilities that inspire them, alternative energy systems such as the one described in the following section are ultimately bound to take shape in line with the ordinary ethics that potential dependants bring to them.

## Green Charcoal

According to an overview of USAID's environment programmes in Madagascar, wood-fuel extraction accounts for up to 20 per cent of 'small-scale forest aggression' (Freudenberger 2010: 65) on the island. The most problematic aspect of this extractive work is associated with the production of charcoal, described as an easily transported and commoditized but 'highly inefficient' (2010: 66) source of wood energy. The report asserts that it would be unrealistic and inadvisable to recommend that 'Madagascar put more emphasis on gas or electricity as energy sources for cooking' (2010: 66). A more realistic and appropriate response to the problem has been to promote the development of new, more efficient and sustainable, ways of making, distributing, and

*Journal of the Royal Anthropological Institute (N.S.)*, 108-123
© Royal Anthropological Institute 2019

using charcoal.[6] One such effort is what I will term the 'Green Charcoal' (*Charbon Vert*) Project, which has been operating in northern Madagascar over the past several decades.[7]

Funded by German International Development (GIZ), developed in co-operation with Malagasy state agencies, and implemented through a number of local NGOs, the Green Charcoal Project has sought to address the threat of the region's existing charcoal industry through interventions and reforms all along the commodity chain. In rural areas, efforts have focused especially on encouraging community partners, organized in 'afforestation associations', to transform communally owned 'degraded' or 'waste' land into plantations of fast-growing eucalyptus that promise a more sustainable source of charcoal. Such plantations are ideally sub-divided into small plots titled to individuals through an easily navigated process that aims, ultimately, to transform 'users [of communal land] to owners' (Etter, Sepp, Ackerman, Plugge & Schaur 2014: 147) and, when possible, to make 'owners' of segments of the population identified as having especially poor access to resources – women and the landless in particular.

The Green Charcoal Project has also aimed to improve the processing of charcoal – through the introduction of higher-efficiency kilns and educating the region's charcoal makers in more efficient methods of production – as well as to 'moderniz[e] the value chain' (Etter *et al.* 2014: 148) by having associations oversee the collection and sale of charcoal in ways that would ensure the efficiency and regularity of its distribution, to streamline members' relations with the state (making it easier for them to secure permits and pay taxes), and add value to what has become the first branded charcoal in the region. As of my most recent visit to the region in July 2018, *Charbon Vert* was not only being offered for sale at special roadside depots and by mobile sellers (in sacks marked with the brand's logo), it was also being advertised in the manner of Coca-Cola and Three Horses Beer with signs on the walls of the restaurants that used it.[8]

In service of a broader 'Regional Modernization Strategy', the Green Charcoal Project has also promoted 'proposals for urgently needed regulatory measures by the forest service to curb the widespread and unregulated production of wood fuel from natural forests' (Etter *et al.* 2014: 149). One of the main challenges faced by this project is the simple fact that charcoal made from freely accessed wood on communal land will always be cheaper than charcoal produced from more sustainable, privately owned and planted, sources (Fleischhauer *et al.* 2008). And so to succeed over the long term, the Green Charcoal Project will have to do more than teach people to plant eucalyptus, build more efficient kilns, and organize themselves in particular ways – it will require them to rethink long-standing relationships with land and neighbours.

The Green Charcoal Project's self-reports are largely positive, indicating not only that it has been a great success, but also that it is worthy of imitation elsewhere; it is 'pro-poor, pro-development, and a potential driver of sustainable economic growth', as well as 'highly valuable in mitigating biodiversity loss and climate change' (Ackerman, Kirtz, Andriamanantseheno & Sepp 2014). What is more, it is described as being especially well suited to the contexts of weak resource governance in which charcoal is most commonly made and used given that it 'relieves governments of the need for organisational and governance interventions'. I am in no position to dispute the central claims of these reports (but see Fleischhauer *et al.* 2008: 53-4 and Raudonis 2012), nor would doing so serve the broader point I hope to make in bringing this project up.

The sensibilities underlying the design and implementation of the Green Charcoal Project have much in common with those underlying other efforts at encouraging the development of better, more sustainable energy systems elsewhere in the world, not least those being undertaken in the wind parks of Mexico's Isthmus of Tehuantepec or in the offices of solar humanitarian start-ups, as described by Howe and Cross, respectively, in their contributions to this volume. Inspired as it is by concerns for both Madagascar's biodiversity and the sustainable development of the country's people, for example, the Green Charcoal Project's successes and/or failures are bound to be assessed in relation to what Howe refers to as a 'rubric of care and concern' expansive enough to include 'human needs, social needs, energy needs, and ecosystems' (Howe, this volume, p. 169) all at once. In pinning its plans on the development of a more efficient charcoal supply chain and a resulting, branded, product that consumers will find appealing, meanwhile, it reveals as fundamental the assumption that the market can serve as a mechanism for changing, transforming, or improving the world. And most fundamentally, as an energy project, it is very much a product of what Frigo terms a 'traditional energy paradigm' constituted by 'norms, values, and principles' derived from 'a *scientific, quantitative,* and *mechanistic* approach' to energy and its production (2017: 7, emphasis in original). Ultimately, however, the sensibilities that will play the biggest part in determining the future of this project are those of the Malagasy people it involves, a point that became especially clear to me in the course of a 2015 interview with a man I will call Jean, the 60-year-old president of a Malagasy afforestation association dedicated to making and marketing Green Charcoal.

Jean described the Green Charcoal Project in much the way that the reports cited above do, focusing especially on the opportunities it had provided to him and others who had benefited from its programmes. As proof of the project's success, he told me of his plans to start selling charcoal made by his association's members from out of a recently built storage shed in his yard, conveniently located along the national highway leading into the city of Antsiranana. He spoke with such conviction that I could almost imagine that the whole thing had been his idea. And then he mentioned his main problem with the Green Charcoal Project: the name. 'I don't know why they call it "Green Charcoal" [i.e. "*Charbon Vert*"]', he noted, 'it's black, just like any charcoal'.

When I explained to Jean the meaning of 'Green' (i.e. '*Vert*') to the people and thinking behind the project, he understood completely. Symbols of global conservationism are nothing new in Madagascar, and certainly not in this region or in the town where Jean lived. The name continued to pose a problem, however. 'People ask me [about the name]', he said 'but I don't know what to tell them'. I asked if there isn't a Malagasy term that could be substituted for the 'Green' in 'Green Charcoal'. He answered that when people don't refer to it by what was meant to be its recognizable and highly valued brand name, they call it '*charbon kininy*' – 'eucalyptus' charcoal. And, as we went on to discuss, this alternative name was even more problematic.

As noted earlier, Malagasy charcoal users know that different kinds of trees make for different qualities of charcoal, and eucalyptus has a reputation for being among the very worst kinds of wood to use. In fact, in the weeks leading up to my conversation with Jean, I learned that *Charbon Vert* branded charcoal has a reputation among its users as being hard to light and easily extinguished, especially during the time of the *varatraza* – a strong wind that buffets the city of Antsiranana over several months every year. A solution to this common problem – a more efficient, high-sided, clay alternative to the metal stoves that most people use – was available (thanks again to the Green

Charcoal Project), but the cooks who complained to me about eucalyptus charcoal weren't convinced or willing to invest in a new stove.

Jean knew about Green Charcoal's bad reputation among cooks, and he admitted that there was something to it. But he also stressed that, thanks to the expert advice of the project's foreign and Malagasy planners and educators, this was not an insurmountable problem. One lesson that had been repeated to Jean and others frequently, for example, was that eucalyptus trees must be harvested and processed after only five years of growth in order to ensure the best-quality finished product. If harvested too early or left to grow too long, the charcoal will be of lower quality. Jean was convinced of this solution, but resolving the problem would require him to convince members of his association to follow the five-year rule, and this was not easy. 'Even in our association', Jean noted,

> there may be some who know this requirement, and they know that their charcoal isn't appropriate, but they send it along [to us for further distribution] anyways because they want the profit. And then the people who use it see that it's not very good. We tell people that they shouldn't produce [charcoal] from older trees, that they should put such trees to other uses, but they do what they want.

Private owners of what had once been communal land were meant to harvest the eucalyptus trees they had planted after five years. Doing so would enable them to fulfil an important part of the Green Charcoal Project's plan, allowing them to make good money by producing better, 'greener', charcoal. Instead, at least some of them opted to harvest their trees too early (in times of need) or let their trees grow longer (in order to have more wood and thus make more money), resulting in worse, unmistakably eucalyptus, charcoal – choices that rippled along the commodity chain in ways that Jean understood. I asked Jean if the members of his association understood that the Green Charcoal Project was meant to be good not just for them but for the environment as well, and that in not following the rules they were undermining the project as a whole – fostering doubts about the quality of the branded product for which all association members are responsible. 'They understand', he said, 'but it generally doesn't matter to them'. What matters to them is what matters to the charcoal makers of Bobaomby, to the independent charcoal traders that more efficient systems of distribution will squeeze out, and to the users of charcoal, 'Green' or not: namely making the best possible lives and livings from the resources and opportunities at hand, and negotiating relationships with neighbours, landscapes, and markets in ways informed more by ordinary ethics than by commitments to the abstract goals of sustainable development and the ideals of global environmentalism.

That the goals of the Green Charcoal Project do not matter to at least some of those who work under its name should not be a surprise. As noted earlier, the 'ethos of conservation' underlying international concern over the future of Malagasy forests is one thing, and the 'ethos of life' with which Malagasy people live often quite another (Keller 2008). If anything, attempts at regulating charcoal production through this project have created new possibilities for charcoal producers to rethink their place in a changing energy system that promises not just new models of production and distribution but also new forms of alienation. Although the Green Charcoal Project was intended to make northern Madagascar's charcoal industry more transparent and manageable, it has also served to anonymize and alienate charcoal producers, making one member of an afforestation association much like any other in producing a relatively generic, branded, product. Were the quality of their output consistent, this would not matter. But quality is seemingly not yet guaranteed, and will not be without further restructuring and scaling up to a more familiar and less engaging system – one that would ideally supply charcoal users with the energy they need *without* so obviously involving them in the messy engagements and entanglements that characterize the existing, artisanal, system in which so many of them participate today.

## Conclusion

By way of concluding, it is worth considering what will be accomplished if the Green Charcoal Project described in the previous section is able to achieve its ultimate aims. Were all of the charcoal for sale in the city of Antsiranana experienced by its users in the same way – i.e. as a relatively generic energy source made from plantation-grown eucalyptus burned in high-efficiency kilns and then distributed only through dependable and well-regulated channels – the habit that cooks have of associating the qualities of particular batches with the characters of those responsible for them would doubtless fall away. Were this same charcoal somehow made consistently easy to light and unlikely to be blown out (perhaps by ensuring that it is made only from five-year-old eucalyptus following strictly policed processes), cooks would be thrilled. And were cooks convinced to invest in the more efficient stoves on offer (and were the stoves to work as advertised), the task of cooking with charcoal would unquestionably be much less frustrating than it appeared in the opening paragraphs of this essay. Although I am certain that some of the Malagasy charcoal makers, collectors, and users with whom I have spoken about the topics raised here might complain about certain aspects of a more efficient and sustainable energy system, I am sure that many, many more would welcome it. Indeed, most of the cooks I know would happily do their daily cooking using propane (provided it could be supplied cheaply and efficiently), and most of the people I have visited in villages in places like Bobaomby long for electricity. Bearing these points in mind, asking 'What will be lost?' in the realization of any of these scenarios is a potentially problematic way of ending this essay. Still, it is a question worth asking. While there are certainly many good arguments to be made for developing more efficient energy delivery systems in Madagascar, given the ultimate goals of these or any other energy transitions, it is worth remembering that there is nothing inherently sustainable about systems that make alienated, disengaged dependents of energy users, allowing them/us to imagine energy dilemmas as extraordinary and, thus, inscrutable to or in light of ordinary ethics.

NOTES

Funding for the research discussed here was provided by the Social Sciences and Humanities Research Council of Canada. Thanks are due to many colleagues, students, and friends in Madagascar, but especially to Hortensia Rasoanandrasana, Élysé Nomenjanahary, and the RAGADS team, to Ian Colquhoun, Alex Totomarovario, and the Western-Université d'Antsiranana class of 2015, and to the many charcoal makers, cooks, and others I have spoken with over the years. Thanks also to Michael Lambek. Finally, thanks to Mette High and Jessica Smith for inviting me to participate in this discussion of energy ethics, and to reviewers of, and fellow contributors to, this special issue for their suggestions and inspiration. Any shortcomings of this essay are my own responsibility.

[1] The processes of the industry described here and elsewhere in this essay are based on observations recorded in field notes during different periods of research in northern Madagascar since the early 1990s, supplemented by focused interviews, surveying, and observations conducted in the Bobaomby region in 2013 (in collaboration with RAGADS, an association of Malagasy students based in Antsiranana) and in 2015 (as part of an ongoing research and teaching collaboration between the University of Western Ontario and the Université d'Antsiranana, co-led by Ian Colquhoun and Alex Totomarovario). For more on the charcoal industry in other parts of Madagacar, see Bertrand (2001), Gardner *et al.* (2016), Minten, Sander & Stifel (2013), and Muttenzer (2012).

[2] For an excellent account of the ethical complexities involved in encounters between low-paid Malagasy conservation workers and their rural neighbours, see Sodikoff (2012).

[3] In these interviews, we heard no reports of corruption among such authorities, but studies conducted in other parts of the island indicate how state-sanctioned efforts at monitoring and regulating the charcoal industry can be undermined by state representatives pursuing their own interests (see, e.g., Minten *et al.* 2013).

[4] For example, although all could name the kinds of trees that produce the best charcoal (relatively slow growing and hard trees like tamarind), they were also aware that cutting such trees was illegal and none admitted to doing so.

[5] Bloch describes a similar encounter with a woman in another region of Madagascar where forests were deemed to be endangered as a result of unsustainable anthropogenic activity. In response to his urging that she admit a fondness for the standing forest, the woman finally acknowledged that she did like the forest, but not for the reason Bloch anticipated. She liked it, she said, 'Because you can cut it down' (1995: 65).

[6] For an excellent overview of key issues and problems (not addressed in this essay) associated with the transfer of natural resource management to communities in the name of conservation and sustainable development, see Pollini, Hockley, Muttenzer & Ramamonjisoa (2014).

[7] The project in question has sometimes gone by the name GREEN-Mad, where GREEN is an acronym for the French phrase 'Gestion Rationnelle de l'Énergie et de l'Environnement' (Fleischhauer, Amend & Eissing 2008: 48) translatable as 'The Rational Management of Energy and Environment'. I have chosen to call it the 'Green Charcoal' Project as this is the best English translation for the French brand name (Charbon Vert) by which the charcoal produced under this project is marketed in the region.

[8] The project has also included efforts to develop and market more efficient stoves 'manufactured locally' and 'compatible with established cooking habits' (Etter *et al.* 2014: 149).

## REFERENCES

ACKERMAN, K., L. KIRTZ, C. ANDRIAMANANTSEHENO & S. SEPP 2014. The Green Charcoal chain. Rural 21, News (available on-line: *http://www.rural21.com/english/news/detail/article/the-green-charcoal-chain-00001053/*, accessed 16 January 2019).

ANTROSIO, J. & R. COLLOREDO-MANSFELD 2015. *Fast, easy, and in cash: artisan hardship and hope in the global economy.* Chicago: University Press.

BERTRAND, A. 2001. La vache laitière et le sac de charbon. *Bois et Forêts des Tropiques* **269**: 3, 43-8.

BLOCH, M. 1995. People into places: Zafimaniry concepts of clarity. In *The anthropology of landscape: perspectives on place and space* (eds) E. Hirsch & M. O'Hanlon, 63-77. Oxford: Clarendon Press.

BOYER, D. 2015. Anthropology electric. *Cultural Anthropology* **30**, 531-9.

CORSON, C.A. 2016. *Corridors of power: the politics of environmental aid to Madagascar.* New Haven: Yale University Press.

ETTER, H., S. SEPP, K. ACKERMAN, D. PLUGGE & M. SCHAUR 2014. Modernization of wood energy in northern Madagascar. In *Towards productive landscapes* (eds) J. Chavez-Tafur & R.J. Zagt, 146-52. Wageningen: ETFRN, Tropenbos International.

FLEISCHHAUER, A., T. AMEND & S. EISSING 2008. *Entre fourneaux et esprits de la forêt: la protection de la nature entre efficience énergétique et vieilles traditions – des idées venues de Madagascar.* Eschborn: Deutsche Gesellschaft für Technische Zusammenarbeit (GTZ) GmbH.

FREUDENBERGER, K. 2010. *Paradise lost? Lessons from 25 years of USAID environment programs in Madagascar.* Washington, D.C.: International Resources Group.

FRIGO, G. 2017. Energy ethics, homogenization, and hegemony: a reflection on the traditional energy paradigm. *Energy Research & Social Science* **30**, 7-17.

GARDNER, C.J., F.U. GABRIEL, F.A.S. JOHN & Z.G. DAVIES 2016. Changing livelihoods and protected area management: a case study of charcoal production in south-west Madagascar. *Oryx* **50**, 495-505.

HUBER, M.T. 2013. *Lifeblood: oil, freedom, and the forces of capital.* Minneapolis: University of Minnesota Press.

HUGHES, D.M. 2017. *Energy without conscience: oil, climate change, and complicity.* Durham, N.C.: Duke University Press.

INGOLD, T. 2012. Toward an ecology of materials. *Annual Review of Anthropology* **41**, 427-42.

KAUFMANN, J.C. 2006. The sad opaqueness of the environmental crisis in Madagascar. *Conservation and Society* **4**, 179-93.

KELLER, E. 2008. The banana plant and the moon: conservation and the Malagasy ethos of life in Masoala, Madagascar. *American Ethnologist* **35**, 650-64.

LAMBEK, M. 2010a. Introduction. In *Ordinary ethics: anthropology, language, and action* (ed.) M. Lambek, 1-36. New York: Fordham University Press.

——— (ed.). 2010b. *Ordinary ethics: anthropology, language, and action.* New York: Fordham University Press.

LATOUR, B. 2014. Anthropology at the time of the Anthropocene – a personal view of what is to be studied. Distinguished lecture delivered at the American Anthropological Association annual meeting, Washington, December (available on-line: *http://sector2337.com/wp-content/uploads/2015/06/Latour_Anthropocene.pdf*, accessed 16 January 2019).

MEYERS, D., B. RAMAMONJISOA, J. SÈVE, M. RAJAFINDRAMANGA & C. BURREN 2006. *Étude sur la consommation et la production en produits ligneux à Madagascar.* JariAla/USAID (available on-line: *https://rmportal.net/library/content/frame/etude-sur-la-consommation-et-la-production-en-produits-forestiers-ligneux-a-madagascar/view*, accessed 17 January 2019).

MINTEN, B., K. SANDER & D. STIFEL 2013. Forest management and economic rents: evidence from the charcoal trade in Madagascar. *Energy for Sustainable Development* **17**, 106-15.

MUTTENZER, F. 2012. Community forest management on the agricultural frontier: charcoal makers, immigrant associations and land claims in Ankarafantsika, North-West Madagascar. *Les Cahiers d'Outre-Mer* **2: 258**, 249-72.

MWAMPAMBA, T.H., A. GHILARDI, K. SANDER & K.J. CHAIX 2013. Dispelling common misconceptions to improve attitudes and policy outlook on charcoal in developing countries. *Energy for Sustainable Development* **17**, 75-85.

POLLINI, J., N. HOCKLEY, F.D. MUTTENZER & B.S. RAMAMONJISOA 2014. The transfer of natural resource management rights to local communities. In *Conservation and environmental management in Madagascar* (ed.) I.R. Scales, 172-92. Abingdon, Oxon: Routledge.

RAUDONIS, D. 2012. Fourteen years of sustainable charcoal: the case of Ankitsakalaninaomby. Independent Study Project (ISP) Collection. Paper 1262 (available on-line: *http://digitalcollections.sit.edu/isp_collection/1262*, accessed 16 January 2019).

SHOVE, E. & G. WALKER 2014. What is energy for? Social practice and energy demand. *Theory, Culture & Society* **31: 5**, 41-58.

SODIKOFF, G.M. 2012. *Forest and labor in Madagascar: from colonial concession to global biosphere.* Bloomington: Indiana University Press.

STRAUSS, S., S. RUPP & T. LOVE 2013. Introduction: Powerlines: cultures of energy in the twenty-first century. In *Cultures of energy: power, practices, technologies* (eds) S. Strauss, S. Rupp & T. Love, 10-38. Walnut Creek, Calif.: Left Coast Press.

WALSH, A. 2002. Responsibility, taboos and 'the freedom to do otherwise' in Ankarana, northern Madagascar. *Journal of the Royal Anthropological Institute (N.S.)* **8**, 451-68.

——— 2006. 'Nobody has a money taboo': situating ethics in a northern Malagasy sapphire mining town. *Anthropology Today* **22: 4**, 4-8.

——— 2009. The grift: getting burned in the northern Malagasy sapphire trade. In *Economics and morality: anthropological approaches* (eds) K. Brown & L. Milgram, 59-76. Lanham, Md: AltaMira Press.

WEYANDT, M. 2013. Learning to cook in Africa. *Nowhere* (available on-line: *http://nowheremag.com/2013/04/learning-to-cook-in-africa/*, accessed 16 January 2019).

## L'éthique ordinaire du charbon de bois dans le nord de Madagascar

*Résumé*

Les producteurs de charbon de bois font partie des entrepreneurs les plus décriés à Madagascar, souvent pointés du doigt comme des ennemis des forêts et écosystèmes menacés de l'île dans les rapports et les mesures de protection de l'environnement. Pourtant, le charbon de bois reste un important combustible pour la cuisine et, de ce fait, une marchandise énergétique primaire pour de nombreux Malgaches. Le présent essai s'intéresse à l'éthique ordinaire de la production et de la consommation de charbon de bois dans le nord de Madagascar, et notamment à la place fondamentale qu'occupent ces processus dans un circuit de l'énergie « artisanal », dans lequel les individus sont impliqués et interagissent de manières caractéristiques.

# 6

# Consulting virtue: from judgement to decision-making in the natural gas industry

ARTHUR MASON *Norwegian University of Science and Technology*

Shifts in the terrain of energy politics have given rise to consultant experts who produce and distribute knowledge of energy futures. Drawing on fieldwork at executive roundtables in global cities across North America, this essay examines the consolidation of this form of expertise and the opulent settings in which it is distributed. By exploring the role of aesthetic judgement in market-orientated decision-making, it contributes to anthropological work on elites, expertise, and energy ethics by highlighting the relationship between credibility and luxury. The essay also considers the enrolment of the expert in a kind of virtue ethics, whereby adherence to neoclassical economic principles is taken to be a character trait worthy of emulation. While clients may not look to consultants for advice coded in terms of ethics, I argue that they regard the person-based qualities of consultants as proxies for their ability to recommend a judicious course of action. By adopting this analytic, the essay sheds new light on the confidence that clients place in consultants by drawing out the relationship between depersonalized, quantitative approaches to energy markets and the virtue of the persons who propose them.

In 2002, Ed Kelly was in his mid-forties and senior economist for the consulting firm Cambridge Energy Research Associates. When asked for his advice on energy issues, he would spin tightly knit sentences from memory and would take pride in the weight that others placed on his predictions. Kelly's statements were couched not just in terms of expert advice, but also in terms of a credible disposition. His immaculate features and slightly wooden manner gave me the impression of a man deeply committed to ideals of excellence.

When I first met Kelly, I was the energy co-ordinator for Alaska Governor Tony Knowles and reporting to Larry Persily, Knowles's assistant on oil and gas development. Kelly, Persily, and I met at the Palace Hotel in San Francisco, where, earlier that day, Kelly had delivered his latest market forecasts to executives at a Cambridge Energy roundtable event. Established during the California gold rush, the Palace Hotel had provided us with a room large enough to accommodate a chaise longue and Old World-style armoire, while stamped on the hotel stationery was a gilded two-headed eagle with the words 'The Luxury Collection'. We had gathered in this opulent setting to discuss strategies for promoting a multibillion-dollar natural gas pipeline that would cross Alaska. Ever since the discovery of a large natural gas reservoir at Prudhoe Bay in the 1960s, state officials have harboured fantasies of delivering Arctic gas to lucrative North American markets thousands of miles away.

Ethnographic research in contexts such as this one raises a number of questions about the social life of energy extraction. What role do consultants play in the promotion of global oil and natural gas development? What is the nature of consultant knowledge, such that it demands to be conveyed in luxurious spaces like the Palace Hotel? What is the broader context for this form of knowledge production in terms of how industry actors understand energy systems? And, finally, how do answers to these questions offer insights into the ethical dimensions of knowledge production in a domain where reliable information is both scarce and prized?

In this essay, I draw attention to a shift in energy planning in the Global North whereby new spokespersons and spaces of knowledge provisioning coexist with older and more established mechanisms for deliberation and oversight. I identify three emergent features of this political landscape: first, the rise of consultant experts who analyse market information to produce knowledge of energy futures; second, the distribution of this knowledge at executive roundtable meetings; and, third, the enrolment of the consultant in a kind of virtue ethics, whereby adherence to neoclassical economic principles is taken to be a character trait of excellence and trust. Taken together, these features suggest a shift in energy planning from calculations based on political judgement to calculations made by economic decision-making.

To grasp the meaning of this shift from judgement to decision-making, I draw inspiration from sociologist Lucian Karpik's (2010) account of qualitative and quantitative choices in commodity purchases. For Karpik, certain types of commodities are unique or singular, including wine, artwork, and the professional services of lawyers and psychologists. Such so-called 'singularities' are marked by uncertainty about quality and therefore do not follow the logic of neoclassical economics by which choices are based on equal access to information about market pricing (see Kopytoff 1986). Neoclassical economic theory attempts to explain prices in terms of interactions between supply and demand, given the substitutability of production inputs. On this view, alternative methods of production exist for each commodity and consumers make rational choices between them on the basis of fully transparent pricing (Garegnani 1990: 76; Morgan 2016). In a letter written to Alaska's revenue commissioner around the time of my meeting with Kelly, Cambridge Energy consultants noted that modelling energy market prices in this way means that 'clients can better understand the forces driving the future'. That is, prices explained in terms of the substitutability of factors of production lay bare how significant uncertainties can affect the future strategically.

By contrast, purchases of what Karpik calls singularities must be made even when the nature of the product and how it is priced remain a mystery (see Appadurai 1986). Such uncertainty calls for qualitative choices, which depend on a synthesis of values and knowledge and for which judgement is ultimately associated with the notion of taste. Here, Karpik draws on the work of Pierre Bourdieu (1984), whose work rescued taste from essentialist doctrines of aesthetics and showed how the everyday judgements it entails are structured by the subject's habitus. That is, while taste may present itself as a naturally occurring phenomenon, Bourdieu reveals it to be a hierarchical, classificatory scheme of judgement with social origins, often shaped and transmitted

*Journal of the Royal Anthropological Institute (N.S.)*, 124-139
© Royal Anthropological Institute 2019

through formal education. According to Karpik, judgement – like taste – mobilizes preferences through 'regulated improvisations' (Bourdieu 1977: 78) that index social relations as they unfold. Importantly, Karpik grounds this concept of judgement in the judicial system, where legal decisions are handed down on a case-by-case basis by figures who remain personalized.

Whereas judgement consists in and is limited by particular points of view, decision-making, for Karpik (2010: 14), is 'lodged in a system of equivalences' set up to produce solutions that are not unique but instead substitutable. While judgement is hierarchical, decisions based on economic calculation assume an egalitarian form in which rational choice is available to all through the transparency of the market. Here, proponents of neoclassical economics align themselves with what Cymene Howe (this volume) describes as the political location of free speech: that is, as a kind of critique that selects 'frankness over persuasion' (Howe, this volume, p. 160).

The idea that decisionist knowledge or quantification has a significant role to play in displacing the idiosyncrasies of judgement is by no means a new one. Theodore Porter (1995) describes the nineteenth-century application of statistics to such diverse fields as the natural sciences, engineering, and accounting, displacing pre-industrial regimes of discretion and negotiation that favoured local interests. The result, for Porter, is the centrality of expressions of quantification to more and more aspects of society, serving as a kind of historical substrate for the rise of twentieth-century modernism and arguably signalling a threshold of modernity itself.

More recent studies of neoliberal governance have also identified a post-war form of decision-making that has had powerful effects in corporate management. Samuel Knafo and his colleagues argue that decisionist knowledge emphasizes quantitative and mathematical precision as an attempt to structure a process in explicit opposition to the privileging of judgement through experience (Knafo, Dutta, Lane & Wyn-Jones 2019). These scholars identify insights from game theory and rational choice theory, initially developed by economists working at the RAND Corporation, who model and quantify the uncertain environments in which organizations operate for the purpose of strategic decision-making. Elsewhere (Mason 2006), I connect futures research developed by RAND to the first comprehensive programme by the US Energy Information Administration (EIA) for producing forecasts on the nation's energy supply system. The purpose of the EIA is to generate reliable data and methods and to produce relevant supply forecasts. Here, *reliable* means faithful representation, verifiability, and neutrality for the purposes of financial accounting, while *relevance* signifies information that has feedback and predictive value as well as timeliness for decision-making. Today, analysts from many of the well-known consulting firms, including Cambridge Energy, began their careers as EIA economists.

Thus, studying energy consultant practices builds on existing scholarship around efforts to promote decisionist knowledge amidst shifting traditional authorities. In this essay, I argue that the spread of consultant-driven neoclassical economic thought can be explained by two interconnected factors: first, *aesthetic judgement* in establishing luxury as a condition for consultant expertise; and, second, a process of emulation rooted in *virtue ethics* as the mechanism for the uptake of consultant expertise.

The growing and perhaps paradoxical importance of aesthetic judgement to decisionist knowledge coincides with a shift over the past few decades towards communicating predictions via new modes of expression for intellectual work. Bourdieu

**Figure 1.** The energy salon. (Photo by the author.)

(1984: 152) suggests that new ways of organizing intellectual life through brains trusts and think tanks as well as new institutionalized modes of communication arise among intellectual producers who are 'more directly subordinated' to economic demands. Neil Pollock and Robin Williams (2015) argue that industry conferences are particularly important in building acceptance of such knowledge and establishing distinctive formats for knowledge production and consumption. Energy development is one of several industries reliant upon such encounters for the alignment of distinct perspectives (Brown, Reed & Yarrow 2017: 15).

As I demonstrate in what follows, the mobilization of Arctic futures has come to require the provisioning of expertise in particular contexts such as executive roundtables, which take place in luxury hotels, art museums, and other elite spaces (Fig. 1). I refer to these settings, where luxurious lifestyles intersect with the work of energy planning, as *the energy salon* (Mason 2015). My use of the term 'salon' is meant to evoke a kind of trading zone where purpose, action, and affect mingle towards both instrumental and unintended ends. In such spaces, judgement does not necessarily entail a concern with the sense of goodness associated with deliberation over a set of possibilities (High & Smith, this volume). In the energy salon, the aesthetics of luxury serve as a 'judgment device' (Karpik 2010: 44) for discerning the quality of market information. What clients do with this information is, of course, susceptible to ethical evaluation by different parties. But in the process, the association of energy planning with neoclassical quantification becomes naturalized as a mode of action that is beyond reproach.

A second factor in the spread of decisionist knowledge is that the consultants I came to know fostered communities of interpretation that subscribed to neoclassical market rationality but derived their persuasive force from a kind of virtue ethics. Briefly, virtue ethics is a category of moral philosophy that emphasizes the character of the ethical actor in contrast to other varieties of normative ethics that emphasize rules or ultimate consequences (see van Hooft 2014). To be clear, clients of Cambridge Energy were not necessarily looking to consultants for advice coded in terms of ethics. Instead, efficacy was their primary overt criterion. But clients seemed to regard the person-based qualities of energy consultants as guarantors of their ability to recommend a judicious course of action. The confidence that clients placed in the consultants was at once rooted in a depersonalized, highly quantitative approach to energy markets and in the matchless singularity or virtue of the person who proposed it.

The ethnographic data I present are drawn primarily from debates over Arctic natural gas development, which took place at the turn of the millennium when expectations began to mount about transporting natural gas from the North Slope of Alaska to continental markets. Proposals for a pipeline that could accomplish this task were first considered during the 1970s, when plans for constructing energy infrastructure led to the passage of the Alaska Natural Gas Transportation Act (ANGTA). By the early 2000s, though, energy consultants had embraced a growth imperative underpinned by a model of unlimited global gas development. Stoking expectations of dramatic industry expansion, consultants seized on legacy infrastructures like the ANGTA system as the raw material out of which new logics and systems of meaning could be elaborated. By 2010, these visions had extended across the Arctic from Alaska to natural gas basins in the Russian Barents Sea.

As I demonstrate in what follows, the rise of energy consultant knowledge and the distribution of this knowledge at executive roundtables function to replace political and legal judgements with economic decision-making. The aim of doing so is to establish conditions for making rational choices in a market of large-scale projects. I argue that consultants drive this shift from the qualitative (as reached through deliberative mechanisms like the legislative process) to the quantitative (based on neoclassical ideas of information about price) in a way that is, crucially, routed through the singularity of their own expertise. Consultants go to great lengths to frame markets as a function of relations between energy supply, demand, and price projection, from which competing actors can then make rational choices. If, for Caura Wood (this volume), it is a set of calculative procedures that makes it possible to render the qualities of prospective hydrocarbon sites into imagined economic assets, I argue that energy consultants and their clients take abstraction one step further by investing the qualitative dimensions of judgement in the figure of the expert. Here, the luxury of the executive roundtable, which requires aesthetic discernment to parse and participate in it, also thematizes the discernment that is needed if clients are to align themselves not just with any expert, but with the right one.

Has the rise of the consultant expert, who can speak in the name of the market, short-circuited a democratic sense of deliberation and oversight that characterized previous regimes of energy regulation? The nostalgic tone that many of my informants slip into when discussing the pre-consulting era might suggest so. I am wary of romanticizing the kind of turf wars between oil companies and federal agencies that I discuss below, because these power struggles were carried out in the context of more fundamental forms of collusion: the closed-circle, backroom arrangements of public utility officials, industry leaders, legislators, and technocratic elites who presided over much of the expansion of twentieth-century energy systems. Yet, analytically speaking, I am convinced that it is important to describe shifts in the terrain of energy politics, even without a normative stance to fall back on. Such an approach to energy ethics seeks to describe the material and epistemic processes by which the contingent becomes normative and even necessary.

*Journal of the Royal Anthropological Institute (N.S.), 124-139*
© Royal Anthropological Institute 2019

## Of quantities and qualities

Energy consultants like Ed Kelly gained prominence during the 1980s during a period of regulatory transition in North American natural gas markets when a highly integrated industry morphed into one composed of distinct, but interlocking segments. Before this restructuring, pipeline companies moved natural gas from producing areas in Western Canada, the Rockies, and the Gulf of Mexico to consumers on the East and West Coasts of the United States. Under the supervision of federal and state regulators, pipeline companies purchased gas at the production source or well-head, then gathered, treated, processed, compressed, stored, and transported it before delivering it to customers. Today, though, pipeline companies provide only transportation; all other merchant activities are performed by independent companies or by pipeline affiliates subject to the new regulatory mandates of open service.

The transition from integrated pipeline service to today's fragmentation has seen the emergence of distinct market segments which provide a host of services along the interconnected pipeline grid system. These segments operate alongside and in conjunction with gas commodity markets and include: gathering and processing; pipeline transportation; marketing and trading; management of market centres or 'hubs'; storage; and packaging of gas-related financial instruments. Each exerts an influence on the prices realized by producers at the well-head, as well as on end-use prices paid by consumers.

If there is one set of actors that straddles all aspects of today's gas industry, it is marketing companies. Gas marketers handle more than 80 per cent of natural gas consumed in North America. Their activities serve to link the production and distribution of natural gas to facilities like power stations that assemble gas supplies, hold and repackage them as necessary, and make deliveries to a portfolio of gas customers. Competition among marketers, coupled with the opportunity to earn unregulated profits, has created a demand for innovative services. The proliferation of marketing firms has spurred growth and innovation in related activities. The marketers' need for information has, in turn, created robust opportunities for firms such as Cambridge Energy which collect, interpret, analyse, and distribute information relevant to gas buyers and sellers, including information about weather, future prices of gas and other fuels, transactions, demand patterns, storage flows and levels, and much more.

Energy consultants rely on abstract models to advance particular market futures. Following Koray Çalışkan and Michel Callon (2009a; 2009b), I understand future-making in terms of an interplay of institutions, material entities, socialization practices, and ways of seeing and speaking that serve to establish authority (see also Boyer 2005; Carr 2010). Susanne Wengle (2012), for instance, also frames this interplay in terms of market-shaping phenomena by describing shifts in the Russian power sector which have contributed to a transnational process of cultural evaluation constructed and configured by agents engaged in valuation practices.

My initial research in this space was structured by my role as a participant observer in the Office of the Governor of Alaska in Washington, D.C., where I worked on legislative issues related to the Alaska natural gas pipeline project. In this role, I became familiar with Cambridge Energy's Member Executive Roundtable Sessions. Following Peter Adey (2014), such events may be considered elite premium networked environments that take place in expensive hotels located in global cities; I have, over time, attended roundtables in Washington, Houston, San Francisco, Calgary, and Mexico City. At each roundtable, six or seven Cambridge Energy experts give individual talks lasting fifteen

*Journal of the Royal Anthropological Institute (N.S.), 124-139*
© Royal Anthropological Institute 2019

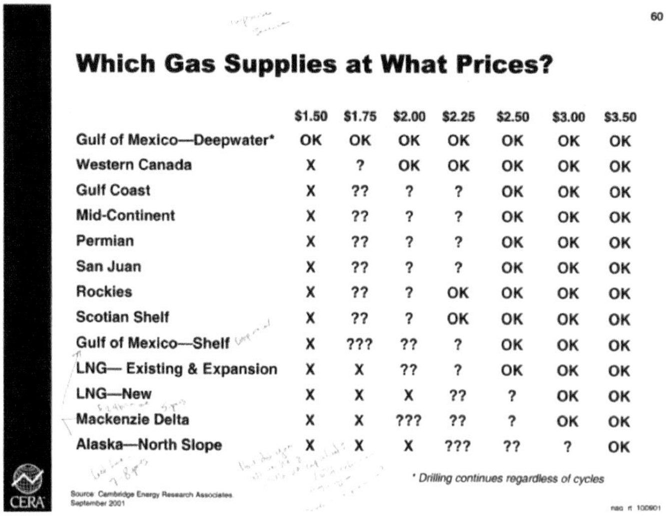

**Which Gas Supplies at What Prices?**

| | $1.50 | $1.75 | $2.00 | $2.25 | $2.50 | $3.00 | $3.50 |
|---|---|---|---|---|---|---|---|
| Gulf of Mexico—Deepwater* | OK | OK | OK | OK | OK | OK | OK |
| Western Canada | X | ? | OK | OK | OK | OK | OK |
| Gulf Coast | X | ?? | ? | ? | OK | OK | OK |
| Mid-Continent | X | ?? | ? | ? | OK | OK | OK |
| Permian | X | ?? | ? | ? | OK | OK | OK |
| San Juan | X | ?? | ? | ? | OK | OK | OK |
| Rockies | X | ?? | ? | OK | OK | OK | OK |
| Scotian Shelf | X | ?? | ? | OK | OK | OK | OK |
| Gulf of Mexico—Shelf | X | ??? | ?? | ? | OK | OK | OK |
| LNG— Existing & Expansion | X | X | ?? | ? | OK | OK | OK |
| LNG—New | X | X | X | ?? | ? | OK | OK |
| Mackenzie Delta | X | X | ??? | ?? | ? | OK | OK |
| Alaska—North Slope | X | X | X | ??? | ?? | ? | OK |

* Drilling continues regardless of cycles

Source: Cambridge Energy Research Associates
September 2001

CERA

**Figure 2.** Natural gas supply regions lodged in a system of equivalences. (Reproduced courtesy of the PanArcticon Energy Archives.)

minutes each. The expert stands near a wall-screen onto which PowerPoint slides are projected. Clients observe and listen, but also follow along in an agenda booklet that they are issued upon arrival. This booklet contains reproductions of the slides that are being shown by the expert. Often clients scribble notes in the booklet, an activity that I came to understand as an effort to elucidate the relationship between the printed material and its meaning as explained by the expert. The tempo of scribbling would often pick up during Q&A sessions, when clients worked to transcribe points of expert clarification.

In Figure 2, I include an example of my own jottings in an agenda booklet. I do so to illustrate that the printed material itself does not tell the whole story, but requires added-value notations that draw on the singular expertise of the speaker. Clients saw the roundtables as encounters with charismatic individuals and not just conduits of information. As Larry Persily, whom I introduced above, explained it:

> You're in a room with people who do this [market analysis] for a living. From that, you get a consensus on where gas supply and demand and price is headed. You get a consensus on what the rest of the world suppliers, users, utilities, are thinking. What are they planning on, what are their expectations, what do they think is going to happen? Because no one knows what's going to happen.

Note the date when the printed graphic was created in the bottom left corner of the page; this indicates the relevance or freshness of data and analysis. The timeliness of Cambridge Energy data series was important in providing adequate and accurate information for market analyses and policy decisions. Price fluctuations impose substantial risk on capital-intensive projects that require long lead times, such as the Alaska natural gas pipeline. Unpredictable pricing was also said to have deleterious consequences for natural gas consumers by increasing the risk associated with the operating costs of natural gas facilities. Restructuring in the industry facilitated the design of new data collection instruments, redoubling efforts by the EIA to assure data quality, accuracy, and timeliness. Cambridge Energy relied on EIA data and often

*Journal of the Royal Anthropological Institute (N.S.)*, 124-139
© Royal Anthropological Institute 2019

cited the organization directly. Yet the comparative advantage for getting this data from Cambridge Energy was the firm's ability to repackage it into market-specific analyses.

In learning to decode the various symbols and words ('X', '?', 'OK') that are put to use in this chart, the client would become acquainted with comparative cost estimates for various developed and proposed natural gas projects. This chart provides a real-time assessment of the cost of bringing units of natural gas to the marketplace. The cheapest paths for natural gas delivery are listed at the top. So, for instance, both Gulf of Mexico and Western Canada natural gas could be delivered to market at $2 per thousand cubic feet of gas (Mcf). These sources are listed at this price with an 'OK'. However, at a cost of $1.75 Mcf, delivering Western Canada gas to market becomes questionable ('?'), while Gulf of Mexico gas remains profitable ('OK'). At the bottom of the chart, Alaska gas is presented as the most costly to deliver to the marketplace. It is shown to be 'OK' only at $3.50 Mcf.

While from a regulatory perspective, these energy regions differ as to how proposed developments might turn a profit, they appear in the chart and at the roundtable as, in Karpik's terms, 'lodged in a system of equivalences' (2010: 14). The basis of equivalence in this case is the relationship between natural gas supply and US energy demand. Most consultants viewed the US gas market as growing incrementally. They would therefore direct clients to protect market prices by avoiding large influxes of supply. Practically speaking, this required an economic environment in which individual supply sources would compete with each other in a sequence of staged developments. From the perspective of officials from Alaska, then, the chart indicated which other sources were most likely to compete with Alaska to fill the incremental gap between North American demand and supply. The development of other supply sources, while it exerted downward pressure on price, also jeopardized the economic fundamentals of demand for Alaska gas.

Each roundtable session that I attended lasted half a day and was given a title referring to the corresponding advisory service provided by Cambridge Energy. Clients, who included high-ranking individuals from private firms, government agencies, and other stakeholders along the energy value chain, sat around a U-shaped table and asked questions in polite, rapid exchanges. In the process, they gained and shared new insight about the functioning of energy markets. For the uninitiated, though, the significance of these exchanges, the visual materials they draw on, and their relation to a market out in the world might not be readily perceived.

At the beginning of my research, the idea of reducing the future to such an arcane set of symbols and acronyms seemed like a vast simplification. For Cambridge Energy experts and their clients, however, the arrangement of these quantifiable elements served to propel their expertise and its material effects into the future. This is because, as Karen Hébert and Samara Brock (2017) have pointed out, quantification enlivens registers of knowledge and experience. By accumulating individual numbers and interchangeable units, experts can build powerful stories of uniqueness. In this way, the qualitative, forward-looking judgements of energy consultants are visible signs of their associated quantities. Indeed, these quantities and the need to constantly refresh them might be said to reproduce the aura of uniqueness of qualitative reasoning by accelerating its depreciation.

Over the course of my work at the Office of the Governor of Alaska, I learned to summarize roundtable sessions. These summaries consisted of three typed pages which addressed whether competing gas supply sources were expected to be developed, the time frames of development, and the elements, forces, movers, and uncertainties that favoured or deterred development. I circulated these reports to other officials in Alaska's state government, particularly at the Departments of Revenue and Natural Resources. Looking back at these documents today, I am struck by the emphasis that I was expected to place on the interplay of quantifiable qualities, measurable units, and quantities expressed as value. These data can be understood as crystallized economic and political relations. Quantities, the anthropologist Paul Friedrich (1989: 298) observed, often 'obsess' our informants during periods of historical change because they enable systematic realignments and reorientations.

Yet if the stakes of quantification were high for energy market actors, executive roundtable events were spaces where numbers could be curated in authoritative ways. The energy futures on offer at these events were commodities whose uncertain value to a great extent relied on trust. Consider this statement by a strategic planning analyst for the gas marketing firm KeySpan whom I met at a Cambridge Energy roundtable:

> Our company needs to look at prices. We need to have supply for the customers [and know] when the prices will go up. We need to know that to let the customers know. We've been working with Cambridge Energy for a long time. We always renew the contract to get the Internet subscription and a spot to attend the roundtables. One time, they came in [to our offices] when we did scenario planning, to project the future and how the company could respond to different scenarios. They've been doing it for a long time, so people trust them in one way or another. Because internally, you're interested in [gas pricing and storage] but you don't have the time to develop that; as a company you only have so much resources and time. A lot of times, price projections and scenarios are important for us. Internally, I don't know if we have enough people to develop certain things so we look out, and [Cambridge Energy analysts] are the ones that we've been looking at.

Since firms like KeySpan lacked the capacity to produce projections of their own or even to validate the forecasts they were presented, assessing the quality of this knowledge required non-expert forms of judgement. Over time, I saw that representatives of such firms seized on the incidental features of luxury found at these roundtables as a way of dispersing judgement about the quality of consultant knowledge so that it was not solely directed at the speaking subject of expertise. In fact, after attending other roundtables that were viewed as insufficiently luxurious by participants, I became convinced that the aesthetic dimensions of these events and, specifically, the performance of luxury served as a proxy for the quality of the expertise on offer.

In moments when outdated technology or the absence of high-end retailers signalled a breakdown in the aesthetics of luxury, attendees openly complained about the quality of the event as a whole. It was as if knowledge provisioning and incidental luxury were bound up in what Marcel Mauss called a 'total social fact' (1990 [1925]: 3). I first became attuned to the linkage between aesthetics and credibility at Cambridge Energy's annual CERAWeek event after it was moved from the ageing Galleria hotel in Houston to the newly built Hilton Americas. Many of the attendees with whom I spoke told me, with a sigh of relief, that CERAWeek was now 'back on the A-list': that is, the expertise on offer at CERAWeek was now more credible because of its adequately luxurious surroundings.

A different connection between credibility and luxury at such events is access to knowledge and networking through the astronomical cost of attendance: $7,000 to $15,000 for three days. This point occurred to me at the Hilton Americas during 2010 CERAWeek when a few energy executives and event participants, myself included, gathered at the hotel bar for after-dinner drinks. In one exchange, Jad Mouawad, then energy reporter for the *New York Times*, deadpanned that the cost of staying at the Hilton Americas was too expensive for his travel budget. More earnestly, he stated that staying at a cheaper off-site hotel in no way compromised his experience of CERAWeek. Unconvinced, the executives began teasing Mouawad over the missed personal exchanges that came from not staying at the hotel and the appearance of professional underachievement as indicated by an inadequate expense account. Staying off-site in a less luxurious hotel threatened the possibilities for achieving the knowledge acquisition and authoritative presentation of self for which roundtable attendance represented a bid.

Like expertise, luxury is distinguished from the world of interchangeable objects and operations. Indeed, it carries a sense of matchlessness (Gundle 2008). As a visible signature that affirms the presence of qualities that are both unique (Klingeis 2011) and superfluous (Featherstone 2016), luxury is taken to say something about the sort of persons who can command it.

## Virtue ethics

What does the ethical life look like in action? Virtue ethicists from Aristotle to the present day have concerned themselves with human excellences that are deep and broad rather than mere habits. These involve 'caring strongly about certain things and reasoning wisely about them' (Russell 2013: 17). Thus, virtue ethics offers guidance not by offering rules to follow but by offering exemplars of how to become the sort of person – or, crucially, organization – that can act rightly. In this way, virtue and its aspirational emulation are distinguished from a prescriptive focus on deeds or rules of conduct (van Zyl 2018).

In a related discussion, the sociologist Steven Brint (1996) has analysed the stratification of ethics and conduct as a shift in social trustee professionalism. Where the highly educated once performed their social role in the name of ethical standards, Brint argues that since the 1960s professionals have become vital in creating market value by applying expert knowledge across industry and political sectors. Porter (1995: 110), too, refers to a narrative about professionals as 'gentlemen of character' as a strategy for legitimacy. Following these scholars, I propose a repurposing of virtue ethics for the theorization of energy expertise. Consultant experts, with both the content and the form of the advice they give, come to embody the right functioning of the market (and, implicitly, the distribution of rewards that justly follows from it). Clients then come to bring both their individual comportment, which must not be dissonant with the luxurious setting in which expertise is imparted, and the business decisions of the organization they represent into alignment with those of the consultant as exemplar.

To illustrate these points, let me return to the private client meeting at the Palace Hotel with which this essay opened. As part of incentivizing construction of a $20 billion natural gas pipeline, state officials in Alaska were at the time advocating for a fiscal instrument that would compensate shippers of natural gas should the price fall below a certain benchmark for profit. This benchmark was known as a 'commodity price floor', and it would trigger a tax credit for the shipper if the price of gas fell below 52 cents per million British thermal units. Members of Congress from other states opposed the commodity price floor, as did competing gas producers and the Canadian government, as an unnecessary corporate subsidy that would inhibit so-called 'organic growth in the market'. Opponents argued that the need for more natural gas should not be used as an excuse to set up an uncompetitive delivery system or to guarantee profits for a specific group of producers well into the future.

*Journal of the Royal Anthropological Institute (N.S.), 124-139*
© Royal Anthropological Institute 2019

In reaching out to Ed Kelly, then, Larry Persily and I were seeking counsel on how to counter these objections to the commodity price floor. Several weeks earlier, the US Senate had voted in favour of a bill whose language included the tax credit mechanism for putting the price floor in place. Days after the bill passed, though, critical responses began to appear, including a letter in the *Wall Street Journal* from Michael Kergin (2002), then Canadian Ambassador to the United States, which singled out the tax credit as 'a vast subsidy providing tens of billions of dollars in transfers from US taxpayers to producers of Alaska gas'. At the Palace Hotel, Larry Persily told Kelly that he wanted feedback on 'how to advocate the commodity price floor'.

At first, our description of the tax provision did not seem to capture Kelly's interest. As a political operative, Persily wanted Kelly to weigh in on what impact the tax provision might have on the overall market outlook. Given the prospect of confrontation with the measure's critics, Persily wanted to know what their arguments were likely to be in terms of Kelly's own neoclassical script. This was a familiar perspective for Cambridge Energy analysts to articulate. Using State of Alaska projections, Persily explained how an abundance of natural gas shipped to market from Alaska would drop prices more than would be paid out by taxpayers through the credit. The precise question he posed to Kelly was: 'Given elasticity with respect to volume, how much would price drop? And if it's large enough, can we promote the statement that "policywise, consumers are winners"?'

Kelly shook his head and let out a sigh. He looked at Persily and, with an air of scepticism, responded: 'That may not be the most intellectually honest argument to make, given that we have three years of organic demand growth'.

Here, Persily interrupted to clarify his reasoning. Yes, he granted, the Alaska pipeline project, if built, would disrupt three years' worth of relatively high-cost natural gas production in Canada and Texas. But that same high-cost production would, he argued, become profitable again because of economic growth and increased demand resulting from the availability of low-cost gas from Alaska. Kelly, speaking with dramatic distinctness, replied: 'But those gas producers are still out 4.5 billion cubic feet [Bcf] no matter what. Right now, it is a 61 Bcf market in the US. The argument that consumers get lower prices because there's a recovery for postponed gas production? We don't actually need the Alaska project until 2015'.

With this, Kelly made the argument that whoever already held market position should not be pushed out by regulatory design. To devise political mechanisms for doing so would be a violation of the market's organic unity, on behalf of which he spoke. But Persily persisted: 'Will existing production be postponed, though? Will there be a price drop on gas from other areas with Alaska gas flooding the market?'

In responding, Kelly conjured a different, more ambivalent energy future than the one Persily had in mind. In doing so, he laid claim to a kind of market-based virtue through his responsibility for caretaking the future of the industry. He told Persily:

> As long as we're playing this conceptual game, there may be very little elasticity. What will actually occur is that prices go down in anticipation of new gas. It comes down to a level where development ceases and enters a fuel-switching layer [at which consumption shifts to a different, usually cheaper fuel]. The assumption is that, with natural gas prices below oil, switching occurs. Let's say there's 2.5 Bcf market capture of natural gas from oil.

As price begins to drop, Kelly forecasted, all industry sectors would take notice. Those sectors using oil or coal would begin to switch fuels in favour of cheaper natural gas. But this shift would increase demand as capacity expanded, which would again force up price. Persily did not want to be sidetracked by such ripple effects, and shot back an actual figure that consumers might save (per thousand cubic feet of natural gas) as a result of the tax credit's implementation: 'So, would you say $0.39?' It was at this moment that Kelly reminded us, with his own virtue on the line, of the value he placed on his own predictions: 'I know better than to say a specific number, where "Cambridge Energy says this is the figure consumers will save", and then it's in all the newspapers'. Here, quantification failed (or was set aside) so as to preserve the qualitative assessment of Cambridge Energy as a trusted arbiter. Besides, Kelly added, returning to his neoclassical catechism, 'the legislation you're talking about is utility supply planning for the benefit of consumers. It's a form of national utility supply procurement'.

Persily protested, with a catch in his voice that acknowledged he'd been beaten: 'Yes, but there are federal price supports for sugar'.

'Not nearly the same thing', Kelly snapped.

By speaking above what he framed as the petty interest mongering of energy-producing regions, Kelly worked to burnish the reputation of Cambridge Energy for transcending industry politics and thus enabling competitors to sit down together and work in their shared interests. But this apparent neutrality is also paradoxical, in that Kelly's desire to avoid committing to a particular number was hardly disinterested. That is, even as Kelly spoke on behalf of an impersonal market, he also spoke from the particular location of Cambridge Energy, a firm deemed to be trustworthy within a field of knowledge producers with its own share of hacks. Thus, Kelly's virtue ethics demands an aesthetics of disinterest as a means of reproducing an image of Cambridge Energy as one of a handful of knowledge leaders whose aim is the monopoly over the legitimate production of neutrality.

## Terms and conditions

It is worthwhile to illustrate how the different regimes of judgement and decision-making in energy planning are bound up with different concerns of contestation and alignment. If, as I have argued, the rise of consultant knowledge and the luxurious spaces of its provisioning have changed how energy planning is undertaken in the Global North, then it is instructive to consider how decisions around the very same pipeline project were adjudicated before they were routed through experts like Ed Kelly. In February 2003, vice-presidents of BP, ConocoPhillips, and ExxonMobil, then sponsors of the pipeline project, sent a jointly signed letter to Alaska's Congressional delegation in support of legislation to expedite construction of the pipeline. Attached to the letter was proposed language that, the writers stressed, should be included in any legislation enacted by Congress. 'There is nothing in the enclosed language that should surprise you', the letter explained, noting that it also appeared in a proposal that passed the Senate the previous year. It went on to say:

> We arrived at this language after a long, substantive process in which *all* interested parties had an opportunity to provide input, including the State of Alaska. Therefore, we strongly urge you to resist any attempt to further wordsmith the language. If the language is opened again, there will be countless efforts to pursue further changes. Considering the cost and risks associated with the Alaska Gas Pipeline, further modifications will weaken support for this legislation and undermine the $20 billion pipeline project. We stand ready to, again, offer all of the assistance we can to move the Alaska Gas Pipeline closer to reality.

How is it that language, whether open or closed, can undermine the reality of a $20 billion energy transportation project? And what is the 'reality' of a $20 billion project that is vulnerable in this way? A crucial distinction, I argue, between the legislative process and the executive roundtable rests on the status of the differences between written and spoken language. If the former operates on a text-based framework that builds on juridical precedent, the latter distributes forecasts and scenarios in the form of visual materials that are assembled, but rarely contested, through economic evaluation. Judgement is deployed in the former through text, while decision-making holds sway in the latter through the interplay of images and virtuous expertise.

To draw out this contrast, consider the ANGTA, and in particular the associated transportation system documents that would define an initial vision for the Alaska pipeline. During the 1970s, the United States confronted energy shortages, including insufficient natural gas supplies. Energy producers seeking ways to bring new supplies to market filed three separate proposals with the Federal Power Commission (FPC) seeking authorization to construct transportation projects for Alaska's North Slope natural gas. The applications set off a contentious and litigious proceeding before the FPC, in which competing applicants vied to be picked to build a natural gas pipeline. The shortcomings in the FPC's process were referred to Congress and resolved, not through an appeal to economic decision-making, but with a debate over and the eventual passage of the statute known as the ANGTA.

One key question around the ANGTA was the role of a federal inspector with the authority to oversee pipeline construction. The first person to occupy this role was John Rhett, a civil engineer. Rhett oversaw construction of the southern segments of the pipeline, which today deliver Canadian gas to the United States and are known as the 'pre-build' in anticipation of the expected construction of an Alaska-to-Alberta pipeline. At the time of Rhett's appointment, one concern of Congress was whether he could adequately monitor inflated construction costs, which would raise the price that consumers would pay for gas. Members of Congress feared that Rhett might become too cosy with the sponsoring firms and forget his responsibility to audit cost controls. In a conversation between Rhett and California Congressman William Dannemeyer during a 1983 hearing (Congressional Record 1983), Dannemeyer asks Rhett: 'Are you a friend of the banker, or a friend of the consumer?'

'Being a portion of the government', Rhett replies, 'I would hope I am a friend of all, trying to do what is in the best interests of the country. I guarantee you, there is no problem [with] our being too cosy with [the bankers]. There is much blood that is lying on the floor in many of those conference rooms'.

Dannemeyer responds: 'You know, you are a very charming man, but you would, I think, give a better impression to this member from California if you would not smile so much when you talk about blood on the floor'.

Reading between the lines of these historical statements, Rhett would seem to be emphasizing his own ethical credentials by associating bankers with blood on the floor. But Dannemeyer reads his own affect back against him, noting that while his words say one thing, his smile says another.

In 1982, the companies sponsoring the Alaska-to-Alberta pipeline segment had difficulty attracting financing and suspended construction. In time, one of Rhett's successors recommended dissolution of the position, noting in a letter to the President that 'times have changed'. Congress agreed and transferred the office's powers to the Department of Energy. But in 2003, with the prospect of restarting pipeline construction on the horizon, the Federal Energy Regulatory Commission (FERC) requested guidance on how, specifically, those powers would be exercised.

At this point, Alaska's Congressional delegation called for legislation that would create a separate Office of the Federal Co-ordinator, with many of the same functions as the previous federal inspector. But FERC did not relish the prospect of being subject to the new co-ordinator's veto power. They made their objections known and a new version of the pipeline legislation was drafted with the co-ordinator's powers cut back significantly. But the sponsoring oil companies began lobbying legislators to include an official on the project whose interest was aligned not with the federal government but with the marketplace, as reflected in the proposed legislative language that they submitted. At one meeting that I attended, a lobbyist argued that a diminished role for the federal co-ordinator would leave FERC with 'virtually unlimited authority to unduly delay and add to the cost of the pipeline'. Moreover, the lobbyist added, 'there would be no check by those putting up the capital, who are taking the economic risk to build the pipeline'. Sceptical, legislators asked lobbyists to provide examples of instances when FERC had imposed 'terms and conditions permitted, but not required, by law' that had delayed other pipeline projects. While the original text of the ANGTA had included this language, the actual dynamics of federal oversight meant that no examples could be found.

This contestation over the role of the federal inspector/co-ordinator illustrates the regime of judgement that I argue precedes the regime of decision-making. Energy planning, in this era, was bound up with the turf wars of different government agencies. Significantly, though, the oil companies were forced to go through the legislative process in hopes of installing a regime of economic decision-making.

**From hearings to roundtables**

In the transformations I have discussed in this essay, I mark a distinction between, on the one hand, economic experts who are said to transcend proprietary attachments to the interests of their clients and, on the other hand, public officials and the technocrats reporting to them, who are said to remain tethered to either local interests or regulatory tidiness in a way that makes them incapable of advocating an industry-wide horizon of expectation.

As the former group has gained influence, knowledge within the energy system is increasingly back-ended and supplied by 'partial intellectuals' (Bauman 1987: 114) on whom both industry and government rely. Economic knowledge, here, emerges as in the vanguard and is presented as capable of making claims on behalf of impersonal forces, including the market and the future. As a result, this knowledge becomes attributed with a prestige value as its independence from local entanglements is positioned as an inherent attribute. In this context, executive roundtables offer the possibility of presenting knowledge as neutral so as to enrol competing parties in a shared setting. Yet, by linking the reliability of that knowledge to the aesthetics of luxury, on the one hand, and the personality-based virtue of the consultant, on the other, relationships of quantity and quality come to depend not only on the assembly of data, but also on its abstraction in the event itself.

In this way, roundtable events complicate the notion of a straightforward turn from qualitative to quantitative decision logics by replacing the rituals of constitutional politics not with the impersonal market, but with a highly crafted stand-in for it. As Thomas Princen (2005) has argued, experts claim that they will dodge the effects of labour market restructuring because expertise is unique and not open to greater efficiencies. As with luxury, expertise is said to be matchless. By staging decisive points of view in elite settings, energy planning thus increasingly appeals to an image of rationality that derives neither from the endeavour to control energy-based power (as in techno-scientific rationality) nor from the competition for regulatory power (as in bureaucratic rationality). Rather, it arises from the calculated display of neoclassical quantification as a form of ethics that is, perversely, beyond critique.

## ACKNOWLEDGEMENTS

I am indebted to Marcel LaFlamme for his thoughtful feedback on the argument and structure of this essay. I also want to thank Mette High, Jessica Smith, and the anonymous reviewers for their detailed and insightful comments on multiple versions of the manuscript.

## REFERENCES

ADEY, P. 2014. Security atmospheres or the crystallisation of worlds. *Environment and Planning D: Society and Space* **32**, 834-51.

APPADURAI, A. (ed.) 1986. *The social life of things: commodities in cultural perspective*. Cambridge: University Press.

BAUMAN, Z. 1987. *Legislators and interpreters: on modernity, post-modernity, and intellectuals*. Ithaca, N.Y.: Cornell University Press.

BOURDIEU, P. 1977. *Outline of a theory of practice* (trans. R. Nice). Cambridge: University Press.

——— 1984. *Distinction: a social critique of the judgement of taste* (trans. R. Nice). Cambridge, Mass.: Harvard University Press.

BOYER, D. 2005. The corporeality of expertise. *Ethnos* **70**, 243-66.

BRINT, S. 1996. *In an age of experts: the changing roles of professionals in politics and public life*. Princeton: University Press.

BROWN, H., A. REED & T. YARROW 2017. Introduction: Towards an ethnography of meeting. *Journal of the Royal Anthropological Institute* (N.S.) **23: SI**, 10-26.

ÇALIŞKAN, K. & M. CALLON 2009a. Economization, part 1: shifting attention from the economy towards processes of economization. *Economy and Society* **38**, 369-98.

——— & ——— 2009b. Economization, part 2: a research programme for the study of markets. *Economy and Society* **39**, 1-32.

CARR, E. 2010. Enactments of expertise. *Annual Review of Anthropology* **39**, 17-32.

CONGRESSIONAL RECORD 1983. Marketing alternatives for Alaska North Slope natural gas: hearing before the Subcommittee on Energy Regulation of the Committee on Energy and Natural Resources, United States Senate, Ninety-Eighth Congress, 16 November.

FEATHERSTONE, M. 2016. The object and art of luxury consumption. In *Critical luxury studies: art, design, media* (eds) J. Armitage & J. Roberts, 108-31. Edinburgh: University Press.

FRIEDRICH, P. 1989. Language, ideology, and political economy. *American Anthropologist* **91**, 295-312.

GAREGNANI, P. 1990. Quantity of capital. In *Capital theory* (eds) J. Eatwell, M. Milgate & P. Newman, 1-78. London: Norton.

GUNDLE, S. 2008. *Glamour: a history*. Oxford: University Press.

HÉBERT, K. & S. BROCK 2017. Counting and counter-mapping: contests over the making of a mining district in Bristol Bay, Alaska. *Science as Culture* **26**, 56-87.

KARPIK, L. 2010. *Valuing the unique: the economics of singularities*. Princeton: University Press.

KERGIN, M. 2002. Trust the market (and Canada). *Wall Street Journal*, 15 May (available on-line: *https://www.wsj.com/articles/SB1021420631470244440*, accessed 17 January 2019).

KLINGEIS, K. 2011. The power of dress in contemporary Russian society: on glamour discourse and the everyday practice of getting dressed in Russian cities. *Laboratorium* **3**, 84-115.

KNAFO, S., S. DUTTA, R. LANE & S. WYN-JONES 2019. The managerial lineages of neoliberalism. *New Political Economy* **24**, 235-51.

KOPYTOFF, I. 1986. The cultural biography of things. In *The social life of things: commodities in cultural perspective* (ed.) A. Appadurai, 64-91. Cambridge: University Press.

MASON, A. 2006. Images of the energy future. *Environmental Research Letters* **1**, 21-5.

———— 2015. Inside the energy salon: installation and illusions of finality. *Journal of Business Anthropology* **4**, 23-39.

MAUSS, M. 1990 [1925]. *The gift: the form and reason for exchange in archaic societies* (trans. W.D. Halls). New York: Norton.

MORGAN, J. (ed.) 2016. *What is neoclassical economics? Debating the origins, meaning and significance.* Cambridge: University Press.

POLLOCK, N. & R. WILLIAMS 2015. The venues of high tech prediction: presenting the future at industry analyst conferences. *Information and Organization* **25**, 115-36.

PORTER, T. 1995. *Trust in numbers: the pursuit of objectivity in science and public life.* Princeton: University Press.

PRINCEN, T. 2005. *The logic of sufficiency.* Cambridge, Mass.: MIT Press.

RUSSELL, D. 2013. *The Cambridge companion to virtue ethics.* Cambridge: University Press.

VAN HOOFT, S. (ed.) 2014. *The handbook of virtue ethics.* London: Routledge.

VAN ZYL, L. 2018. *Virtue ethics: a contemporary introduction.* London: Routledge.

WENGLE, S. 2012. Engineers versus managers: experts, market-making and state-building in Putin's Russia. *Economy and Society* **41**, 435-67.

## La vertu de la consultation : du jugement à la prise de décision dans le secteur du gaz naturel

*Résumé*

L'évolution des politiques énergétiques a suscité l'apparition d'experts consultants qui produisent et diffusent un savoir sur le futur énergétique. Une ethnographie de tables rondes réunissant des cadres d'entreprises dans des grandes métropoles d'Amérique du Nord permet l'examen de la cristallisation de cette forme d'expertise et du cadre opulent dans lequel elle est dispensée. En explorant le rôle du jugement esthétique dans la prise de décisions concernant les marchés, l'article contribue au travail anthropologique sur les élites, l'expertise et l'éthique de l'énergie, en mettant en lumière le lien entre luxe et crédibilité. L'analyse porte également sur l'engagement de l'expert dans une sorte d'éthique de la vertu, dans laquelle l'adhésion à des principes économiques néoclassiques est considérée comme un trait de caractère digne d'être imité. Bien que les clients ne demandent pas aux consultants de formuler leurs conseils suivant des principes éthiques, ils considèrent les qualités personnelles des experts comme un substitut de leur propre capacité à recommander des mesures judicieuses. Cette approche analytique éclaire d'un jour nouveau la confiance que les clients font aux consultants en dépeignant les liens entre les approches quantitatives et dépersonnalisées des marchés de l'énergie, d'une part, et d'autre part la vertu des personnes qui les proposent.

# 7

# Fuel of fear and force: gasoline's energetic power and its entanglement in composite ethics

AMY PENFIELD *University of Bristol*

Energy is far more than a resource exploited by states and corporations. Yet, at the level of consumption it is generally thought to be a difficult phenomenon to examine because it is so familiar that we barely notice its role in our lives; or at the very least, its production becomes obscured by this pragmatic daily engagement. The other side to the story – the one in which energy is a provision distributed to and experienced by people in intimate and unanticipated ways — is distinctly perceptible in locales like the Amazon rain forest where conventional energy provisions are absent. This essay explores how everyday encounters with gasoline offer insights into ethical judgements among the Sanema of Venezuelan Amazonia. The fuel is so pervasive that it is increasingly present in numerous facets of daily life, including gold mining, dilemmas of kinship, the animist world of vengeful spirit masters, and ethically infused rumours of disaster. Being a volatile substance – simultaneously vaporous, explosive, narcotic, and caustic – gasoline is also a vital entity that holds a particularly intriguing place in the Sanema's understanding of personhood and ethics. Indeed, its mysterious and unsettling qualities cause it to become entangled within a composite form of ethics that defines Sanema social worlds.

The significance of gasoline in Venezuelan Amazonia struck me profoundly one day during my doctoral fieldwork. It was a humid afternoon and I was lazily swinging in my hammock while other members of my Sanema host family lay similarly idle nearby. Suddenly we were jolted from our languor by the sound of screaming in the adjacent house, and as was the normal response, we all grabbed our machetes and ran towards the sound of the commotion. I had expected to see the familiar sight of an inebriated fight, but was alarmed by what I actually did see. A young boy had been tied to a post and his father was repeatedly striking him with the broad side of his machete as the boy squirmed and screeched. His father emitted a bellowing, 'You must not drink gasoline!' with each blow, and when he finally desisted with his punishment, he threw down the machete and thundered off. The sobbing and trembling boy was released from his constraints as his weeping female kin inspected the red welts that covered his body. I had never before witnessed such severe castigation among the Sanema, particularly of pre-teens, who are still granted a much-valued autonomy. It was evident that some others present also considered this punishment unduly grave by the fact that the boy's grandmother sought revenge on his behalf (Sa. *noa kua*), imparting equal injury to the father, although with a rope rather than a machete. Yet, after the incident, many residents suggested that it was to be expected given that the boy had enacted improper behaviour by 'drinking', or rather inhaling, gasoline (also known as huffing gasoline). 'This never happened before', one woman lamented, 'this is now'.

The event occurred during a time when gasoline was gaining immense significance in Sanema lives as the material dispensation of Venezuelan petroleum wealth, as an indispensable energy-based substance in daily life, and – through its sale in informal forest gold mines – as a source of potentially limitless wealth. The embodied intimacy between gasoline and humans in this context was striking, creating a visceral encounter that provoked regular contemplation and discussion on the unusual substance. It was handled, inhaled, siphoned, poured, hauled, and spilled several times a day and it had become so intricately interwoven into my hosts' lives that existence without it was increasingly considered unthinkable. What was most interesting about this new development was that affective narratives (see also High, this volume) emerged over and over again of gasoline's beguiling performance and its association with ethical assessments in daily life.

The thrashing incident I witnessed, which I shall explore in greater detail later in the essay, was startling in that the perceived pathological effects of gasoline could be so deeply terrifying for my hosts. They spoke often of how the boy had behaved badly (Sa. *salia bai*) and had 'let demons inside' by inhaling gasoline, a statement that alludes to the growing phenomenon of substance abuse that accompanies an encroaching capitalist economy (see Gracey 1998; Taussig 1980). Seen in this light, the proclaimed transgressions surrounding gasoline in this context could be interpreted as a fear of the gradually expanding presence of the Venezuelan petroleum economy. Yet the moral terrain that this oil derivative occupies is far more complex. In this essay, I shall introduce vernacular notions of ethics in order to reveal how gasoline becomes actively entangled in an intricate web of social arrangements; revealing not merely sublimated anxieties about an ethically depraved capitalist economy, but simultaneously deeply rooted ideas about a broad and composite form of ethical action that is expanded to include nonhuman entities.

In what follows, I will show how gasoline emerges in discussions as a volatile substance that impinges on 'proper thinking' as an intoxicant, but also as a lively entity that is morally reactive in similar ways to other forest beings. Consequently, it becomes a key player in a sophisticated schema of ethical actions and reflections, rather than being met solely with resistance and underlying apprehension. Exploring unanticipated experiential accounts such as these enables us to overcome the 'blind spots in our disciplinary understanding' (High & Smith, this volume, p. 20) in studies of energy dilemmas and the appropriation of hydrocarbons in everyday life. This is not a story about the global inequalities created through energy production and consumption, but about the wonderment (see Scott 2016) generated at sites of energetic encounter, in this case the Sanema's perception of gasoline's lively and vital force.[1]

The Sanema are the northernmost branch of the wider Yanomami ethnic group, a customarily semi-nomadic hunting and foraging indigenous people who inhabit the forests of southern Venezuela and northern Brazil. Over a period of twenty-four months between 2009 and 2011, a time of relative economic stability in Venezuela owing to high oil prices, I conducted multi-sited fieldwork in two forest communities and

*Journal of the Royal Anthropological Institute (N.S.), 140-159*
© Royal Anthropological Institute 2019

**Figure 1.** Barrels of gasoline are never far away. (Photo by the author.)

a Sanema encampment in a frontier town in southern Venezuela.[2] The abundance of gasoline in this region of Venezuela has coincided with indigenous people's increased participation in state initiatives such as voting in elections and establishing state-funded development initiatives known as communal councils (see Penfield 2018). This process of inclusion emerges out of an indissoluble link between citizenship and the nation's immense petroleum wealth. In Amazonia in particular, the presence of the petroleum economy is materialized as an influx of gasoline-run machinery obtained through political clientelism or as part of the aforementioned state-funded development

*Journal of the Royal Anthropological Institute (N.S.), 140-159*
© Royal Anthropological Institute 2019

initiatives. However, as the ethnography will demonstrate, energy's twofold bearing in Sanema lives – both its political and experiential presence – is met with an intricate mix of curiosity, desire, and fear. I shall return to the reasons behind the ubiquity of this energy source in Venezuelan Amazonia in a moment, but first I will reflect on theories of ethics, in order to propose that we think in more detail about the role that personhood and nonhumans play within this field of inquiry.

## Ethics meets dividuality

A Foucauldian approach to the ethical self has been fruitful for scholars seeking to understand reflexive moral judgements, but also as a way to understand how the self comes into existence through power relations (see Faubion 2013). Significantly, Foucault's notion of the 'care of the self' foregrounds agentive self-mastery as an alternative to a Durkheimian normative mode of morality which has led some to regard social theory as a 'science of unfreedom' (Laidlaw 2014). Yet the care of the self is distinctly individualistic. Although there have been discussions regarding Foucault's neglect of 'the social' in his approach to ethics, Laidlaw dismisses this as a misreading, because, he argues, the 'individual' and the 'social' remain inextricably linked; Foucault 'takes for granted that [an ethical life] is lived with others, and that relations with others are constitutive of it' (Laidlaw 2014: 116; see also Faubion 2012: 76). It is, he stresses, a deeply relational modality. I will propose in this essay, however, that we instead think about ethics as composite rather than relational. The relational approach presupposes an oppositional juxtaposition between 'self' and 'other', and is hinged on the idea that the former is a bounded and discrete subject engaging in an individual pursuit of ethical self-mastery through relations with other bounded subjects. A composite approach, which I will demonstrate in this essay, is premised on collective personhood in which ethics does not depend on relationality but is prior to it. In other words, ethical principles should be seen not as emerging out of interactions between discrete persons, but rather as a pre-existing moral unity that defines personhood.

The term 'composite personhood' can undoubtedly be attributed to the work of Strathern, whose approach focuses primarily on the body 'imagined as a social microcosm' (1988: 13). Beyond this corporeal dimension, however, dividual personhood also includes nonhuman entities because items exchanged, and the relationships they represent, also comprise detachable parts of the self (1988: 204). In this context, gifts of ceremonial exchange relations – predominantly pigs – are 'multiply authored' (1988: 159), inalienable parts of the pluralized self because they are grown and nurtured by women, using the land and labour of their husbands (both spouses together forming a dyad). Moreover, through acts of care, nurtured things, including crops, children, and pigs, become internal multiplications of the body (although ultimately detachable) (1988: 250), a manifestation of shared labour, and a 'product of the relationship between the conjugal partners' (1988: 160). Nevertheless, the objects of exchange that constitute composite personhood in this context seem to do no more than mediate relationships, rather than perform, behave, or engage in any significant way:

> This construction thus produces objects (the person as a 'part' of a person him- or herself or another) which can circulate between persons and mediate their relationship. As parts, then, these objects create *mediated* relations. They are not, of course, apprehended as standing for persons: that is our construction. They are apprehended as extracted from one and absorbed by another (1988: 178, original emphasis).

These nonhuman components of composite personhood embody relations between persons; they are not themselves persons. In this essay, I similarly explore the role of nonhuman entities in personhood; however, these entities participate actively and morally in this broader sociality. The flipside of this endeavour is to propose a more nuanced approach to the field of ethics by drawing on theories of unbounded personhood, thus propounding a view of ethics beyond a mere relational arrangement between individuals. Strathern's model of dividuality remains useful in this respect as morality is inherent in her relational schema; as she states, 'The criteria that I have been calling aesthetic with regard to form can also be called moral: the self is judged by the way it activates its relationships' (1988: 277; see also Mosko 2015).

We might ask, however, how one can make sense of nonhuman participation in ethical life. While Foucault explored the relationship between power and materiality in his earlier work (2002a [1966]; 2002b [1969]), material or nonhuman entities do not appear in his later writings on ethics. Clearly Latour's work is particularly important when considering the role of nonhuman material entities in social and ethical life. Latour developed his *actor-network-theory* as a way to reconfigure the post-enlightenment separation between subject and object, in which nonhumans were invariably relegated to mere 'hapless bearers of symbolic projection' (2005: 10). His approach prompts us to consider how anything that modifies 'a state of affairs by making a difference' (2005: 71) is an actor, or in his terms, an actant.[3] In his earlier work, Latour (1992) asks more specifically where morality is located in social life, whether solely in humans, or possibly also located in the material world that impels one to act morally. In so doing, he turns our attention to the role of the 'nonhuman masses' such as alarmed seatbelts, speed bumps, and automated door closers that either force us to act responsibly or embody moral behaviour *for* humans. This, in turn, demonstrates how 'we have been able to delegate to nonhumans not only force as we have known it for centuries but also values, duties and ethics' (1992: 232). Nevertheless, this approach, much like Strathern's described above, presupposes that nonhuman entities merely mediate ethical intentionality in order to facilitate human meaning-making.

Notwithstanding my earlier scepticism regarding the egocentric stance of Foucauldian ethics and Laidlaw's claim that it is nonetheless a relational modality, Laidlaw does elsewhere offer a more subtle concession to the emphasis on individual agency in ethical action. Analogous in many ways to Latour's actant, Laidlaw (2010) grants the material world a role when propounding a notion of responsibility. When it comes to ethical action, he states, authorship of that action can take place through – often nonhuman – mediating entities. This approach similarly asserts that, in enabling a form of 'third-party' responsibility for action, these extrinsic entities are mere conduits, 'responsible' only in that they 'act as an agent on our behalf' (2010: 152). This is made possible by virtue of a capacity for ownership by the 'agentive' party, who somehow relocates his or her autonomous (i.e. individual) agency elsewhere. It is not insignificant that most examples offered by Laidlaw stem from legal cases profoundly conditioned by the concept of bounded right-bearing selves (2010: 154). As such, it seems that both Latour's and Laidlaw's accounts follow lines of deflected intentionality, rather than dispersed responsibility per se.[4]

The question remains, then: could we envisage an ethics that expands the bounds of a human-centred approach, in which nonhumans are something more than inert mediators? Verbeek (2011) attempts this approach by considering ethics as 'hybrid intentionality', specifically calling for a broadening of the 'humanist' foundation of ethics and moral action in order to further an approach to humanity beyond humanism.[5] This hybrid moral agency, he argues, is 'distributed among human beings and nonhuman entities' (2011: 38) to become a human-thing amalgam. Although his terminology is productive, the extent to which Verbeek's ethics amalgam is truly possible – particularly given his less than persuasive examples of cars, mobile phones, and ultrasound equipment – is certainly questionable (and indeed restates Latour's approach). Yet this does not mean that finding an ethical hybrid, so to speak, is an impossible task, particularly if we take the lead from our research participants, many of whom describe nonhumans as acting and reacting to broader human-nonhuman behaviour.

When it comes to the theme of energy, ethics, and nonhumans, Howe's contribution to this volume does seek to explore 'other-than-human lives and their intertanglement with energy infrastructures' (Howe, this volume, p. 163) in order to provide 'a broader analytic of ethics, energy, and socioecological environments' (Howe, this volume, p. 165). Applying Foucault's theory of parrhesia ('free speech' from one in a subaltern position) to her work, she explores the communicative role (a 'being-as-message') of animal life in proposed wind turbine sites in Mexico. This approach shifts the frame from Foucauldian ethics and the care of the self back to a sense of collective moral responsibility, since 'speaking truth to power' assists the progress of the 'greater good'. In this sense, parrhesia may even recover a non-coercive Durkheimian rights-centred view of society.[6] However, the nonhuman entities that Howe describes 'act' only insofar as their threatened extinction draws attention to – or indexes – broader environmental concerns: '[O]ther-than-human beings appear to "speak" a kind of parrhesia: indexing their imperilled state of being as a message from "below" and enunciating an ethical challenge' (Howe, this volume, p. 172). Gasoline, by contrast, is seen by the Sanema to *actively* respond to immoral behaviour. Indeed, it is precisely its vitality – which empowers gasoline as a fuel – that also grants it a place alongside human ethical subjects.

Despite some shortcomings, the above theoretical stances demonstrate that numerous scholars have contemplated ethics as a composite phenomenon. But what precisely do we mean when we say composite, and what form does it take? Welker's approach to corporations (2014) is useful when thinking about an anti-essentialist composite ethics, as she shows 'how corporate identity and interests are distributed and contextual, produced through interactions and temporary associations between humans, animals, and objects in particular places' (2014: 5; see also Mol 2003). Welker demonstrates how the subject – the resulting whole – is an entity made up of both human and nonhuman parts; a 'hanging together' of disparate components. Furthermore, rather than exploring composite entities as co-ordinated and harmonious wholes, Welker shows how they emerge as contested and somewhat incidental manifestations of internal struggles. Though the context she presents is considerably different to the case of gasoline offered in this essay, the resulting arrangement of unbounded personhood is not altogether dissimilar: a combined human and nonhuman phenomenon that is constituted through a degree of tension and conflict.

Returning, then, to my earlier assertion that the study of ethics must move beyond an individual or relational approach, composite ethics – constituted of both human and nonhuman entities – may offer a productive alternative. In what follows, I shall explore in detail how Sanema encounters with the intriguing energy source of gasoline may help conceptualize how their particular view of composite personhood is central to understandings of both energy and ethics, but also to the relationship between the two. Before I describe this Sanema composite ethics in detail, I shall consider the wider backdrop in which the Sanema and their gasoline are situated: the Venezuelan petro-state.

## Magical oil and its ubiquitous derivatives

In *The magical state* (1997), Coronil illustrates that, since the birth of Venezuela's oil industry in 1908, fossil fuels have been central to its democratic institutions and public sphere, both of which were founded on the relationship between natural resources and the people; or the natural body and the social body, as he described it. This dynamic is upheld by the illusion, performed by state leaders, of oil's power to manufacture 'dazzling development projects that engender collective fantasies of progress' (1997: 5), a phenomenon Coronil encapsulates with the term 'magical state'. These magical chimeras that oil proffers stem from its apparent supernatural qualities associated with the fiscal abundance that accrues from its natural and miraculous fecundity. In this way, petroleum creates 'hallucinations' that modernity is somehow pulled out of a hat (1997: 68). Yet the magic of oil also stems from its capacity to veil its role – both marvellous and disastrous – in political actions; Coronil describes this as 'the visible embodiments of the invisible powers of oil money' (1997: 2). Importantly, whether conscious or not, national imaginaries and subject formation are intimately and unmistakably bound up with the substance of oil in Venezuela.

But there is something even more unique about Venezuela's position as a petro-state and the public relationship with oil. Not only does the country possess the world's largest proven oil reserves, but the most pervasive petroleum derivative – gasoline – remains the cheapest in the world owing to a subsidy introduced in the 1940s when Venezuela was emerging as one of the world's main suppliers of oil. During the time of my fieldwork, for instance, the receptacle most often used by indigenous peoples to transport fuel back to their remote communities – the 200-litre oil drum – could be filled with gasoline for less than £1. As such, it was often gasoline, rather than crude oil, that was the material manifestation of citizens' proclamations of right to petroleum wealth in Venezuela. This powerful privilege came to a head most starkly when attempts were made to raise the price of gasoline during a period of neoliberal reforms in 1989. The public response was to protest, but demonstrations soon spiralled into a period of riots that led to a violent military crackdown and numerous deaths known as *El Caracazo*, or 'The Caracas Smash'.

In Amazonia, citizens' relationship with gasoline is even more intimate because the fuel is interwoven in practical and visceral experiences of daily life. Like solar energy (see Cross, this volume), this 'off-grid' energy source is used to power the increasingly prolific items of machinery – generators, outboard motors, chainsaws, yucca-grating machines, grass trimmers, two-way radios, and water pumps – that have no reliable power source besides gasoline in these remote forest locations. This fluid has become so inescapable that barrels forever lurk in the background, small jerry cans are often seen stashed in the shadowy corners of houses, and cumbersome rows of oil drums solemnly wait at the river's edge for the next trip with the outboard motor.

This deluge of gasoline-run machinery and its fuel into this region of Venezuelan Amazonia has its roots in a long history of political patronage and the flow of petro-dollars into Venezuelan public life. Oil-powered politics took a new turn after the Revolution in 1998 and the subsequent era of so-called 'Bolivarianism'. This socialist regime, forged by the late Hugo Chávez, was also bolstered by the same illusion of progress that defines oil's power. This time the magic was channelled into grass-roots projects, free education and healthcare, and subsidized food for millions of previously excluded Venezuelans. Indeed, this endeavour weaves the 1930s Venezuelan motto of 'sembrar el petróleo' (sow the oil) – which describes the use of oil wealth for productive agricultural and industrial investments – with the revolutionary slogan 'Venezuela ahora es de todos' (now Venezuela belongs to everyone). As far as indigenous people were concerned, the election of Chávez also accelerated their engagement with state initiatives, as he proclaimed his commitment to indigenous peoples and their recognition. In 1999, the Venezuelan Constitution was adapted to reflect the inclusionary socialist political ideology and introduced a new section devoted to native peoples,[7] with clauses that espouse rights to collective land ownership, native education and health practices, and prior consultation for natural resource extraction in their territory. Notwithstanding this multi-ethnic vision, Chávez simultaneously directed attention to indigenous peoples' history of exclusion and thus promoted their incorporation into broader Venezuelan development initiatives, engagement in party politics, and their equal participation in the grassroots projects of Bolivarianism.

Nevertheless, it is gasoline – the everyday energy source derived from oil – that encapsulates and materializes indigenous peoples' relations with the state. It is made readily available to them and is guzzled by the outboard motors that transport them to the cities in order to engage in the political processes of Venezuelan citizenship: namely the procurement of ID cards as a precursor to voter registration, which thereafter leads to the bestowal of outboard motors, yucca-grating machines, and chainsaws from local politicians (see Penfield 2016). All of this machinery is run on highly subsidized fuel.

To make this to-ing and fro-ing more intense still, only indigenous communities (i.e. not criollo/non-indigenous peoples) are allocated a licence to purchase gasoline in monthly quotas (Sp. un cupo) – dispensed into several 200-litre drums – as well as the valuable paperwork that grants the legal transit of fuel within indigenous territory (Sp. la guía). This combination of concessions, licences, and forms facilitates continued use of gasoline-run machinery but also provides indigenous citizens with considerable power over the purchase and movement of gasoline within their territory. As a subtle form of enrolment in the petro-state, the prolific use of gasoline and the appropriation of its accompanying paperwork further impel indigenous peoples to regularly travel to the cities, and in the process expend and procure more gasoline. Even travelling to the city with an outboard motor to obtain gasoline requires gasoline, and so indigenous people find themselves returning to the cities to replenish supplies sooner than they expect. The bountiful presence of this evanescent fluid in Venezuelan Amazonia has thus arisen from the multicultural vision of the new socialist nation, along with indigenous peoples' budding apprenticeship in political patronage and the increased mobility that results.[8]

Notwithstanding this political milieu, I was astonished to see the quantity of gasoline being procured on a daily basis by the native Amazonians of this region, beyond even its pervasive presence in communities. The frontier town where indigenous peoples travel to collect their fuel at the local gas station was strewn with abundant orange-painted oil drums filled with gasoline. This landscape of barrels was evidence of an altogether more distinct purpose: the need for gasoline to run the clandestine gold mines in the hinterlands of the forest. The mining that was taking place in this region of Venezuela was part of the now common practice of illegal small-scale mining in lowland South America, composed of extensive invasions by thousands of independent prospectors seeking riches. The mine's high consumption of gasoline was due to the reliance on

**Figure 2.** Indigenous Venezuelans speed upriver in their canoe with an outboard motor donated by the regional government. One man wears a jacket with the words: 'Socialist Indigenous Warrior. Charge!' (Photo by the author.)

high-pressure water hoses used to access the colluvial gold deposits. After the land is deforested, these large gasoline-powered hydraulic cannons blast away the topsoil to create cavities of muddy water, which is then passed over a crude carpet-lined sluice box that separates the heavier sediment, the gold being later extracted with the use of mercury.[9] Reports emerged that there were up to a thousand hydraulic machines at work at any given time, and while these numbers were difficult to confirm, it was certainly true that the demand for gasoline at the mine site was exceedingly high.

Many local people, indigenous and non-indigenous alike, were involved in mining in this region. Very few, however, were troubled by the environmental degradation or violent incursions that preoccupied those inhabiting Yanomami lands further south (Kopenawa & Albert 2013: chap. 16; Rocha 1999). Most Sanema do not mine for gold directly for fear of the evil tutelary spirits that guard the mineral (Sa. *orotil töpö*), as described by one of my Sanema contacts: 'You can't get the gold, you can't work with the gold. You will die like that. That's what our forefathers warned'. Instead, most spend only brief moments at the mine site, arriving specifically to supply gasoline to the *criollo* (non-indigenous) machine owners (Sp. *dueños*), who pay with gold. In this sense, the gold rush, for the Sanema, can better be understood as a scramble for gasoline, which saw many attempting any means possible to acquire large quantities of the fuel, with some residing permanently in the towns for this purpose. Many Sanema saw the mine as a place to make astronomical riches, and rumours circulated that one could earn tens of thousands of dollars in each trip if enough gasoline could be procured, delivered, and traded.[10]

These activities were, on the surface, peripheral to the petro-state because they were deregulated and took place at the edges of state power. However, the influx of highly subsidized free-flowing gasoline into the area – intended for indigenous consumption – inadvertently assisted the smooth running of the mine and its hydraulic machines, while at the same time the petro-state's strategy of co-opting the local indigenous population made them essential actors in mining activities. Native inhabitants have a unique access to the *cupos* (quotas) that allow them to purchase gasoline in vast quantities, and to the paperwork (Sp. *la guía*) that authorizes them to transport it within indigenous territory (see Penfield 2016). *Criollos* travelling in these territories with large volumes of gasoline without the associated paperwork are likely to have their fuel confiscated at one of the military checkpoints that now line the river as part of an ineffectual government endeavour to eradicate illegal mining.

When it comes to analysing the ethical encounters that emerge from the increasingly indispensable energy source of gasoline, one possible approach is to draw out the social ruptures that are occasioned by the copious dispensation of this remarkable fluid. During the end of my fieldwork period, people did indeed begin to hoard gasoline and hide their barrels more regularly, and the term 'stingy' (Sa. *umi ipö*) – a reviled and even dangerous trait – was used with greater frequency in relation to fuel and its capacity to become a medium of power and control. In spite of these evident concerns, this essay will explore how gasoline becomes interwoven with social life as much as how it disrupts it.

## Lively gasoline

In my fieldsite, gasoline was spoken about with an undertone of mystery, and was treated as a substance beyond the ordinary. Its volatile energy was utilized to suffocate the overabundance of cockroaches that scuttle beneath belongings, or to set fire to a trail of ants making their way towards a cassava bread stash. Its potency was regularly harnessed for medicinal purposes: to stifle the itch of scabies, to douse feet riddled with jiggers, or even to pour over the hair to rid one of lice. I was also shocked to hear that a young man had drenched a deep machete wound on his wrist with gasoline to, as he said, 'make it better' (Sp. *hacer que mejore*). In addition, gasoline is thought to possess a kind of liveliness beyond mere chemical potency. The volatility and transformative nature of the fluid was often remarked on, but frequently in terms of some kind of capricious and malicious conduct (Sa. *salia bai*), as though acting with intentional 'fierceness' (Sa. *waitili*). Narratives of the substance declared how it expanded, surged, and leaped without warning or when left unattended for long periods, more often than not resulting in abrasions and burns. It was said to have many 'friends' (Sa. *nohimo*), the machines to whom it gave a 'voice', allowing them to groan away when they are brought to life. This equipment was not said to speak in the oratory sense, but rather to murmur or sing through the feeding of gasoline. As one described it: 'Gasoline is the friend of the motor. If you always use gasoline, the motor will always go. If water enters the motor, it will no longer sing'.

Like humans, for whom the state of being *tökö* – 'alive' and in good health – is sustained by meat and cassava gruel, and evidenced through the warmth and movement at the centre of the body, the warmth, movement, and health of machinery depend on the nourishment offered by its special 'friend' gasoline. The category of 'friend' in Amazonia is highly significant and suggestive of gasoline's burgeoning role in Sanema worlds. Friendship is necessary to social reproduction in the region (see, e.g., Killick 2009), but not without a degree of apprehension. Moreover, the fact that gasoline nourishes and stimulates – in the process giving life and life-force – is not dissimilar to other reactive substances created from organic forest matter among the Sanema, such as tobacco, manioc beer, sorcery poison, and *sakuná* (a hallucinogenic snuff). All such substances have, in one form or another, their own tutelary spirit masters who bestow them with potency and vital properties. One woman even described gasoline as possessing spirits not dissimilar to shaman spirit allies (*hikula*) that appear upon consumption of *sakuná*. She stated that 'gasoline also has spirits, because when you sniff it you see Sanema men. But they are not men, they are the spirits of gasoline'.

An example of gasoline's vital potential is its use within a repertoire of ritual substances known as *alawalia*. These are objects and elements prepared for divination rites, most commonly nail or hair clippings taken from a sick person combined with plant cuttings from species 'known to have spirits'. These fragments of matter are assembled into bundles and hung above the hearth, or stuffed into a hole of a special tree for a number of nights to allow the spirit of the *alawalia* to enter the dreams of the woman conducting the prognosis. *Alawalia* is also the term used for substances and items utilized in assault sorcery, such as tiny darts that are propelled into the bodies of unsuspecting victims (see also Walker 2015). These substances can be magically extracted by particularly powerful shamans, who then vomit up the fragments for others to see. Assault sorcery can also take the form of revenge spells that form widespread rituals in response to unexplained fatalities, including the throwing of reactive substances on cremation fires (rock and plant fragments) to bring about the death of unidentified or distant murderers. This is where gasoline joins the array of *alawalia* substances, as it was increasingly used to pour over dead bodies to intensify funerary fires and accelerate the agonizing, feverish demise of the elusive enemy. What is significant here is that the category of *alawalia* includes fragments of sentient persons or animist beings that have been removed and used for their vital capacities, yet still retain the spirit of the 'distributed' personhood from which they emerged (Gell 1998: 104). *Alawalia* itself is also a partible composite.

Gasoline is fundamentally recognized as a reactive and, in turn, socially catalytic substance; an agitator rather than an inert conduit. This social dimension of gasoline's influence was evident in the young boy's punishment described at the beginning of the essay. The explicit reason given for the whipping he endured was that he had 'let demons inside'.[11] One friend later described the Sanema term for demon – *ai pupo* – as 'one who is disguised' (Sp. *alguien que está disfrazado*), or 'transformed into a bad person' (Sp. *transformado en una mala persona*).[12] The implication is that by letting bad things inside, one wilfully transmutes oneself into the unrecognizable 'other'. Indeed, this phrase – letting demons inside – was often used to describe excessive drunkenness, a state that indexes violent upstream others, and which precipitates unchecked fierceness, capricious behaviour, and a general obstruction to community well-being. Many residents of my host community described alcohol consumption as troubling because being drunk – *polemo* (literally meaning 'to be like a dog') – causes one to forget one's kin and act unpredictably. Alcohol consumption triggers one to name the dead, have numerous illicit affairs, act aggressively towards kin, and unwittingly entice evil spirits (Sa. *sai töpö*) and raiders (Sa. *oka töpö*) to the community. The incorporation of harmful essences in this way is also analogous to descriptions of the onset of illness, in which vengeful animal spirits enter the body; although the difference here is that the spirit is intentionally granted entrance – *letting* demons inside – rather than invading against one's will.

Like alcohol, then, huffing gasoline can cause a solipsism that obstructs the fragile balance of conviviality (see also Santos-Granero 2000: 277). Unlike alcohol, however, gasoline sniffing was once described to me as causing '*permanent* damage to the mind' (Sp. *daño permanente a la mente*) where 'proper thinking is' (Sp. *donde está el pensamiento verdadero*). Many of my Sanema interlocutors believed that excessive exposure to gasoline could cause serious derangement because such conduct was personified by a local man from the neighbouring Ye'kwana who was famous throughout the region for his regular 'consumption' of the fluid. He was renowned for his inappropriate behaviour, gibberish talk, voluntary isolation, and aggression (see also Vilaça 2011: 251-2). Often described as 'going around without a place, and without people', he would spend weeks at a time wandering the streets of the *criollo* frontier town, and then drifting from community to community with seemingly no awareness of kinship rules, the importance of sharing, and other social interdictions.[13] As rumour had it, he was abandoned as a child and left on his own, causing him to 'drink' gasoline in solace, which in turn resulted in his madness and the further intensification of his alienated and anomalous behaviour. It is clear, then, that gasoline acts as a physical, social, and occult stimulant, and that its power in Sanema lives is multifaceted and complex. To show how this potency intermingles with human ethics, however, we must next look in detail at Sanema moral personhood.

## Sanema moral personhood

Each Sanema person has multiple components, both internal and external, to the self. Besides the corporeal form, the Sanema have a shadow soul (Sa. *nonoshia*) which is a discrete animal alter ego living its distinct but lateral life far away in another part of the forest. They also have a core soul (Sa. *oshitö*) that manifests as gentle movement at the centre of the body (the heartbeat), and a spirit of vengeance (Sa. *okola*) which moves beyond the body in order to avenge illusory sorcerers (Colchester 1982: 449; see also Vilaça 2005: 453). Personhood is also constituent of one's kin network. The term *aitö* – which is used to refer to kin – literally means 'other', although more in the sense of similar than strictly 'other'. When a Sanema person talks of 'my similars' (Sa. *ipa aitö*, 'my family'), it is inferred that their kin are versions or parts of themselves, and that together they form a whole. Gow observes a similar logic among the Piro, who consider both humanity and kinship as multiplicities, and that selfhood constitutes a 'multiplication of identical entities' (2001: 49; see also Kohn 2013: 64-8; Strathern 1988: 14).[14] This is a relationship not between individual discrete units, but between parts of a whole – a composite. This notion is made most salient when actions towards or between kin are considered equivalent, as when women breastfeed their sisters' infants, when taboo breaking can seriously harm the transgressor's children, and when vengeance is carried out against the brothers of a murderer.

Importantly, this form of personhood plays out most notably in relation to behaviour, which can critically affect the well-being of kin. Perhaps one of the best ways to demonstrate this is through the case of *onihamo* among the Sanema. As my host brother described it, *onihamo* is the unwitting or uncontrolled desire to amass possessions, or a voracity in hunting that causes illness among family members. Although no historical data have been published on this concept, discussions on the topic suggest that it is tightly bound up with transforming notions of ethics and personhood, particularly as they relate to Sanema ideas of ethnic difference and shifting economic activities. Like myth, this transformational concept serves to make sense of the dynamic lived world that the Sanema inhabit (see also Gow 2001). It was once a term used to describe the dangers of hunting large numbers of game animals in one trip, and the cosmic counter-response to such actions, but now also refers to the uncertainties of contemporary economic activities such as procuring all available gasoline portage work to the mine, or obtaining more gold than anyone else (see also High 2017). When I asked my host brother the meaning of the term, he responded with a blended description of its transforming economic significance, both in hunting and in gold mining:

> If six men go to the mine and five of them only make 4 grams of gold and you make 20 grams, you are *onihamo*: someone in your family will die. It is the same with hunting. A hunter can't help himself and will continue to kill until he has lots because he needs meat for his family. He doesn't avoid it; he thinks only of killing. He doesn't think it's bad at the time, but others will say behind his back that he is *onihamo*.

He went on to explain that he had unintentionally caused the death of his young niece after greedily grabbing all the fish during a barbasco fishing trip when all the other participants came away with nothing.[15] This phenomenon, then, relates to transforming ideas of auspicious circumstances when one fails to maintain social relationships through generosity and compassion. Most importantly, excessive procurement or consumption by a single person threatens the health of any member of the kin group as a whole. This case shows how ethics must be seen as a collective phenomenon, as one's behaviour determines the health and well-being of one's kin. Indeed, it is somewhat telling that other community members describe inward-looking people as *onihamo* 'behind their backs', as though the individuals themselves fail to notice both the gossip and their tragic fate, so wrapped up are they in their solipsistic desires.

A parallel case of a young trainee shaman, Eudin, illustrates well how ethics in this case concerns not merely care for the self, but also care for one's similars. I noticed that Eudin, who was around 15 at the time of fieldwork, occasionally acted in a very peculiar and erratic manner. Most days he would be quietly sitting with his family eating or fishing, but on others he ran around the community shrieking with arms outstretched, or entered my household to imitate animals in front of my ageing host father. One evening I found Eudin telling an awe-struck audience how he had flown over the forests one night in search of the mine site. I suspected he must be a shaman in training, so asked my friend Teo if this was the case. It was true, he had been on the way to becoming a very special shaman, I was told. 'Eudin was born with the umbilical cord wrapped around his neck so they knew he was going to be a powerful shaman with mighty spirit allies to accompany him', Teo began. 'He was the sort who could vomit up lumps of *alawalia* [harmful sorcery substances] that he had extracted from sick people. He knew about everything and flew all over the place at night'. But then the story took a sinister turn. Eudin had started to fall in love with women, and it was at this point that his spirit allies left him, 'They wanted to get as far away from him as possible because they don't like the smell of women. Eudin abused their trust'. On his return home after shamanizing one day, he was choking and unable to breathe. Teo recounted the episode with a burdened expression. 'It was as though they had grabbed his neck and were suffocating him. The next day his sister's new-born baby died. It was the spirits gaining revenge'. Stories like this were common, and demonstrate how ethical action is not merely a means for self-improvement, even if achieved through relationality. Ethics can be a composite form of responsibility, with all entities forming an integrated whole. But there is more to it than this. Not only does the behaviour of one person affect the well-being of another, but in fact any being in the animist cosmos can respond to conduct. In the final section that follows, I will bring together the ideas of energy and ethics explored thus far to consider how gasoline becomes interwoven into Sanema composite ethics.

## Energy and composite ethics

My Sanema friend Wilfredo sat at the hearth looking extremely irritated. He had just returned from a two-month trip trading gasoline at the gold mines upstream, and evidently not all had gone to plan. 'There are a lot of problems if we can't sell gasoline', Wilfredo snapped at his brother Cesar who was sitting opposite him at the hearth. 'You sit here in the community waiting for your gold, behaving badly. But I cannot sell this gasoline if you behave badly'. This snippet from a tense exchange that I had unwittingly encountered while passing by the family hearth stuck in my mind for a while afterwards. It had certainly seemed that Wilfredo was suggesting that the sale of gasoline was contingent on kin behaviour. But what piqued my interest further was that in the days following Wilfredo's return, numerous rumours circulated as to why the sale of his gasoline had failed, all of which led back to the question of kin moral behaviour; depraved or deceptive acts that had somehow impeded his success.

Some time after his return from the mine, I was finally able to ask Wilfredo directly what had happened. He told me that he always worked hard for his kin and this was why he went to sell gasoline in the mine. But, he added bitterly, he had failed because of their waywardness. He described the numerous attempts he had made to transport gasoline to the mine, each time failing to pass the military checkpoints owing to lack of the requisite paperwork. Finally, he and his brothers had managed to buy the documentation from a Ye'kwana contact, and this time he sailed up the river with ease, optimistically reaching the mine with his several barrels to sell to the non-indigenous owners of the hydraulic machinery. When he arrived, he noticed that other traders had arrived directly before him, exchanged their barrels, and blissfully walked off with their gold. Wilfredo delivered his gasoline, but the machine bosses did not pay. Then some other fuel traders arrived after him, passed over their gasoline, and again happily departed with their riches. Wilfredo waited for his payment but received nothing, slowly suspecting that something unusual was occurring.[16] In that moment, he realized what was going on. 'Aha!' he said to himself, 'My brother, or my wife's younger sister, they are behaving badly. That is why the miners aren't paying quickly'. I later confirmed this with another research participant, who expounded as follows:

> People are like that. Wilfredo goes to sell gasoline in the mine. He sells it but they don't pay well, or don't pay quickly. 'When are you going to pay?' you ask and they say 'the day after tomorrow', but this day passes and again you ask, and they say 'tomorrow' and again the day passes. This is because your family is misbehaving.

He elucidated further by describing how immoral behaviour (Sa. *salia bai*) can result in misfortune. For example, he explained, if a man goes fishing and his family are misbehaving, then he will catch no fish.[17] While it was not explicitly stated that the gasoline and the fish were 'resisting' exchange, both were becoming entangled in human social and moral relationships rather than mere practical acts of procurement and exchange, or as mediators in purely human ethics. Just as fish and peccaries are believed to be deliberately evasive in cunning ways as intentional beings who are active players in a broader human/nonhuman social field, so too can gasoline – already viewed as highly unusual – become drawn into these same webs of ethical action.

Beyond this apparent resistance to being traded, the volatile fuel was often portrayed as intentionally carrying out malicious or predatory acts in response to conduct, taking centre stage in many accounts of disaster and fascination. Large heavy barrels of fuel appear in many Sanema narratives as wicked travel companions. One man, Mario, lost his wife and three children when a heavy drum of gasoline had caused the canoe they were travelling in to topple over when passing through some strong rapids. The 'gasoline had dragged them under', as one person described it. The story was also accompanied by hushed suggestions that the incident had been the result of their *salia bai*, their bad behaviour. Both Mario and his wife, I was told, had been engaging in extra-marital affairs at the time. In another story, a Ye'kwana man who had been transporting many barrels of gasoline to the mine had arrived above a series of large waterfalls and eagerly boarded his canoe with the huge drums, despite the water threateningly licking the rim of the boat. The motor did not have sufficient power for such weight, and so had choked and failed. As the story goes, the Ye'kwana man had desperately pulled the starter cord over and over to no avail as his canoe slowly drifted towards the precipice. His hefty gasoline pulled him over the waterfall and down to his death. Talk of the incident was accompanied by the suggestion that he perished because of his stinginess and that gasoline was somehow responding to his depraved conduct. His downfall was not merely an indication of his greed, but also a broader social and cosmic reaction to it. Other cases regularly emerged in which gasoline sat at the centre of horrific narratives of *salia bai* and the inevitable doomed consequences.

When considering these assessments of gasoline and its placement within the cosmos of intentional beings, it is important to keep in mind that the Sanema have no notion that death comes about through natural or accidental causes. Fatalities are the result of the agency of harmful forces and the will of vengeful beings (see similar cases in Storrie 2006: 229; A.C. Taylor 1996: 202; Whitehead & Wright 2004). Indeed, as argued by Howell in the Malaysian context, the entire cosmos is a web of 'cosmo-rules' in which the agency of nonhuman beings is 'activated in the wake of a human transgression' (2012: 136). The inauspicious repercussions brought about by both *onihamo* and evasive game animals are testament to this morally reactionary cosmos. Recall that gasoline is also an *alawalia* substance, utilized for sorcery and divination specifically because it has both fiery qualities and potent faculties like other intentional beings. It possesses a 'personhood' that can be distributed but with regard to which one must also be vigilant. In many of these cases, one might argue that the active moral capacity of humans is what impinges upon a mute material world, or that nonhuman entities happen to be conduits through which human morality is realized. This would be different from suggesting that the material world itself acts. Yet precisely because gasoline exhibits unusual 'energetic' properties – the Sanema perceive that it has a lively and vital force – it is seen to be something more than an inert material.

## Conclusion

Given the political context of contemporary Venezuela, where gasoline is heavily subsidized and increasingly widespread, the Sanema experience the petro-state through this tangible, energy-producing fluid. In scholarly literature, everyday ethical encounters within oil economies invariably result in societal breakdown resulting from increased individualism and greed, what Kirsch has described as 'the microeconomics of the resource curse' (2014: 33). The same could be said for the Sanema context, as they are engaging in the magical state for material – petro-funded – ends. There is a temptation to draw parallels between the Sanema's belief that gasoline 'lets demons inside' with Taussig's (1980) association between capitalist modes of production and demonic metaphors among peasants in the Cauca Valley of Colombia, a juxtaposition that creates a 'stunningly apt symbol of alienation' (1980: xi; see also Gamburd 2004; High 2013: 677; Kirsch 2006: 108; Shipton 1989; Walker 2012). In such cases, the capitalist economy and resource wealth are viewed as morally contaminating; a dystopia entirely divergent from the 'solar humanitarianism' of *renewable* off-grid energy (Cross, this volume). In some ways, the Sanema find they must negotiate the moral ambivalence of what emerges from the powerful petroleum economy on a daily basis, and anxieties clearly fringe the general threat of dangerous excess thought to exist as part of this economy – much like the unwitting overhunting that causes *onihamo*. In an analogous way, the act of supplying the illegal gold mines upstream with huge quantities of gasoline carries with it the opportunity for gratuitous riches, with yet again the potential for lurking, and highly ominous, individual desires. Nevertheless, attention to gasoline reveals that Sanema ideas of right or wrong that surround this energy source are not entirely correlated with a perceived immorality of the encroaching market economy, but are also associated with notions of personhood, sociality, and the cosmic order.

I have argued that current theorizations of ethics rely excessively on individualist models of the self. I furthermore suggested that ethical principles should not be seen as premised merely on intersubjectivity (which implies relationality), nor as deflected responsibility (which suggests possessorship over supposedly extrinsic agents). Composite ethics, by contrast, is an intentionality that cannot automatically be separated out from other associated parties. My critique of works such as those of Latour and Laidlaw above stems from the idea that – in animist societies in particular – ethical intentionality is not *deflected* through nonhuman entities merely for the purpose of serving human societies. Rather, moral arrangements encompass entities whose intentionality forms part of a broader (both human and nonhuman) composite ethics, rather than *facilitating* human individual ethics. In other words, nonhuman entities do not just act 'for us as our proxy' (Laidlaw 2010: 148) because, in certain contexts, they can form part of a broader ethical 'human-thing amalgam' (Verbeek 2011).

As has been shown, because gasoline is so intimately intertwined with Sanema social life, it might be viewed as a key player in this composite form of ethics, reacting in mysterious and at times frightful ways. Its energy-based qualities make it something other than inert material, and like other animist agents with generative and energetic capacities, it participates in ethical action together with humans. As such, gasoline, for the Sanema, is indeed something extraordinary; not merely a substance for the use in and 'symbolic projection' of Sanema worlds, but something that has vital power in its own right, and thus perhaps also ethical intentionality.[18] An approach to ethics that points to composite action in this way enables us to better appreciate the intense fear of inhaling gasoline, as well as Wilfredo's problem with selling it at the mine, because as a generative substance, this unique fuel becomes entangled in – and in turn responds to – a broader ethical action. Because my Sanema research associates viewed gasoline as socially potent in this way, we are forced to see ethics not as an exclusively individual human action, but as composite and nonhuman too. Even beyond the Sanema context, an unconventional approach such as this draws attention to our preoccupation with individual ethics and agency that obscures alternative forms of ethical action both in our fieldsites and closer to home.

*Journal of the Royal Anthropological Institute (N.S.), 140-159*
© Royal Anthropological Institute 2019

NOTES

This work was made possible with the support of the Economic and Social Research Council. All personal names have been changed to protect the identity of actors portrayed. This essay is a version of a paper presented at the Energy Ethics conference in St Andrews in March 2016. It also includes components of papers I presented at the London School of Economics, University College London, the University of Kent, the University of Manchester, and the University of St Andrews. I thank the seminar participants for their insightful comments. I am particularly grateful to the Editors of this special issue – Mette High and Jessica Smith – for their insightful and detailed feedback throughout the process. I also thank the anonymous reviewers for their comments, as well as Agustin Diz, Ana Gutierrez Garza, Tamara Hale, Evan Killick, Francesca Mezzenzana, Michael Scott, Katherine Swancutt, Anna Tuckett, Harry Walker, Johanna Whiteley, and Matt Wilde for their comments and advice during different stages of preparing this essay.

[1] The Sanema's experiences with energy are the inverse of other encounters outlined in this volume. Gasoline is not routinely experienced as an opaque energy source such as the 'invisibilities produced by the vast electricity infrastructure' (Smith, this volume, p. 98). Neither is it completely understood, unlike the charcoal produced by the Malagasy (Walsh, this volume). It is an extraordinary foreign fluid that, for the Sanema, is shrouded in mystery and thus received in diverse ways.

[2] The current political and economic crisis in Venezuela will certainly have changed the context. The situation escalated to critical pitch at the time of completing copy-editing for this essay (February 2019), as opposition leader Juan Guaidó declared himself interim president and demanded fresh elections. These circumstances also inevitably affect access to energy sources. Telephone conversations I have had with my research associates in recent years have confirmed that the volatility of the economy is paralleled by volatility in gasoline supplies. In this way, boom-and-bust mineral cycles are evident in the snapshots we observe when doing fieldwork.

[3] Latour's theory has been criticized, specifically with regard to his use of the category of nonhumans, which can constitute a broad range of living and non-living entities. Ingold (2011), for instance, takes issue with the disregard for a nuanced understanding of life in descriptions of actants. While I agree with this critique, the intriguing thing about gasoline is the fact that it does seem to have a unique form of liveliness and unpredictability that other inert objects lack.

[4] Laidlaw's notion of responsibility parallels Gell's (1998) theory of 'distributed personhood', in which the agency of the primary agent (i.e. artist) is distributed through secondary agents (i.e. artefacts and art works). Most of the authors outlined here, including Verbeek and Welker, do not make a clear distinction between ideas of collective, unbounded, distributed, and composite, often using the terms interchangeably. This is in part because the difference is subtle and variable depending on the argument advanced. The main point I wish to make here is that ethics is not an individual phenomenon, but also that nonhuman entities are more than mere conduits of human capacities. The Sanema case highlights how, in some cases, nonhuman entities are themselves seen to be key players in ethical action.

[5] Verbeek refers to the 'humanist' or 'modernist' approach to ethics as one that divides the world into human subjects on one side and everything else on the other, denying in the process any form of moral significance to nonhumans.

[6] Although perhaps these ideas might be analogous to a 'morality of choice' rather than a 'morality of reproduction' (Robbins 2007).

[7] Capitulo VIII: De los derechos de los pueblos indígenas.

[8] In many ways, this scenario is not dissimilar to the automobile-enabled lifestyles and associated dependence on fuel in the 1930s and 1940s United States, outlined by Huber (2013). This, too, was a political project – predominantly on the part of petrochemical and automobile industries – in which an 'addiction to oil' became intimately tied up with American values of freedom, status, contentment, and even 'life' itself.

[9] In Venezuela, a different term is used for gold panning (*minería artisanal*), which is permitted. Mining with high-pressure water hoses (*minería illegal/informal*) is illegal as it is far more destructive to the environment.

[10] When my interlocutors managed to transport and trade gasoline, however, it was rather infrequent, and normally only consisted of a few barrels of gasoline traded for about 50 grams of gold each. I was told that 50 grams could be traded for approximately 16,300BF, which at the exchange rate at the time was US$2,037.

[11] Note that these terms are different to those that refer to the Christian devil, for which they use *satana* in Spanish and *sai ton* in Sanema.

[12] Kenneth Taylor (1979: 213) describes the Sanema term for transformation as *išwanižo*, which refers to illness and the primordial transformation from humanoid bodies to animals, normally as a consequence of improper behaviour.

[13] Although this abnormality might be indicative of his closeness to the spirit world (see Pedersen 2011), there was no mention of this man being a shaman. Most saw him as damaged by gasoline.

[14] A similar definition is evident in the Yanomami word *mashi*, meaning brothers and parallel cousins of the same sex, but also 'to be of the same class or species, or one side of an object' (Lizot 2004: 206).

[15] Barbasco fishing, which is normally undertaken in groups, involves pounding the bark from a poisonous tree into a pulp. The fluid from the mashed bark is then added to a stream, temporarily stunning its fish, which float to the surface, at which point people grab as many as they can.

[16] Although Wilfredo describes the machine owners as not paying, anxiety seems to revolve around the refusal to pay directly or miscommunication and confusion concerning *criollo* trading practices.

[17] This phenomenon seems in some ways to be the inverse of *onihamo*: instead of reacting to overhunting and stinginess, here game animals refuse to be caught. In both cases, however, animist beings are reacting to immoral behaviour.

[18] This idea follows Howell's (2012) notion of 'cosmo-rules', in which causality is tightly interlaced with cosmology. Forest beings, in this context, respond maliciously to immoral behaviour in humans (such as a disastrous thunderstorm described by Howell). Whether this implies that beings with intentionality act on impulse or sentiment (i.e. actively contemplating right and wrong) is not explored by Howell, nor by others who describe similar cases (e.g. Cruikshank 2012). My Sanema research associates rarely explained disastrous phenomena as meticulous responses by animist beings; rather they viewed them as a series of spontaneous and somewhat perplexing events. In other words, there is no indication that these 'responding' entities ponder ethics and responsibility, even though they act according to them.

## REFERENCES

COLCHESTER, M. 1982. The economy, ecology and ethnobiology of the Sanema Indians of South Venezuela. Ph.D. dissertation, University of Oxford.

CORONIL, F. 1997. *The magical state: nature, money, and modernity in Venezuela*. Chicago: University Press.

CRUIKSHANK, J. 2012. Are glaciers 'good to think with'? Recognising indigenous environmental knowledge. *Anthropological Forum* **22**, 239-50.

FAUBION, J.D. 2012. Foucault and the genealogy of ethics. In *A companion to moral anthropology* (ed.) D. Fassin, 67-84. Malden, Mass.: Wiley-Blackwell.

——— 2013. Foucault's ontology and epistemology of ethics. In *A companion to Foucault* (eds) C. Falzon, T. O'Leary & J. Sawicki, 491-509. Malden, Mass.: Wiley-Blackwell.

FOUCAULT, M. 2002*a* [1966]. *The order of things: an archaeology of the human sciences*. London: Routledge.

——— 2002*b* [1969]. *Archaeology of knowledge* (trans. A.M. Sheridan Smith). London: Routledge.

GAMBURD, M.R. 2004. Money that burns like oil: a Sri Lankan cultural logic of morality and agency. *Ethnology* **43**, 167-84.

GELL, A. 1998. *Art and agency: an anthropological theory*. Oxford: Clarendon Press.

GOW, P. 2001. *An Amazonian myth and its history*. Oxford: University Press.

GRACEY, M. 1998. Substance misuse in Aboriginal Australians. *Addiction Biology* **3**, 29-46.

HIGH, M.M. 2013. Polluted money, polluted wealth: emerging regimes of value in the Mongolian gold rush. *American Ethnologist* **40**, 676-88.

——— 2017. *Fear and fortune: spirit worlds and emerging economies in the Mongolian gold rush*. Ithaca, N.Y.: Cornell University Press.

HOWELL, S. 2012. Knowledge, morality, and causality in a luckless society: the case of the Chewong in the Malaysian rain forest. *Social Analysis* **56**, 133-47.

HUBER, M.T. 2013. *Lifeblood: oil, freedom, and the forces of capital*. Minneapolis: University of Minnesota Press.

INGOLD, T. 2011. *Being alive: essays on movement, knowledge and description*. New York: Routledge.

KILLICK, E. 2009. Ashéninka amity: a study of social relations in an Amazonian society. *Journal of the Royal Anthropological Institute* (N.S.) **15**, 701-18.

KIRSCH, S. 2006. *Reverse anthropology: indigenous analysis of social and environmental relations in New Guinea*. Stanford: University Press.

——— 2014. *Mining capitalism: the relationship between corporations and their critics*. Berkeley: University of California Press.

KOHN, E. 2013. *How forests think: toward an anthropology beyond the human*. Berkeley: University of California Press.

KOPENAWA, D. & B. ALBERT 2013. *The falling sky: words of a Yanomami shaman*. Cambridge, Mass.: Harvard University Press.

LAIDLAW, J. 2010. Agency and responsibility: perhaps you can have too much of a good thing. In *Ordinary ethics: anthropology, language, and action* (ed.) M. Lambek, 143-64. New York: Fordham University Press.

——— 2014. *The subject of virtue: an anthropology of ethics and freedom.* Cambridge: University Press.

LATOUR, B. 1992. Where are the missing masses? The sociology of a few mundane artifacts. In *Shaping technology/building society: studies in sociotechnical change* (eds) W. E. Bijker & J. Law, 225-58. Cambridge, Mass.: MIT Press.

——— 2005. *Reassembling the social: an introduction to actor-network-theory.* Oxford: University Press.

LIZOT, J. 2004. *Diccionario enciclopededico de la lengua Yanomami.* Puerto Ayacucho: Vicariato Apostolico de Puerto Ayacucho.

MOL, A. 2003. *The body multiple: ontology in medical practice.* Durham, N.C.: Duke University Press.

MOSKO, M.S. 2015. Unbecoming individuals: the partible character of the Christian person. *Hau: Journal of Ethnographic Theory* **5**, 361-93.

PEDERSEN, M.A. 2011. *Not quite shamans: spirit worlds and political lives in northern Mongolia.* Ithaca, N.Y.: Cornell University Press.

PENFIELD, A. 2016. Maneuvering for paper: physical and social experiences of bureaucracy in Venezuelan Amazonia. *Journal of Latin American and Caribbean Anthropology* **21**, 457-77.

——— 2018. Extractive pluralities: the intersection of oil wealth and informal gold mining in Venezuelan Amazonia. In *Indigenous life projects and extractivism: ethnographies from South America* (eds) C.V. Ødegaard & J.J. Rivera Andía, 75-94. Basingstoke: Palgrave Macmillan.

ROBBINS, J. 2007. Between reproduction and freedom: morality, value, and radical cultural change. *Ethnos* **72**, 293-314.

ROCHA, J. 1999. *Murder in the rainforest: the Yanomami, the gold miners and the Amazon.* London: Latin American Bureau.

SANTOS-GRANERO, F. 2000. The Sisyphus Syndrome, or the struggle for conviviality in native Amazonia. In *The anthropology of love and anger: the aesthetics of conviviality in native Amazonia* (eds) J. Overing & A. Passes, 268-87. London: Routledge.

SCOTT, M.W. 2016. To be Makiran is to see like Mr Parrot: the anthropology of wonder in Solomon Islands. *Journal of the Royal Anthropological Institute* (N.S.) **22**, 474-95.

SHIPTON, P.M. 1989. *Bitter money: cultural economy and some African meanings of forbidden commodities.* Washington, D.C.: American Anthropological Association Monograph Series.

STORRIE, R. 2006. The politics of shamanism and the limits of fear. *Tipití* **4**, 223-46.

STRATHERN, M. 1988. *The gender of the gift: problems with women and problems with society in Melanesia.* Berkeley: University of California Press.

TAUSSIG, M.T. 1980. *The devil and commodity fetishism in South America.* Chapel Hill: University of North Carolina Press.

TAYLOR, A.C. 1996. The soul's body and its states: an Amazonian perspective on the nature of being human. *Journal of the Royal Anthropological Institute* (N.S.) **2**, 201-15.

TAYLOR, K.I. 1979. Body and spirit among the Sanumá (Yaнoama) of North Brazil. In *Spirits, shamans, and stars: perspectives from South America* (eds) D.L. Browman & R.A. Schwarz, 201-22. Amsterdam: Mouton.

VERBEEK, P.-P. 2011. *Moralizing technology: understanding and designing the morality of things.* Chicago: University Press.

VILAÇA, A. 2005. Chronically unstable bodies: reflections on Amazonian corporalities. *Journal of the Royal Anthropological Insitute* (N.S.) **11**, 445-64.

——— 2011. Dividuality in Amazonia: God, the Devil, and the constitution of personhood in Wari' Christianity. *Journal of the Royal Anthropological Institute* (N.S.) **17**, 243-62.

WALKER, H. 2012. Demonic trade: debt, materiality, and agency in Amazonia. *Journal of the Royal Anthropological Institute* (N.S.) **18**, 140-59.

——— 2015. Justice and the dark arts: law and shamanism in Amazonia. *American Anthropologist* **117**, 47-58.

WELKER, M. 2014. *Enacting the corporation: an American mining firm in post-authoritarian Indonesia.* Berkeley: University of California Press.

WHITEHEAD, N.L. & R. WRIGHT 2004. *In darkness and secrecy: the anthropology of assault sorcery and witchcraft in Amazonia.* Durham, N.C.: Duke University Press.

# Le carburant de la crainte et de la force : le pouvoir énergétique de l'essence et son imbrication dans une éthique composite

*Résumé*

L'énergie est bien plus qu'une ressource exploitée par les États et les entreprises. Sa consommation est souvent considérée comme un phénomène difficile à analyser parce qu'elle est tellement familière que l'on remarque à peine son rôle dans nos vies ou, à tout le moins, que sa production est occultée par son utilisation pragmatique au quotidien. L'autre côté de l'histoire, celui dans lequel l'énergie est une marchandise distribuée aux gens et avec laquelle ils vivent des relations intimes et inattendues, est clairement visible dans des lieux tels que la forêt humide amazonienne, d'où les modalités habituelles de fourniture de l'énergie sont absentes. Cet article explore la manière dont les rencontres quotidiennes avec l'essence éclairent les jugements éthiques chez les Sanémas d'Amazonie vénézuélienne. Le carburant est de plus en plus omniprésent et s'insinue dans de nombreux aspects de la vie quotidienne : extraction d'or, dilemmes de parenté, univers animiste des maîtres des esprits vengeurs et rumeurs de catastrophes au sous-texte éthique. Par sa nature volatile (à la fois vaporeuse, explosive, narcotique et caustique), l'essence est aussi une entité vitale qui tient une place particulièrement intrigante dans la compréhension de la personne et de l'éthique chez les Sanémas. De fait, ses qualités mystérieuses et troublantes lui valent de s'intégrer dans une forme composite d'éthique qui définit les mondes sociaux des Sanémas.

# 8

# Greater goods: ethics, energy, and other-than-human speech

CYMENE HOWE *Rice University*

Renewable energy projects are ethically laudable for their cleansing intentions, but they also produce effects upon other-than-human beings in their orbit. Taking the case of Mexico's Isthmus of Tehuantepec, which is home to the densest concentration of on-shore wind parks anywhere in the world, and following Foucault's reading of the speech form 'parrhesia', this essay argues that the bodies of affected nonhuman beings, particularly those whose existence is actively balanced against a 'greater good' for humanity, enact a form of other-than-human speech, first in their threatened status and, secondly, through environmental management regimes that seek to synchronize human and nonhuman lives in settings of both local and global ecological failures.

## Free speech

In one of his lesser-known theoretical fascinations, Michel Foucault contemplated a Greek speech form called parrhesia. His notes tell us that this term is ordinarily translated into English as 'free speech'. In its subjective usage, the parrhesiastes is s/he/they who utilize parrhesia, the one who speaks her/his/their truth. Parrhesia is the articulation of a genuine belief, unencumbered by rhetoric and thus purified in its honesty. The parrhesiastes uses their freedom to choose frankness over persuasion, or flattery over morality, selecting veracity in place of falsehoods.[1] Foucault further reminds us that the free speech of parrhesia always comes from 'below' and it is always a critique. It may be self-critical and it may be personally or politically directed, but the quality it preserves is that of assessment and evaluation. The parrhesiastes helps people recognize their 'blindness', a blindness that is a consequence of what Foucault calls 'moral fault' (2011: 16).[2] Parrhesia is a critical project, but a decidedly moral task as well. Finally, the free speech of parrhesia is not simply speaking truth, but telling that lived truth to power. Parrhesia is an enactment that involves risk and danger. Sometimes that risk is bodily, permanent, or fatal, and other times it is less dramatic but perilous nonetheless.[3]

To be a parrhesiastes, one must be in a subordinated state, similar to what Spivak might call a subaltern position, at least in respect to the person whom one is addressing.[4]

*Journal of the Royal Anthropological Institute (N.S.)*, 160-176
© Royal Anthropological Institute 2019

Foucault puts it quite simply when he writes, 'The parrhesiastes is always less powerful than the one with whom he or she speaks. The parrhesia comes from "below", as it were, and is directed towards "above"' (1999: para. 19).[5] A philosopher may speak against a tyrant or a student critique their teacher, but never the other way around. It becomes readily apparent, however, that he who can exercise parrhesia is never fully 'from below', because it is in almost all cases only 'a male [Greek] citizen' who can undertake such speech. Above all, parrhesia is a human project: whether between one another or to the gods, it is Man who enunciates these transparent truths.

Parrhesia is an index of who, or what, is capable of speaking the truth. It is, for Foucault, a decidedly human act. But what if parrhesia were not solely an occupation of the human? What if we were to consider nonhuman beings as 'speeching' (freely)? Remember that: (a) the parrhesiastes has a special relationship to truth because their life may be endangered; (b) the parrhesiastes is synonymous with their message, a living virtue, and a transparent truth that also surfaces ethical concerns;[6] and, finally, (c) the parrhesiastes always comes from 'below'.

### Parrhesia in the wind

In the examples assembled here, I draw from my research on the massive expansion of wind parks in Mexico's Isthmus of Tehuantepec.[7] Mexico's foray into super-dense wind park development is predicated on a desire for greener forms of profit as well as cleaner power sources meant to better the global climatological commons. But although renewable energy projects are ethically laudable for their cleansing intentions, they also, like all infrastructural works, have effects upon humans and nonhuman beings in their orbit. In this context, I would like to propose that there is in fact a form of parrhesia at work in the bodies of affected nonhuman beings, particularly those whose existence is actively balanced against a 'greater good' for humanity, as in the case of endangered species proximate to renewable energy endeavours. Parrhesia is here enunciated first in these creatures' threatened status, or the probability of their extinction, and, secondly, through environmental management regimes that seek to synchronize human and nonhuman life in settings of both local and global ecological failures. I will argue that as nonhuman beings appear in representational forms (like legal protections), as they are produced through environmental management (as in environmental impact reports), and, finally, as they become present (ironically) in their perishing, this can be taken as a kind of parrhesia an imperilled being-as-message that comes from below. But before encountering our other-than-human parrhesiastes, let me first set the stage in southern Mexico, and within a series of conversations in the anthropology of energy, ethics, and multispecies studies.

### Inhabiting the wind

Mexico's Isthmus of Tehuantepec is a place where eighteen-wheel semi-trucks are regularly overturned, blown, and battered by gusts of *El Norte* (the north wind). Home to a meteorological ontology that makes it one of the best places on the planet to generate renewable electricity (Fig. 1), the Mexican Isthmus has also become home to the densest concentration of on-shore wind parks anywhere in the world. Turbines began to appear in the Isthmus when its windy potential was paired with policy measures to ensure that Mexico would reduce its carbon footprint. Under the guidance of President Felipe Calderón (2006-12), the country came to exemplify ambitious possibilities for climate remediation, setting legally binding targets for clean energy sources to provide

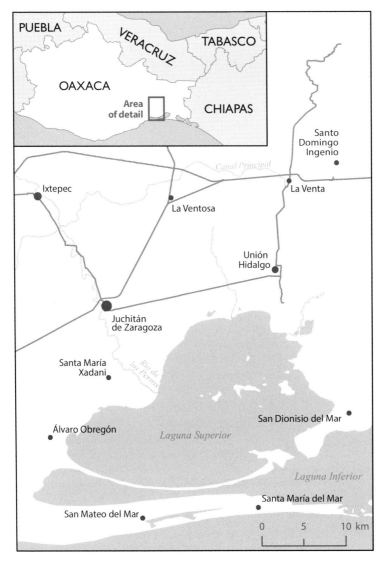

**Figure 1.** Map of Isthmus of Tehuantepec's core wind zone. (Created by Jean Aroom with assistance from Jackson Stiles and Hannah Krusleski.)

35 per cent of the nation's electricity by 2024 (Booth 2010). Thanks to the barometric pressure differential between the Gulf of Mexico and the Pacific Ocean, the winds of the Isthmus would come to be the hub of that renewable dream, captured through the revolutions of blades and their kinetic powers (Aiello, Valencia, Caldera Muñoz & Gómez 1983; Alonso Serna 2014; Elliott, Schwartz, Haymes, Heimiller & George 2003).

The same biogeography that makes Isthmus winds so potent for the production of renewable energy also makes the region an important migratory corridor for birds. This is a rich avian space, a crossing point between the lowlands of the Atlantic and the Pacific where migrating flocks and keen-eyed raptors avail themselves of draughts and favourable currents. With turbines in their paths, these birds, along with other animals, encounter potentially deadly obstacles in the form of lopping blades or habitat encroachment. The Isthmus wind pulls many lives through it, both in the form of flighted creatures and among the terrestrial human occupants who hope to achieve better levels of development – such as health centres, schools and prosperity – through the income that new energy infrastructures might bring (Escobar 1994).

If some Isthmus residents have profited from the arrival of the turbines, they are not the only people who see the growth of renewable energy as an ethical project of unqualified good. Investors in renewable energy ventures and Mexican state officials at all levels of governance also recognize the financial and developmental potential of renewable energy in the region, one of the country's most impoverished. Moreover, in a time of ecological precarity and a rapidly changing climate, the need to ameliorate anthropogenic harm by reducing carbon emissions is recognized as a concern affecting all biotic life, human and otherwise. In the Isthmus, as in other elsewheres where turbines and creatures meet, an ethical dilemma emerges (Crate & Nuttall 2009). Is the betterment of a global climate – through the tools of renewable power – to be prioritized over localized ecological spaces where that energy is produced and conveyed? Is there reason to forsake places like the Isthmus for the greater good of the climatological commons? And what sorts of ethical paradoxes are produced between human desires for energy and proximate creatures' desires to survive and thrive? Some response to these questions, I believe, can be found at the nexus of anthropological work on other-than-human lives and their intertanglement with energy infrastructures, both physical and bureaucratic (Howe 2019). Anthropological work that treats multispecies dynamics and energy forms in combination offers a unique analytical take on nonhuman speech, as a form of parrhesia enacted in environmentally troubled and ethically charged times.

### Energy ethics, multispecies ethics

The Anthropocene[8] – the dramatic anthropogenic morphing of Earth systems – hails particular conditions of possibility for other-than-human species. It is an opportunity, in one sense, to imagine new calibrations of vitality and its loss, as well as enunciations of risk and danger. Following several years of conclusive evidence from natural scientists that humans have radically altered essential Earth systems and are continuing to do so, many conversations across the social sciences and humanities have centred attention on the consequential relationships emerging between energy and environment (Barry 2015; Kirby 2011; Klieman 2008; LeMenager 2015; Petrocultures Research Group 2016; Szeman & Boyer 2017; Walsh, this volume). Among anthropologists and others, an increasing attunement to energy and its effects now shapes the epistemic ecology that we inhabit. Renewed attention to energy and environment has emerged in parallel with increased ecological precarity and anxieties surrounding extinctions both floral and faunal (Kolbert 2013). A growing recognition of anthropogenic harm has also worked to accentuate interspecies relationships and dependencies, producing innovations of theorizing from the post- or other-than-human (Blaser 2016; Candea 2010; Lien 2015; Matsutake Worlds Research Group 2009; Raffles 2010; Wolfe 2009) to the neo-materialist (Barad 2007; Bennett 2010) and to the post-technological (Haraway 1996; Latour 2013).

In parallel with environmental inquiries, a (re-)emerging subfield, the anthropology of energy, has expanded and deepened in recent years along with global initiatives regarding power generation, greenhouse gas reduction, and related ecological issues. Although an anthropology of energy has existed for some time,[9] the most recent generation of research has explicitly indexed the coeval relationship between energy forms and environmental systems (Behrends, Reyna & Schlee 2011; Breglia 2013; Cepek 2012). So too have many of these projects underscored human inequalities that are often produced in particular energy regimes (Howe 2015; Howe & Boyer 2016; Mason and Stoilkova 2012; Rolston 2014). Suzana Sawyer's (2004) study of US corporate oil operations in the Amazon, for example, details how economic disparities and lack of adequate healthcare are magnified through energy extraction. Combining Marxian political economic and Foucauldian approaches to biopower, Sawyer focuses critical attention on the subjugation of indigenous peoples and *campesino* mestizos whose worlds have been contaminated by the quest for oil.[10] Where extraction has certainly caused multiple kinds of harm in many parts of the world, the securing of energy must also be recognized as a component of energy infrastructures that also compel certain kinds of work and relationship (Smith, this volume) as well as complex investments – both literal and figurative – of finance capital and valuations of energy forms (High and also Wood, this volume). Energy, in other words, is a complex meshwork of human, material, and other-than-human encounter, open to multiple sociocultural interpretations.

Timothy Mitchell's (2011) influential historical account of 'carbon democracy' offers a critical framework within which carbon, as a fuel source, can be taken as a diagnostic of the broader social, political, and economic outcomes of energy production and consumption. The physical form of energy sources, Mitchell suggests, has in part determined the political and economic status of particular fuels over the last two centuries. Politically organized coalminers, beginning in the late nineteenth century, for example, were able to effectively 'choke' the distribution of the increasingly valuable resource they controlled by halting rail shipments of coal to cities in both the United States and the United Kingdom. Derailing carbon energy in this way led to critical political leverage for labourers that, for Mitchell, fomented the rise of the welfare state and a more equitable distribution of social wealth. Oil, he writes, had a wholly different political economic life. It provided a seemingly endless supply of viscous power, floating around the world by ship, and profoundly shaping politics in the Middle East as well as in Northern countries that had steadily become democracies whose growth and stability was dependent upon cheap oil.

Global inequalities are thus produced through forms of energy, their extraction, and their uneven distribution. Inequalities, in both social and environmental forms, have inspired much of the social scientific work on energy over the last decade. However, as High and Smith (this volume) acknowledge, we cannot limit our analytics to corporate and state critique, or to advocacy positions for more sustainable forms of energy production. Each is important, perhaps even crucial, but in the absence of recognizing a full range of human motivation and valuations of energy as a form (see Mason, this volume), we may leave ourselves unable to contend with greater ethical quandaries that appear on the horizon of energy futures. Contingent morality is implied across accounts of energy and its produced inequalities, but to sit only with political economic questions regarding energy leaves largely untapped the broad ethical implications of energy forms. Human desires find many outlets in the domain of energy, whether 'ecologically entrepreneurial' (Cross, this volume), caring for 'orphaned' energy assets (Wood, this volume), or inspired by a new imaginary of energy ethics that seriously engage with the costs of production and utilization from multiple points of view.

*Journal of the Royal Anthropological Institute (N.S.), 160-176*
© Royal Anthropological Institute 2019

Energy is power materialized but it is likewise ethically charged. In his *An anthropology of ethics* (2011), James Faubion uncovers the carefully layered sense of ethics that Foucault (1997) developed, demonstrating that ethical practice is not atomic but relational. Ethics are not individuated but instead *environmentally* conditioned. The 'interpretive universe of ethical forms', Faubion writes, 'is one of subjects *in*, or passing *through*, positions *in environments* (2011: 119, emphasis in original). If we take ethics as constitutionally shaped by relata, interaction, and the social environments in which they are enacted, then any ecoenergic dynamics of the present should also be read through an ethical account. By extending Foucault's and Faubion's social environment – which is composed of human beings exclusively – to a broader ethical ecosystem that includes nonhuman others, a broader analytic of ethics, energy, and socioecological environments may emerge. Accounting for the more-than-human moves us closer to that broader plane of ethical contact, allowing for a 'more capacious' (High & Smith, this volume, p. 11) rethinking of energy ethics.

Humans and other-than-human beings are in ethical relationships with one another, even if humans often prioritize their own (inter-human) ethical projects. In his 2013 book *How forests think*, Eduardo Kohn seeks to unravel the singularity of human communicational practice and to enlarge the scope of ethical encounter. Kohn reads the pragmatist philosopher Charles Peirce across human, forest, and animal interactions, advocating the importance of a semiological approach to more-than-human figures. Focusing attention on Peirce's signs, icons, indexes, and symbols, Kohn argues that the communicational labour between humans and their others is key to disassembling anthropocentricism. After all, it has long been the conceit of anthropos that it is He who is the sole master of language. In Kohn's work, forests and dogs would argue differently. What is of interest here, in the context of energy regimes and other-than-human lives, is the power of cross-species communication; this is not solely a matter of signs and their objects, but rather communication as a *mode of conduct* and behaviour that produces effects. By surfacing interspecies communicative potential, Kohn's brand of semiotic realism suggests an ethical practice that is not bound to humans alone but one which has extensional possibilities to other-than-human worlds.[11] Communication is, in this context, an invitation for humans to enter a habitat of icons and indexes shared by animals and other living beings.

This habitat, however, need not be limited to living beings alone (de la Cadena 2015; Li 2015). Elizabeth Povinelli's principle of 'geontology' (2016) asks for us to push beyond the (much fetishized) divide between life and death and instead recognize juxtapositions between life and non-life. Working with indigenous Australians, Povinelli shows how figures that appear to the settler colonial mind as land formations are in fact beings for Karrabing people. An important quality of the Two Sisters – or what some would take as paired mountains – is their ability to qualify distinctions of epistemic awareness between those who can recognize them as Two Sisters, as opposed to those who can only ever see two mountains. The aliveness of the Two Sisters is not in question for this is not a rehearsal of animism. Povinelli is instead seeking a concerted distance from the biopolitics of Life and Death; she is drawn towards what she calls 'the geontological'.[12] In Australian courtrooms, the Two Sisters have a geontological voice. Through the legal pronouncements of human interlocutors, they are poised as sites of cultural heritage and their preservation is thus ensured. The Two Sisters' speech form is their existence, their being there, even as they are translated by legal experts in order to be understood by those who can only ever see two mountains (and not Two Sisters). Certain forms of

*Journal of the Royal Anthropological Institute (N.S.), 160-176*
© Royal Anthropological Institute 2019

other-than-human existence are semiotically charged and communicatively significant in the protocols of law and policy.[13]

While the logics of settler-colonial modernity and enduring species hierarchies have, in some sense, always compelled nonhuman beings to 'speak from below', contemporary conditions of anthropogenic environmental degradation accentuate the precarity of nonhuman beings. Anthropocenic conditions thus open a space for a particular form of speech between human populations, nonhuman beings, and, in some cases, entities that are commonly taken to be without life, but that may, nonetheless, 'possess a kind of liveliness' (Penfield, this volume, p. 149). In the examples that follow, and drawing from the communicational possibilities laid out above in other-than-human speech forms, I will suggest that the communicational labour of other-than-human animals operates as a form of parrhesia. Where energy infrastructures infringe upon biotic spaces, it is hares and bats and birds whose being and bodily presence function as indexical lives (a) that come from below, (b) that are necessarily at risk, and (c) whose message of 'truth' in bodily form works as a speech act that troubles and interrupts the operative logics of energy extraction, even in its greener forms. Affected nonhumans that occupy the roads in the rush to new forms of energy thus enact a form of speech now (and especially) in a context of climate precarity. Their bodily being-there (presence), or their not-being-there (extinction or displacement), functions as a parrhesiaic 'true speech', coming from 'below' and imperilled. While many (or most) nonhuman animals have been subjugated to human interests and thus regularly made to occupy a subaltern space, the Anthropocene condition presents a unique set of conditions where increasingly vivid environmental degradation and species loss may in fact amplify the subordinated 'voice' of other-than-human parrhesiastes just as they occupy an increasingly precarious place in the biotic and energic worlds that humans continue to remake. And if particular creatures are threatened at the nexus of purer power and global anthropogenic harm, I would additionally ask whether this condition is not paradigmatic of the ethical challenges faced by humanity and our others: 'our' skies vs 'their' lives.

Now, finally, we are back to the wind.

## Hares

The Tehuantepec jackrabbit is the kind of animal that would scarcely be missed. It is not a predator responsible for culling some population of insects, rodents, or other vermin. As a source of prey, it is meagre, skinny, and now numbering so few that it would scarcely feed anyone or anything. Those likeliest to feast on it are stray dogs or a hungry human, both of whom would be lucky to even find, much less kill, this little hare. Wiry and dune coloured like its arid home, the Tehuantepec jackrabbit resembles its North American kindred in the southwestern United States. With its slightly transparent sunset pink ears cocked and nostrils ready for scents carried across the wind, it does not look remarkable, just another long-legged rabbit on its way to the end of days. *Lepus flavigularis* – also known by multiple other names: the Tehuantepec (or Tehuana) hare, the tropical hare, the *Liebre de Tehuantepec* (or *Liebre Tehuana*) – was named or 'discovered' by a nineteenth-century biologist; he called it the 'beautiful-eared jackrabbit'. The Tehuana hare has no recognized subspecies – meaning that there are no taxonomic ranks below it that can be designated with a distinct nomenclature. It is at the end of its line in its taxonominality.

The Tehuana hare has suffered a population decline of over 50 per cent in recent years, more than half of its biotic corpus. Its total numbers are less than a thousand

**Figure 2.** Computer-generated depiction of what the Mareña park might have looked like. (Illustration by the Mareña Corporation.)

and dropping. To make its way in the world, the hare now occupies only a fraction of its original territory, somewhere between 67 and 100 square kilometres. Four small, separate and separated populations make a patchwork of hare habitat – one of which is on a peninsular stretch of land where a portion of a wind park was set to be built: 30 of 132 total turbines, each of which would reach 105 meters (32 storeys) into the sky and weigh 285 tons. The home of the hare was set to become home to the Mareña Renovables project, the largest wind park ever erected in Latin America (Fig. 2). And the hares' habitat was about to become scarcer still as turbines, cement, and rebar would come to occupy their little remaining spaces. The jackrabbit is, however, protected by Mexican law as an endangered species. And when the law functions as it ought to, the little creature should receive respite.

While regulations are often prone to slippage and non-compliance in places like the Isthmus that lie at the margins of the nation-state, in this case, the little hare proved victorious. Saul Ramírez, an environmental impact specialist with many years of experience in the Isthmus region, explained that the presence of protected or endangered species was a 'definitive reason' to compel the developer to 'move the road, move the substation, move whatever'. In these cases, Saul noted, it is the ethical and legal obligation of government agencies, contracted researchers, and project developers to shift the co-ordinates of a project. Following another series of studies, the park was in fact moved, relocated owing to the presence of the withering jackrabbit.

Speaking from below with their bodily presence, hares articulated the fact of their existence and thus their endangerment in the planned path of the gigantic wind park. Although this truth may have been enunciated in human terms of impact reports and policy protocols, the presence of threatened hares had a parrhesiatic effect: exhibiting a unique relationship to truth because their lives were at risk. The presence of hares, and the speech effect this produced, however, need to be understood in parallel with the documents and legislative acts that made this speech possible. If hares are able to speak themselves through their bodily presence, their bureaucratic, legal, and actionable existence is made legible through the documents, reports, and statements that shape the condition of possibility for a wind park (or by that logic, any other infrastructural megaproject). The jackrabbits' vulnerability is enunciated through human mediators, often those who work in government agencies or environmental protection organizations. In other words, the body of the hare speaks only to the extent that regulatory devices of environmental preservation, and the human managers of those regulations, are able to also articulate themselves.[14]

## Environmental impact

The Mexican Secretariat of Environmental and Natural Resources (SEMARNAT) is a building filled with managers, overseers, and administrators whose job it is to ensure adherence to the laws governing the environment and natural resources. Located in a relatively prosperous commercial neighbourhood in Mexico City, the building itself is homage to high, concrete modernity. Alberto Villa is the Director of Evaluation for the Energy and Industrial Sectors, and he has an office set high in the SEMARNAT complex. In our meeting together in the autumn of 2012, he pulled out a massive tome that SEMARNAT has authored to ensure that legal obedience to the nation's environmental laws and resource regulations is assiduously followed. With the volume at his side, Alberto began to explain the intricacies of protections. Other-than-human species were clearly subject to the human machinery of bureaucracy, teetering between the protocols of oversight, care, and legality as well as the inertia of institutional practice.

A megaproject cannot be born, Alberto assured us, without first producing an environmental impact statement, known as a *manifestación de impacto ambiental* (or MIA). The MIA must be contracted by the developer of the structure and executed by third-party consultants. The *manifestación* describes the proposed project – its dimensions and duration, materials and magnitude. It must evaluate and speculate on a proposed project's potential impacts, as well as offer mitigation and prevention measures for those.[15] It also needs to situate each element of the proposed infrastructure within an 'environmental system'. The MIA includes the site's current state of 'degradation' as well as the 'environmental services' (*servicios ambientales*) provided by 'the system' in question. Each must be described and enumerated. Systems logic surfaces here by conscripting networks, actors, and interrelated actants, both human and nonhuman, in a kind of cybernetic dance among species.

If the baseline of the MIA is to reflect what is environmentally extant and what kinds of injury currently prevail, its true purpose is predictive. It is poised to proffer a future and to be an exercise in the possibilities of risk attenuation (Beck 2008; Masco 2014). It is a prognostication about human-imposed future damage and a detailed portrait of the plausible outcomes to be expected. In other words, the MIA is a prospecting device. Its scenarios are creatural extinctions and displacements and its idiom is regulatory and enacted through the state. Hares and bats and birds speak from below, in danger, and in their truth, through the MIA.

*Journal of the Royal Anthropological Institute (N.S.), 160-176*
© Royal Anthropological Institute 2019

Alberto, in his executive position at SEMARNAT, struggles with what appears to be a sacrificial offering: the local environment for the maintenance of a somewhat ambiguous global one. He is aware that creatures and places, materials and flows are systemically linked, and his attunement to the burgeoning of protections and the prevention of extinctions – which includes slowing the pace of global floral and faunal demise – is part of his conscious presentation of self. He stresses that government agencies, 'as a rule, assent only to conditional approval for a project'. They are prone to argue for more intervention, not less, before agreeing to industrial developments like wind parks. 'Vigilance is important' because, as Alberto pointedly remarked, 'sometimes the local impact [of a project] is much more environmentally detrimental than climate change is' (see Eakin 2006). And it is towards these sorts of ethical questions that Alberto has been slowly moving us, leafing through the many calculations, measurements, and validations pertaining to species that live in the region where a wind park would be installed.

Saul Ramírez is also someone who ably navigates the details of environmental impact reports, but from the other end of the process, as a contracted assessor. 'To build a wind park', Saul begins, 'you need two key permissions: an environmental impact permit [from SEMARNAT] and a *cambio de uso de suelo* [change of land use] permit that attends to effects on native vegetation', especially forests (Hecht, Morrison & Padoch 2014; Mathews 2011). The first is a description of the project and its physical footprint, including roads and turbine siting. The second is a discussion of interrelated 'mediums': the *medio físico* (the physical setting and context) and the *medio biótico* (the biotic setting). In the case of wind developments in the Isthmus, Saul notes, these mediums are lagoons, forests, and (human) communities, including people's 'customs and population demographics'.[16] The biotic setting, in good species-tracking form, includes human populations and their quantifiable 'demographic presence'.

When we raised the question of rumours that environmental impact reports have been cut-and-pasted from other studies in other regions, or 'bought and paid for' and then delivered in place of legitimate environmental reports, Saul rejected such speculation. 'That would be unethical', he declared. 'And in any case, the legislation is very clear that the data must be specific to the project site'. But he paused for a moment and reflected. 'Pirating' studies might happen, he admitted, but it is utterly unethical. Nonetheless, the question of graft and obfuscations muddied the transparency of species protections.

In the role of conservation professional, and in the job of 'environmental management', the rubric of care and concern is expanded. It becomes more crowded: human needs, social needs, energy needs, and ecosystems that will be allowed to continue to flow in continuity. With the scope of species awareness extended, other-than-human beings, like those that Alberto and Saul must account for, become increasingly wrapped up in human worlds. This kind of awareness is perhaps especially clear for those who are thinking with other-than-human species day in and day out. Even as they count themselves as belonging to a world of 'moderns', the care exercised by Saul and Alberto for other-than-humans reflects a certain kind of urgency, a more complicated condition where it is not just 'other' creatures that are in harm's way, but humans as well. New demands on soils, waters, and skies appear via spreadsheets and carefully thumbed-through manuals, lists, and precautions. But each turn of the page indexes competing interests between creatures and plant life, energy and

*Journal of the Royal Anthropological Institute (N.S.), 160-176*
© Royal Anthropological Institute 2019

uncorrupted skies, local environmental stability and translocal measures to clear the air. This process is, as Fabiana Li (2015: 92-4) has described it, an enactment of 'equivalence' where expertise and technical tools combine with political conditions and authoritative knowledge in order to shape value and determine comparable metrics of harm and remediation. Alberto, Saul, and others working in these spheres of care and management seem to be deeply aware of their role. Signs of disappearance and the ongoing development of power provoke a condition of creatural and habitational care and the associated horizons of risk. In these horizons of risk, the MIAs must be trained on the presence of endangered life, both floral and faunal, in a nexus of ethical concerns.

## Bats

Barotrauma is a fatal phenomenon for bats swerving through corridors of turbines. Many dead bats that litter the grounds of wind parks have suffered no apparent external physical trauma, but inside their lungs have exploded. Unlike birds, which have rigid lungs, a bat's lungs are pliable. When these more fragile lungs are exposed to a sudden change of atmospheric pressure – such as that occurring directly in front of a rotor in operation – they will expand quickly beyond their capacity and the creature will literally drop dead.

Various hypotheses have been offered as to why bats would be drawn to wind turbines. In Canada and the United States, thermal imaging has documented bats attempting to land on the blades, which they may perceive as roosting trees. The structures may also be seen as a source of food since the blades and rotor area are peppered with dead insects. Another pull may be the heat generated by turbines. Or it may be that sound frequencies and electromagnetic waves produced by turbines disrupt echolocation, causing bats to inadvertently hurtle towards the towers and blades. According to comparative data from wind parks in North America, Europe, and other Interamerican Development Bank-financed parks in Mexico, bat mortalities outnumber those of birds. Despite these comparative reports, the final assessment for the giant wind park slated to be built in the Isthmus nevertheless concluded – in a final glum deferral – that ultimately 'there is no way to know' if bat populations would be adversely affected by the growth of wind parks in the region. Dead bats had piled up in other places where turbines were, but in this case they were simply assigned to the column of the unknowable. Whether they would survive the infrastructural apparatuses of clean energy was left as a question rather than a compelling impetus for protection. Perhaps dead bodies do not speak as well from below. Or maybe bats do not enunciate a particular kind of charismatic truth in their existence. In time, killed bats would provide comparative data for future parks in similar lands; their fatalities would speak to science in number and form. Bird bodies, too, enable similar acts of true speech.

## Birds

Environmental impact assessments may report potential dangers, but they can also serve as opaque prognostications that obscure rather than reveal. In a 2004 report on bird life in the area that would be affected by the Mareña wind park's installation, it was noted that, 'given the lack of studies, the extent of nesting displacement is hard to predict'. And 'significant questions remain as to how flight strategies vary in different wind conditions and how migrating hawks use the site during spring migration'. Spring migration patterns themselves were qualified as 'unknown' and nocturnal migration studies in the region were non-existent. Birds were quantified and identified throughout the studies but ultimately bird appearances in the wind zones became less an object of conservation than they were a calculable, and calculated, data stream.

Indeed, each prognosis found that bird mortalities that might occur with the installation of wind parks would render valuable scientific data. Killed birds would, the report explained, provide 'a baseline for future wind park developments across Mexico and Central America'. 'Collision fatalities' that would be documented once parks were in operation would, in a macabre twist of environmental authority, offer statistical information about bird deaths in the land of the turbines. 'Monitoring results of bird mortalities in Eurus and La Ventosa [two other sites of wind parks in the Isthmus of Tehuantepec]', it was noted, when 'combined with the results of this Project will be helpful in determining the extent of cumulative impacts'. Wind parks could become an experimental lab, testing the necrotic potential of turbines with Isthmus bird deaths serving as baselines, an animal 'testing' of a different kind (Stengers 2011). Birds were to be placed at the centre of an authorizing practice that would establish boundaries and designations of 'biolegitimacy' (Fassin & Pandolfi 2010): a politics of policing the limits of who or what can die and what kinds of lives are eligible for exceptional protection (Jackson & Warren 2005).[17]

In many settings, birds have been understood to have predictive virtues and the ability to illustrate futures (van Dooren 2014), sometimes able to speak in human registers (Kirsch 2014: 104).[18] In many North American indigenous communities, writes Vine Deloria (2006), birds would sketch pictures in the sky, moved in one arc or another by the spirit of the place over which they flew. Birds' prophetic powers are an enduring form of communication across human and animal communities, and examples of birds' perception of future events can be found around the world and across time. Roman divinations were drawn from the observation of bird flight (*auspices*) and were integral to foundational legends. They often preceded political decisions, and no important judgements were made without consulting the *auguri*. Roman oracles were likewise consulted for their *omen*, or 'true speech', a truth predicated not on the present but on an emerging future (Keck & Lakoff 2013).

Weaving across the sky in the same way they did centuries ago, in the renewable age, species of birds and bats seem to offer similar revelations and prognostications: a form of truth enunciated with the presence of their being, openly in the wind.[19] They may be unwilling gauges interpreted through human estimations of harm and risk, but their presence, or disappearance, speaks to ethical concerns created by new energy infrastructures. Certain creatural deaths get caught up in the rotations of power moving forward and these lives are quantified, and thus qualified, on a scale of importance. Dead bats and birds tell a story, from below, with their lives, in a transparent truth that also demands attention to ethical concerns. Hares, birds, and bats perform speech in their indexical being and this speech can be heard, and translated, by humans who are actively thinking with other species as their part of their quotidian lives and studied expertise.

## Greater goods

Mexico's road to the wind in climatologically imperilled times is a move towards purging the carbon congestion that urban-industrial modernity has brought. But it is also a test of weighing local deaths – in the form of hares, bats, and birds – against global data under the auspices of climatological risk reduction. This is where dead birds and bats speak, like the parrhesiastes. It is where hares are pardoned, heard in a different register, and spared. As they appear in representational forms (like policies and regulations), and as they are produced through environmental management (as in their role in environmental impact assessments), and, finally, as they become present in their threatened extinction, other-than-human beings appear to 'speak' a kind of parrhesia: indexing their imperilled state of being as a message from 'below' and enunciating an ethical challenge. The ethical conundrum to which they speak is a question of how to balance local life and global sustainability.

As we stage the survival of species in the Anthropocene, and look to sites of renewable energy generation that are meant to ensure that survival, we occupy a pivotal moment: a tipping of what Isabelle Stengers (2011) describes as 'value scales': the relational balance between human interests for the (so-called) 'greater good' and the suffering inflicted upon other creatures.[20] For Stengers, value scales get revealed in the mix of science, experimentation, and animal testing in scientific labs.[21] Here, value scales become articulated across spheres of life processes and the biopolitical management of species that are, collectively, caught up in the wind. Being caught up in the wind means also, in some cases, finding a true voice, a parrhesiaic truth expressed in the bodies of nonhuman beings, made especially dramatic when their existence (or extinction) is being actively balanced against humanity's 'greater good'.

## NOTES

I would like to thank the Editors of this special issue, Mette High and Jessica Smith, for their insightful comments on previous drafts and for their efforts to bring together critical work on energy and ethics. Funding for this research was provided by the National Science Foundation (Cultural Anthropology grant #1127246) and the Social Science Research Institute, Rice University, and was conducted in a collaborative effort with Dominic Boyer. Matei Candea's masterclass on parrhesia at the University of Cambridge (October 2016) and my ongoing conversations with James Faubion have also provided critical inspiration for the ideas in this essay.

[1] Parrhesia may have a derogatory meaning, according to Foucault, roughly designating someone as a 'chatterbox' who prattles on about nothing of consequence. However, in the positive sense of parrhesia that he explores at length, the parrhesiastes is both frank and illuminative of his truth. 'Parrhesia is therefore "telling all", but tied to the truth: telling the whole truth, hiding nothing of the truth, telling the truth without hiding it behind anything' (2011: 10).

[2] 'The parrhesiast does not help people somehow to step beyond some threshold in the ontological structure of the human being and of time which separates them from their future. He helps them in their blindness, but their blindness about what they are, about themselves, and so not the blindness due to an ontological structure, but due to some moral fault, distraction, or lack of discipline, the consequence of inattention, laxity, or weakness. It is in this interplay between human beings and their blindness due to inattention, complacency, weakness, and moral distraction that the parrhesiast performs his role, which, as you can see, is consequently a revelatory role very different from that of the prophet, who stands at the point where human finitude and the structure of time are conjoined' (Foucault 2011: 16).

[3] In Foucault's terms, 'Parrhesia therefore not only puts the relationship between the person who speaks and the person to whom he addresses the truth at risk, but it may go so far as to put the very life of the person who speaks at risk, at least if his interlocutor has power over him and cannot bear being told the truth' (2011: 12). And the relationship established is, for Foucault, both game and pact. 'This kind of pact, between the person who takes the risk of telling the truth and the person who agrees to listen to it, is at the heart of what could be called the parrhesiastic game' (2011: 13).

[4] But of course for Spivak the subaltern cannot speak (through western academic representation) whereas Foucault's Greek citizen can.

[5] The power differential of the parrhesiastes and his or her audience is critical, just as parrhesia is itself earnest critique. 'Parrhesia is a form of criticism, either towards another or towards oneself, but always in a situation where the speaker or confessor is in a position of inferiority with respect to the interlocutor' (Foucault 1999: para. 19).

[6] Foucault puts it this way. 'It is a stance, a way of being which is akin to a virtue, a mode of action' (2011: 14).

[7] The ethnographic research that I detail here was a collaborative project carried out with Dominic Boyer that sought to reveal how wind power might operate as a 'salvational object': a social and technical apparatus to mitigate climate change in environmentally precarious times. The ways in which wind power was being located – epistemically, infrastructurally, and politically – were the abiding questions that our research team of two set out to answer over the course of sixteen months of fieldwork in the Isthmus of Tehuantepec, as well as Oaxaca City and the country's capital, Mexico City.

[8] A fair amount of controversy surrounds the term 'Anthropocene', which I do not have space here to elaborate (but see, e.g., Haraway 2015; Moore 2016; Tsing 2012; 2015).

[9] The anthropology of energy has been with us for a long time, beginning with Leslie White's mid-twentieth-century theory that linked cultural evolution to fuel sources, efficiency, and human management of energy forms (see White 2007 [1959]). In the days of the early 1970s global oil crisis, anthropologists were again drawn to questions of energy, most comprehensively in the work of Laura Nader (see Nader & Beckerman 1978). Then came the lull, the materialist legacy of energy studies perhaps ill suited to post-structuralist analytics that typified the 1980s and 1990s.

[10] Anthropologists have explored the impacts of energy infrastructures following a similar set of political economic principles, articulating disparities, local and global, among humans around the world who are caught in the political and economic vicissitudes of carbon harvesting and its subsequent incineration. Inequalities and contamination figure heavily in many of these anthropological analyses of energy forms and their effects. Contingent morality is implied throughout, and particularly faulted (perhaps unsurprisingly) are transnational energy corporations. And rightly so, since these institutions have been at the centre of the risky entanglement of biotic lives and carbon combustion.

[11] Forests' and dogs' thinking is conveyed metonymically in the signs they use: icons (signs that share a likeness with what they represent) and indexes (signs that are in relation, contiguous in time, space, and action with what they represent). Indexes, inasmuch as they are deeply in relational and contiguous time with what they mark, share a kinship with Foucault's parrhesia; indexes are coeval with their message. So too with parrhesiastes.

[12] Povinelli is interested in value questions that proceed not from life and death but from the possibility of non-life. This is specifically not extinction. It is non-life.

[13] Similar cases are found in Peruvian Earth beings in Marisol de la Cadena's (2015) work and in the relationship between humans and *atiku* (or caribou) described by Mario Blaser (2016). What gives each of these analytics cohesion is the way in which particular dyads operate (in Kohn's case dog/human, in Povinelli's and de la Cadena's examples earthform/human, or in Blaser's account caribou/human).

[14] In Foucault's formulation, the parrhesiastes does not utilize an interlocutor, or mediator, of their voice.

[15] Developers are responsible for reforestation of areas beyond what is removed for a project. SEMARNAT is also specific about species: Alberto notes, 'you cannot just do the reforestation ad hoc, go plant a bunch of little pine trees in a deciduous forest . . . your proposal would be invalid in that case'.

[16] Attached to the biotic medium of human populations in this calculus are also their 'customs', their culture. Here, humans are consummately 'specied' despite cultural aptitudes. If 'culture' has long been used to distinguish humans from our animal others, here it is merely a quality of species behaviour, or practices that may have effects, but are only important to the extent that they condition the biotic setting and the environmental system. In small ways, the permit process itself demands that humans relinquish their species exceptionalism; culture is here not unique but subordinated to the greater conditions of the species maintenance system.

[17] Or who can be killed but not sacrificed (Agamben 1998; see also Fassin & Pandolfi 2010; Jackson & Warren 2005).

[18] For instance, Yonggom people of Papua New Guinea recognize the predictive qualities of birds, whose visions often come in dreams, offering omens and openings for communication between birds and humans through magic spells. In *Mining capitalism*, Stuart Kirsch (2014) describes how following the disaster at the Ok Tedi gold and copper mine in PNG, the disappearance of animal and bird life from the region not only resulted in diminished biodiversity but also foreclosed the possibility of human/bird dialogues.

[19] In his essay 'Earth, sky, wind, and weather' (2007), Tim Ingold sketches the qualities of an 'open' world where persons and things do not relate as closed, separate autonomous forms reacting to one another, but are instead constituted by their common immersion in a medium of generative flux. That medium, for Ingold, is air, wind, and weather. He asks if earth and sky are viewed as separate, if complementary, hemispheres

furnished with 'environment' – for example, trees, rocks, mountains – then we face a phenomenological dilemma: 'If we are *out* in the open, how can we also be *in* the wind?' (2007: S19, emphasis in original).

[20] For Donna Haraway (2008) as for Stengers, this is a suffering that has never been properly shared.

[21] For Stengers, this is linked to the cosmopolitical proposal. The cosmos, she writes, 'corresponds to no condition, establishes no requirements. It creates the question of possible nonhierarchical modes of coexistences among the ensemble of inventions of nonequivalence, among the diverging values and obligations through which the entangled existences that compose it are affirmed ... thus [integrating] an ecology of practices [that involves multiple domains of living]' (2011: 356).

## REFERENCES

AGAMBEN, G. 1998. *Homo sacer: sovereign power and bare life*. Stanford: University Press.

AIELLO, J.L., J. VALENCIA, E. CALDERA MUÑOZ & V.L. GÓMEZ 1983. *Atlas Eolico Preliminar de America Latina y el Caribe*. Quito: OLADE.

ALONSO SERNA, L. 2014. La energía eólica y los espacios de poder en el Istmo de Tehuantepec: ponencia presentada en el II Congreso Internacional de Pueblos Indios de América Latina. In *Siglos XIX-XXI: avances, perspectivas y retos*. Oaxaca.

BARAD, K. 2007. *Meeting the universe halfway: quantum physics and the entanglement of matter*. Durham, N.C.: Duke University Press.

BARRY, A. 2015. The oil archives. In *Subterranean estates: life worlds of oil and gas* (eds) H. Appel, A. Mason & M. Watts, 95-107. Ithaca, N.Y.: Cornell University Press.

BECK, U. 2008. *The world at risk*. Cambridge: Polity.

BEHRENDS, A., S. REYNA & G. SCHLEE (eds) 2011. *Crude domination: the anthropology of oil*. New York: Berghahn Books.

BENNETT, J. 2010. *Vibrant matter: a political ecology of things*. Durham, N.C.: Duke University Press.

BLASER, M. 2016. Is another cosmopolitics possible? *Cultural Anthropology* **31**, 545-70.

BOOTH, W. 2010. Mexico aims to be a leader in emissions reduction. *Washington Post*, 29 November (available on-line: *http://www.washingtonpost.com/wp-dyn/content/article/2010/11/28/AR2010112803284.html*, accessed 22 January 2019).

BREGLIA, L. 2013. *Living with oil: promises, peaks and declines on Mexico's Gulf Coast*. Austin: University of Texas Press.

CANDEA, M. 2010. 'I fell in love with Carlos the Meerkat': engagement and detachment in human-animal relations. *American Ethnologist* **37**, 241-58.

CEPEK, M.L. 2012. The loss of oil: constituting disaster in Amazonian Ecuador. *Journal of Latin American and Caribbean Anthropology* **17**, 393-412.

CRATE, S.A. & M. NUTTALL (eds) 2009. *Anthropology and climate change: from encounters to actions*. Walnut Creek, Calif.: Left Coast Press.

DE LA CADENA, M. 2015. *Earth beings: ecologies of practice across Andean worlds*. Durham, N.C.: Duke University Press.

DELORIA, V. 2006. *The world we used to live in: remembering the powers of the medicine men*. Golden, Colo.: Fulcrum Publishing.

EAKIN, H. 2006. *Weathering risk in rural Mexico: climatic, institutional, and economic change*. Tucson: University of Arizona Press.

ELLIOTT, D., M. SCHWARTZ, S. HAYMES, D. HEIMILLER & R. GEORGE 2003. *Wind energy resource atlas of Oaxaca*. Oak Ridge, Tenn.: NREL, US Department of Energy.

ESCOBAR, A. 1994. *Encountering development: the making and unmaking of the Third World*. Princeton: University Press.

FASSIN, D. & M. PANDOLFI 2010. *Contemporary states of emergency: the politics of military and humanitarian intervention*. Cambridge, Mass.: Zone Books.

FAUBION, J. 2011. *An anthropology of ethics*. Cambridge: University Press.

FOUCAULT, M. 1997. On the genealogy of ethics: an overview of the work in progress. In *The essential works of Foucault, 1954-1984, vol. 1: Ethics, subjectivity and truth* (ed. P. Rabinow, trans. R. Hurley *et al.*), 253-80. New York: New Press.

——— 1999. The meaning and evolution of the word parrhesia. In *Discourse and truth: the problematization of parrhesia* (ed. J. Pearson). Digital Archive: Foucault.info (available on-line: *https://foucault.info/doc/documents/parrhesia/foucault-dt1-wordparrhesia-en-html*, accessed 22 January 2019).

———— 2011. 1 February 1984: first hour. *The courage of the truth (the government of self and others II): lectures at the Collège de France, 1983-1984* (ed. F. Gros, trans. G. Burchell), 1-22. New York: Palgrave Macmillan.

HARAWAY, D.J. 1996. *SecondMillennium.FemaleMan©MeetsOncoMouseTM*[TM]: *feminism and technoscience.* New York: Routledge.

———— 2008. *When species meet.* Minneapolis: University of Minnesota Press.

———— 2015. Anthropocene, Capitalocene, Plantationocene, Chthulucene: making kin. *Environmental Humanities* **6**, 159-65.

HECHT, S.B., K. MORRISON & C. PADOCH (eds) 2014. *The social lives of forests: past, present, and future of woodland resurgence.* Chicago: University Press.

HOWE, C. 2015. Introduction: Energy, transition and climate change in Latin America. Special Section: Energy, transition and climate change in Latin America. *Journal of Latin American and Caribbean Anthropology* **20**, 231-41.

———— 2019. *Ecologics: wind and power in the Anthropocene.* Durham, N.C.: Duke University Press.

———— & D. BOYER 2016. Aeolian extractivism and community wind in Southern Mexico. *Public Culture* **28**, 215-35.

INGOLD, T. 2007. Earth, sky, wind, and weather. *Journal of the Royal Anthropological Institute* **13**: SI, S19-38.

JACKSON, J.E. & K.B. WARREN 2005. Indigenous movements in Latin America, 1992-2004: controversies, ironies, new directions. *Annual Review of Anthropology* **34**, 549-73.

KECK, F. & A. LAKOFF 2013. Figures of warning. *Limn* **3** (available on-line: *https://limn.it/articles/figures-of-warning/*, accessed 22 January 2019).

KIRBY, V. 2011. *Quantum anthropologies: life at large.* Durham, N.C.: Duke University Press.

KIRSCH, S. 2014. *Mining capitalism: the relationship between corporations and their critics.* Berkeley: University of California Press (ibook edition).

KLIEMAN, K. 2008. Oil, politics, and development in the formation of a state: the Congolese petroleum wars, 1963-68. *International Journal of African Historical Studies* **41**, 169-202.

KOHN, E. 2013. *How forests think: toward an anthropology beyond the human.* Berkeley: University of California Press.

KOLBERT, E. 2013. *The sixth great extinction: an unnatural history.* New York: Picador.

LATOUR, B. 2013. *An inquiry into modes of existence: an anthropology of the moderns* (trans. C. Porter). Cambridge, Mass.: Harvard University Press.

LEMENAGER, S. 2015. *Living oil: petroleum in the American century.* Oxford: University Press.

LI, F. 2015. *Unearthing conflict: corporate mining, activism, and expertise in Peru.* Durham, N.C.: Duke University Press (ibook edition).

LIEN, M. 2015. *Becoming salmon: aquaculture and the domestication of a fish.* Berkeley: University of California Press.

MASCO, J. 2014. *The theater of operations: national security affect from the Cold War to the War on Terror.* Durham, N.C.: Duke University Press.

MASON, A. & M. STOILKOVA 2012. Corporeality of consultant expertise in Arctic natural gas development. *Journal of Northern Studies* **6**: **2**, 83-96.

MATHEWS, A. 2011. *Instituting nature: authority, expertise and power in Mexican forests.* Cambridge, Mass.: The MIT Press.

MATSUTAKE WORLDS RESEARCH GROUP 2009. A new form of collaboration in cultural anthropology: Matsutake worlds. *American Ethnologist* **36**, 380-403.

MITCHELL, T. 2011. *Carbon democracy: political power in the age of oil.* New York: Verso.

MOORE, J. 2016. *Anthropocene or Capitalocene? Nature, history and the crisis of capitalism.* New York: PM Press.

NADER, L. & S. BECKERMAN 1978. Energy as it relates to the quality and style of life. *Annual Review of Energy* **3**, 1-28.

PETROCULTURES RESEARCH GROUP 2016. *After oil.* Edmonton: Petrocultures Research Group.

POVINELLI, E. 2016. *Geontologies: a requiem to late liberalism.* Durham, N.C.: Duke University Press.

RAFFLES, H. 2010. *Insectopedia.* New York: Pantheon.

ROLSTON, J.S. 2014. *Mining coal and undermining gender: Rhythms of work and family in the American West.* New Brunswick, N.J.: Rutgers University Press.

SAWYER, S. 2004. *Crude chronicles: indigenous politics, multinational oil, and neoliberalism in Ecuador.* Durham, N.C.: Duke University Press.

STENGERS, I. 2011. *Cosmopolitics I and II.* Minneapolis: University of Minnesota Press.

SZEMAN, I. & D. BOYER (eds) 2017. *Energy humanities: an anthology*. Baltimore, Md: Johns Hopkins University Press.

TSING, A.L. 2012. Unruly edges: mushrooms as companion species. *Environmental Humanities* **1**, 141-54.

——— 2015. *The mushroom at the end of the world: on the possibility of life in capitalist ruins*. Princeton: University Press.

VAN DOOREN, T. 2014. *Flightways: life and loss at the edge of extinction*. New York: Columbia University Press.

WHITE, L.A. 1959. *The evolution of culture: the development of civilization to the fall of Rome*. London: Routledge [2007 reprint].

WOLFE, C. 2009. *What is posthumanism?* Minneapolis: University of Minnesota Press.

## Biens suprêmes : éthique, énergie et parole non humaine

*Résumé*

Les projets d'énergies renouvelables sont louables du point de vue éthique parce qu'ils veulent lutter contre la pollution, mais ils entraînent aussi des conséquences sur les êtres vivants non humains. Cet article prend appui sur le cas de l'isthme de Tehuantepec au Mexique, qui abrite la plus forte concentration d'éoliennes terrestres au monde. Suivant l'acception par Foucault de la forme de rhétorique dite « parrhésie », l'auteure avance que les corps des êtres vivants non humains affectés, notamment ceux dont l'existence est délibérément mise dans la balance par rapport au « bien suprême » de l'humanité, réalisent une forme de parole non humaine, d'abord par leur statut d'espèces menacées et aussi par le biais de régimes de gestion de l'environnement qui cherchent à synchroniser les existences humaines et non humaines dans des contextes d'échecs écologiques locaux et planétaires.

# Conclusion: Energy ethics and ethical worlds

HANNAH APPEL *University of California*

What happens when the effects of our ethical actions stretch beyond, often far beyond, first- and second-person phenomena? What happens when one person's richly textured ethical world is another's profound violation? Energy offers a particularly useful empirical terrain on which to think through the questions posed by ethical worlds. Ethical worlds gesture both to the supra-individual, supra-present contexts in which we all craft quotidian ethics, and to the expansive geographies and timescapes in which the effects of our ethical practices ramify. Ethical worlds, fields, or landscapes are not bordered by first- or second-person experiences, but rather they intersect and interfere with one another often at great distance, often over multiple generations, and certainly not equally. Ethical practices in more powerful fields spill out, invade, and give shape to ethical practices in other ethical fields. What does it mean to start to see and feel and analyse at these ethical crossroads? In particular, what might it mean to acknowledge that structure, power, and interest – which are too often arrayed against close ethnographic attention to individual and shared experience – are not 'larger forces' but other ethical worlds, equally amenable to ethnographic attention?

> How does it feel to change the climate?
>
> Hughes 2017: 1

From wind parks in Mexico's Isthmus of Tehuantepec to the opulent roundtables of global energy experts; from subsidized gasoline for Sanema people in Venezuelan Amazonia to the moral and often godly ambitions of oil workers in Colorado; from the making and using of charcoal in Madagascar to coal miners' ethical self-narration in Wyoming's Powder River Basin; from novel forms of solar humanitarianism in South Asia to the intimacy of the corporate form in the relationship between debtors, creditors, and abandoned wells in Alberta's oil industry, this special issue on 'Energy and Ethics?' offers a stunning array of empirical sites and energy dilemmas. Across this array, contributors stay with one theme: the ethical. More specifically, the Editors offer a provocation in the issue's introduction. They write, '[M]uch of the existing anthropological literature on energy has been framed by two overarching concerns: the first with critiquing state and corporate power; and the second with advocating energy transitions that cast fossil fuel resources as necessarily immoral and renewable

*Journal of the Royal Anthropological Institute (N.S.)*, 177-190

resources as their assumed opposites' (High & Smith, this volume, p. 10). Through close attention to the ethical worlds of both carbon-intensive fuels – charcoal, oil, coal – and their renewable counterparts – wind, solar, Green Charcoal – the essays in this volume demand that anthropologists rethink instinctive and often undertheorized moral binaries in which immoral : moral is mapped on to carbon-intensive : renewable :: the makers of carbon-intensive energy : affected environments and communities, and beyond. Each essay demonstrates the capacity of ethnography to unsettle taken-for-granted assumptions, including hasty moralizing in what Howe calls 'environmentally troubled and ethically charged times' (Howe, this volume, p. 163).

The Editors and contributors position their approach to this volume – in which papers engage with the ethics of energy without a priori taking analytical positions of critique – in dialogue with anthropological work in the ethical turn.[1] For instance, one can hear Michael Lambek's (2010) approach to ordinary ethics in the Editors' framing of the volume, in particular his wariness of a common theoretical approach in anthropology. As he writes:

> Ethnographers commonly find that the people they encounter are trying to do what they consider right or good, are evaluated according to criteria of what is right and good, or are in some debate about what constitutes the human good. Yet anthropological theory tends to overlook all this in favour of analyses that emphasize structure, power, and interest (2010: 1).

The point in the literature on the ethical turn, as I read it, is not to deny the existence of structure, power, and interest, but rather to ensure that the contours of individual moral experience and relational being-in-the-world are fully and deeply accounted for in ethnographic work, not effaced by always-already constituted explanations via structures of power. As Zigon and Throop put it,

> While fully recognizing the significance of such larger-scale phenomena as historic, economic, and political conditions, as well as the variable forms of sharedness entailed in collective experiences, [we] make the strong claim that an anthropological concern with morality/ethics must be sensitive to the everyday moral lives and experiences of the persons we study, analyze, and write about (2014: 3).[2]

This sensitivity to people's everyday moral lives and experiences suggests methodological entailments. For phenomenologically informed approaches in particular, to attend closely to people's experience is 'to draw attention to the *first-person stance* of the embodied experiencing subject who is always-already a relational being . . . It is the focus on experience – on life as lived – *that gives primacy to first- and second-person positions* in phenomenology' (Mattingly & Throop 2018: 482-3 emphasis mine). As I understand it, this methodological focus on first- and second-person positions aims at a full account of the contours of individual experience articulated in the terms people use to understand and live their own lives, rather than in terms of always-already known intersectional categories including race, class, gender, sexuality, ability, and so on. As Mattingly and Throop put it, '[W]e do not experience ourselves, ontologically, as being mere tokens of a type' (2018: 482).

But what happens when the effects of our ethical actions stretch beyond, often far beyond, first- and second-person phenomena? What happens when one person's richly textured ethical world is another's profound violation? To give an extreme but illustrative example, I imagine that Donald Trump would not describe himself as misogynist, racist, or classist. But he clearly crafts his ethical practices – the reflexive choices he makes about the right and the good – in and through these categories. Is it consequential, analytically and politically, that he himself wouldn't use these terms? Certainly. But should that restrict *our* analysis of the contours and effects of his moral experience? I would argue, certainly not. A full account of Trump's ethical world would show the intersubjective productivity of these categories, the consequences of his refusal to *feel* his situatedness within them, and the radical effects of his ethical practices far beyond first- and second-person stances.

Energy offers a particularly useful empirical terrain on which to think through the questions posed by *ethical worlds*. What happens when the reflexive ethical practices of shale oil workers in Colorado, for instance, contribute to the groundwater chemicals that poison others in shared watersheds? Or, further afield, to the atmospheric carbon dioxide that has already displaced Kivalina (a small Alaskan city), Tuvalu, or much of the Sahel? To start, we might simply say that what Zigon and Throop refer to as 'larger-scale phenomena' – historic, economic, and political conditions – in fact take shape in and through people's ethical actions, not above or outside them. So too with Lambek's 'structure, power, interest', which move through deeply textured biographies, and do not simply impinge upon them as if from above or outside (Ahmed 2017; Fassin 2013; Hartman 1997; Latour 2004; Ralph 2014). I use *ethical worlds*, then, or later ethical fields or landscapes, to gesture both to the supra-individual, supra-present contexts in which we all craft quotidian ethics, and to the expansive geographies and timescapes in which the *effects* of our ethical practices ramify. Ethical worlds, fields, or landscapes are not bordered by first- or second-person experiences, but rather they intersect and interfere with one another often at great distance, often over multiple generations, and certainly not equally. Ethical practices in more powerful fields – Oxford MBAs eager to fulfil both the environmental and market promises of solar energy; prognistication on remaining reserves at a luxurious energy industry event – spill out, invade, and give shape to ethical practices in other ethical fields: the viability of coal mining in Wyoming; the future of state oil subsidies to the Sanema in the face of a turn to renewables.

The essays in this special issue offer richly textured ethnographic accounts of ethical worlds, and I want to walk quickly back through the energy dilemmas posed in each. When we begin to look at multiple ethical worlds and multiple energy dilemmas, we begin to see the relationships between them – perhaps adjacent or overlapping, in conflict with one another or mutually unacknowledged, and, of course, differently positioned and unequally constituted in global political economies of energy. My aim in bringing us from the ethical dilemmas of each essay towards the question of coexistent ethical worlds, often at quite a distance from one another, is to ask: what does it mean to start to see and feel and analyse at these ethical crossroads? What might it mean both for our interlocutors and for our own work? In particular, what might it mean to acknowledge that structure, power, and interest – which are too often arrayed *against* close ethnographic attention to individual and shared experience – are not 'larger forces' but other ethical worlds, equally amenable to ethnographic attention? As we juxtapose the performative PowerPoints of energy consultants presented at $10,000 per ticket conferences with Wyoming coal miners' accounts of their own centrality to keeping the lights on, or the ordinary ethics of Tehuantepec wind farms with a custom-made Colorado oilfield Bible, we can begin to see these ethical fields in relation to one another, *not* via abstractions of structure, power, and interest, but through an unevenly shared world in which we must all begin to imagine new arrangements.

First, then, the situated ethical dilemmas. Four authors – Walsh, Penfield, High, and Smith – walk us through the social thickness/ethical good that local communities derive from engagement with carbon-intensive energy sources.[3] Walsh brings us to Madagascar, where the felling of forests for charcoal production has received extensive international criticism. While acknowledging the fact of deforestation, Walsh notes that it is not a central preoccupation of the Malagasy charcoal makers and users with whom he has worked for nearly three decades. Rather, he suggests that by attending closely to their ethical worlds, we may find, counterintuitively, that charcoal 'offers opportunities for observing and reflecting on certain key processes that, although inherent in *any* energy system, are not always so obvious as they are in the commodity chain that links charcoal makers and users in Madagascar' (Walsh, this volume, p. 110, original emphasis). In part, this is because charcoal in Madagascar is a socially productive commodity. The social life of charcoal, Walsh tells us, knits makers, collectors, market sellers, and users, in addition to their kin, ancestors, and neighbours, into networks of artisanal use and practice. '[A]s a commodity', Walsh tells us, charcoal 'is never fully alienated'.

> Makers know the uses to which charcoal will be put, and some may even know at least some of the users for whom their charcoal is destined, keeping part of what they produce for urban kin as they might do with the rice they harvest. Users, meanwhile, generally know charcoal's sources. They know not only that it comes from trees and that, in fact, its quality depends on what kinds of trees it comes from, but also that it comes from *people*, maybe even *know* people they know, and certainly people they are familiar with – people who are, like them, 'looking for money' (*mitady vola*) in places of limited opportunity (Walsh, this volume, p. 113, original emphasis).

The energy ethics dilemma Walsh presents us with, then, is the ethical good of a socially thick commodity chain, an un-alienated commodity chain, vs either 'the abstract goals of sustainable development and the ideals of global environmentalism' (Walsh, this volume, p. 120) or even a more local project for Green Charcoal that would standardize and regulate the commodity chain in new ways.

Penfield, too, writes of the social thickness of carbon-intensive energy in the Venezuelan Amazon. Here, the Venezuelan state offers indigenous communities monthly quotas of heavily subsidized gasoline. For the Sanema people with whom Penfield works, reselling the surplus gasoline at a profit to regional gold miners enables local visions of contentment and the good life, including the circulation and bestowal of material things, as distinct from the poverty and suffering experienced in their absence. Close attention to their ethical world reveals a form of 'composite ethics', grounded in 'composite personhood', that challenges 'theorizations of ethics [that] rely excessively on individualist models of the self' (Penfield, this volume, p. 155). At the same time, composite ethics also makes an intervention into dominant accounts of extractive economies, suggesting that 'Sanema ideas of right or wrong that surround this energy source are not entirely correlated with a perceived immorality of the encroaching market economy, but rather are also associated with notions of personhood, sociality, and the cosmic order' (Penfield, this volume, p. 155).

In High's and Smith's accounts of oil workers in Colorado and coal miners in Wyoming, respectively, we remain with questions of the situated ethical experiences of carbon-intensive lifeworlds. These hydrocarbon workers in the western United States articulate remarkably resonant ethical landscapes. To illustrate, I juxtapose a fantasy commercial recounted to High by a Colorado oil worker with the descriptions three Wyoming coal workers offered to Smith about the centrality of their work in the US energy landscape (Table 1).

Table 1.

| Colorado oil worker (High) | Wyoming coal workers (Smith) |
| --- | --- |
| A man and a woman are driving on a city road into Denver. The woman is heavily pregnant and they are rushing to the hospital. But suddenly everything starts to change: The car runs out of gas ... It comes to a halt, can't go any further. Then the tyres slowly evaporate – they disappear. Then the plastic steering wheel disappears. Then the seats, the safety belts, even their clothes. The woman is just lying there on the ground, going to give birth. There's *nothing* without oil! Nothing! There's no hospital. No bed. No car. Nothing! (High, this volume, p. 34, original emphasis) | What we do is important because the nation depends on coal to turn their lights on ... Coal is affordable, it's very efficient. It powers this nation and we take a lot of pride in that (Smith, this volume, p. 96).<br><br>It's nice to be able to help millions of people out, you know, in their daily life. So they can see at night, alarm clocks go off in the morning, they can fix their breakfast (Smith, this volume, p. 96).<br><br>The bed of one 320-ton haul truck carries enough coal to supply one American home for forty years (Smith, this volume, p. 96). |

In these juxtaposed narratives, hydrocarbon-based fossil fuels are the indispensable energy of social reproduction. While these narratives don't have the kin-based intimacy of the Sanema gas sellers or Malagasy charcoal makers and users, we are still very much with kinship, family, and the conditions of possibility for (in this case national) sociality. Without oil or coal – and by extension the people who produce them – birth itself, let alone transport, clothing, meals, electrical light, *the entire American home*, would be radically altered if not impossible as we know them. Moreover, for both the oil worker and the coal miners, these narratives are not only about the centrality of their work to the reproduction of sociality, but also about their profound desire for the *recognition* of their centrality, for an empathetic encounter between ethical worlds that seem opposed but are in fact mutually reliant. Thus, High's oil worker concludes her narrative of the fantasy commercial by declaring, 'This commercial might make people think twice before criticizing us for the work we do' (High, this volume, p. 34). Similarly, Smith explains that Wyoming miners 'wished for electricity consumers to see a charged cell phone, a lit home, or an outlet, and look beyond it to see Wyoming miners and their labour' (Smith, this volume, p. 98). In other words, both sets of actors wish for an acknowledgement of their ethical worlds, not only as ethical in and of themselves, but as the *conditions of possibility* for what they perceive to be a separate but not unrelated ethical world – of hybrid cars, regulation of extractive industries, and a perceived eagerness to put their forms of labour and expertise in the past. Finally, and for the purposes of the coexistent ethical worlds discussion to come, the ethical lives of both coal miners and oil workers are, in these pieces, framed by the price volatility and radical uncertainty that typifies nearly all extractive commodities sold on global markets. Smith brings us to Wyoming's Powder River Basin in 2016, just as 10 per cent of full-time coal workers in the region had been laid off, and High's piece is framed by the most recent boom-and-bust cycle of oil production in the western United States. In both cases, our ethnographic gaze is trained on 'how industry actors confronted with the fundamental uncertainty of the [hydrocarbon] economy pursue projects of devotion, negotiating "the human predicament of trying to live a life that one is somehow responsible for but is in many respects out of one's control"' (High, this volume, p. 31, quoting Mattingly 2012b: 179). Again, the ethical dilemma we are left with is hydrocarbons as 'catalysts ... of human flourishing' (High, this volume, p. 41) and the substance of social reproduction, on the one hand, and, on the other, their anthropogenic effects that spatially, materially, and socially exceed those forms of ethical being in the world.

The four authors discussed above direct us, often counterintuitively, to the rich ethical worlds that accrete around carbon-intensive energy sources – assemblages of materialities, supply chains, and the people who animate them which, the authors collectively argue, are too often reflexively dismissed as fundamentally immoral. The authors I turn to now – Howe and Cross – make a mirrored counterintuitive move, directing our attention to the ethical knots presented by renewable energy assemblages, which, perhaps, are too often reflexively accepted as essentially moral.[4] Howe's account of the Tehuantepec Isthmus draws us into a set of ethical juxtapositions in the more-than-human world of wind farms. From endangering hare habitats to exploding bat lungs, Howe's account not only is about which species can felicitously enact a form of parrhesia in response to their own destruction, but more broadly narrates a situated test of 'weighing local death – in the form of hares, bats, and birds – against global data under the auspices of climatological risk reduction' (Howe, this volume, p. 171). Alberto Villa, a director in Mexico's Secretariat of Environmental and Natural Resources to whom Howe introduces us, puts the ethical dilemma starkly: '[S]ometimes the local impact [of a project] is much more environmentally detrimental than climate change is' (Howe, this volume, p. 169). While Villa's unequivocal statement may be jarring to the kinds of tacit anthropological sensibilities the Editors of this special issue are out to unsettle, Howe's interrogative version is equally disquieting: 'Is the betterment of a global climate – through the tools of renewable power – to be prioritized over localized ecological spaces where that energy is produced and conveyed?' (Howe, this volume, p. 163). Both Villa's and Howe's formulations of the ethical conundrums stirred up by wind turbines are in fact classically anthropological questions. *The betterment of a global climate* should sound suspiciously like *the betterment of global poverty*, or, only slightly further back in time, *the betterment of the backward and primitive peoples of the world*. My point here is not loose conflation, but to draw our attention to the long history of global interventions based on unquestioned good – development, poverty alleviation, humanitarian intervention – and anthropology's role in often showing how much more complicated these efforts are on the ground.

This is precisely the terrain Cross brings us into, with his account of an emergent solar humanitarianism that is often market-based and 'morally encoded with a spirit of ecological entrepreneurialism' (Cross, this volume, p. 49).

> Solar-powered lanterns designed in the United States, manufactured in China, and distributed in rural India or post-earthquake Haiti ... are celebrated for simultaneously delivering cheap and clean energy, safeguarding health, reducing carbon emissions, improving educational outcomes, and fostering economic productivity. Across sub-Saharan Africa and South Asia, these small solar objects fuse ecological, social, and economic imperatives, mandates of sustainability, and mantras of growth and gain (Cross, this volume, pp. 53–54).

Here, we have familiarly problematic forms of global intervention: technological fixes for political problems, natural explanations (earthquake) for imperial histories (the United States and Haiti), and the raced, classed, and gendered assemblage of people and things with the power to intervene in global poverty, crisis, and underdevelopment. Cross's account of solar humanitarianism also shows how multiple (adjacent, jostling, contradictory, complementary) ethical worlds already accompany photovoltaic technologies and the people who design and sell them. Rather than disentangle these multiple ethical worlds when they don't present as disentangled in the ethnographic material, Cross uses Robbins' (2013) inquiry into the anthropology of the good to ask, 'What might it mean to pursue an anthropology of the good in a *double sense*, by focusing both on the attempts by people to fashion and pursue the good in their practices of care for others and on the ways that these ideals are inscribed or materialized in a mass-produced commodity?' (Cross, this volume, p. 55, emphasis mine).

One might object here that in pursuing the anthropology of the good in this double sense, Cross is stretching the conceit of the volume. Guy and Logan, after all, do not seem to see this doubling – the pursuit of moral selves; the pursuit of capitalist gain – in the same way he does. Rather, they have come to Hyderabad with 'an explicit ideological defence of what has been called "compassionate capitalism" (Benioff & Southwick 2004) and "philanthrocapitalism" (Bishop & Green 2008), or what we might also call "humanitarian capitalism"' (Cross, this volume, p. 48). But they have *also* come to Hyderabad as participants in other ethical worlds: the worlds of postcolonial racial politics, the worlds of credentialled expertise, the worlds of liberation technology. I do not offer these as etic gestures to structure, power, and interest, Throop and Zigon's 'larger-scale phenomena [including] historic, economic, and political conditions', but rather as *ethnographic descriptors*, along with Cross, of the annual meeting of the Global Off-Grid Lighting Association:

> The event was dominated by young, white, English-speaking men [who established] themselves as leaders of this, the golden age of solar photovoltaics. Some noticed my University of Edinburgh name badge and introduced themselves. Two men remembered their days as students in Edinburgh, where they had taken introductory classes in social anthropology before becoming lawyers or financial brokers, joining or starting firms working in the carbon-offset market with trading offices in Nairobi or companies with links to mining companies in Mozambique and Tanzania. Like others, they were looking to get a foothold in sub-Saharan Africa's emerging off-grid solar industry, seeking out contacts and links (Cross, this volume, p. 56).

In this description, whiteness, masculinity, the symbolic and financial capital conferred by law degrees or positions in finance, and postcolonial geographies of power are not 'larger-scale phenomena' but ethnographic detail – *themselves* ethical worlds of humanitarian intervention and potential profit. In other words, the ethical dilemmas Cross presents, as with Mason's and Wood's essays to follow, open us out into the question of ethical worlds as *ethnographically co-present*. Where Zigon and Throop, and much of the literature in the ethical turn, guides us 'to situate our ethnographic gaze on the lived predicaments, uncertainties, and quandaries that arise in particular moments, events, actions, and situations … to locate our analysis within the singular realities that arise from such moments' (2014: 7), Cross's, Mason's, and Wood's essays ask us to question what we might mean by singular ethical realities. Particularly because these three contributions study up, in many ways they bring us against the empirical limits of apparently singular ethical worlds, and show how the ethical worlds of the powerful spill out through the porous boundaries of imagined singularity.

Mason's essay introduces us to the luxurious material conditions in which experts produce energy market knowledge that bypasses democratic processes. For instance,

CERAWeek ($8,000 to attend), the Oslo Energy Forum ($15,000 to attend), The Arctic Energy Summit, and the Annual Meeting of the International Association of Energy Economics are each held at luxury hotels, with a repeating structure of receptions, plenary sessions, and gala dinners. Representatives from federal energy agencies mingle with independent researchers and bank personnel, oil service firms, and energy media makers. Here, virtue is expressed through luxury, which imbues the forecasts provided by high-profile energy consultants with a quality of singularity, producing consultants and their knowledge as expert. The energy industry is infamous for data manipulation, radically contingent future prognostication, and unnecessary confidentiality: '[D]ata and narrative are at once malleable, convincing, contingent, confidential, and indeterminate. Elasticity, fungibility, and agnotology are often the order of the day' (Appel, Mason & Watts 2015: 91). The elite 'energy salons', such as the roundtables studied by Mason, produce an image of rationality grounded in the 'calculated display of neoclassical quantification as a form of ethics that is, perversely, beyond critique' (Mason, this volume, p. 138). And indeed, it is in no small part through the knowledge propagated at these events, and then passed beyond their walls into the corridors of federal agencies, the world's largest energy corporations, the energy media, banks, and beyond, that shapes the contours of many of the ethical worlds we have seen so far in this volume: the regulatory or market viability of coal in the US West, the ability of a given state (Venezuela, Mexico) to provide subsidized gasoline or to consider the balance between investment in state-run oil companies and emerging wind farms, and, indeed, the ability of small companies like Challenge Energy in Alberta to offload mature assets and still secure bank loans that might enable employee's pensions, salaries, and stock options to still pay out (as we will see in Wood's essay). In short, Mason's energy events are, like all the other essays in this volume, ethical fields. And again, rather than Zigon and Throop's 'larger-scale phenomena [including] historic, economic, and political conditions', what Mason presents us with are relational ethnographic scenes in which groups of experts share information forged in ethical worlds – worlds of credentials, expertise, knowledge production, government service – that will spill out through the porous boundaries of luxury hotels and into the wider world of ethical energy dilemmas, like those Wood recounts.

Challenge Energy, like so many other small oil and gas companies, was insolvent in the wake of the halving of oil prices in 2014. As both a consultant in corporate governance and an anthropologist, Wood was ideally positioned to understand the ethical worlds of corporate actors who feel and attempt to act on their deep senses of duty and obligation: to pay down debts, to ensure invested relatives don't lose everything they committed, to make banks see their worthiness and continue lending. Wood traces what she in an earlier draft referred to as 'the moral work of facing and saving face, of giving an account, of making good on a promise, of perseverance'. Her essay offers a deeply empathetic account of William, Challenge's CEO, who asks her,

> How am I going to look my shareholders in the face? These shareholders aren't just hedge funds. My friends and family are invested … This is their retirement money and their kids' educations. Heck, it's my retirement too … What will [my employees] do? There's no jobs out there right now. We have to try to do something (Wood, this volume, p. 78).

Again, we can hear Wyoming coal miners or Colorado oil workers who are, with William, involved in 'the human predicament of trying to live a life that one is somehow responsible for but is in many respects out of one's control' (to quote Mattingly again).

*Journal of the Royal Anthropological Institute (N.S.), 177-190*
© Royal Anthropological Institute 2019

Like Cross, however, Wood is attuned to the multiplicities *within* and *constitutive of* William's ethical worlds. For instance, she notes that Alberta is 'hyperpermeable' to capital investment of the kind William sought and relied on because of 'systems of rule and land tenure that make oil and gas production zones out of (un)willing citizens and landholders, through colonial settler relations' (Wood, this volume, p. 78).[5] Like the luxury halls of price prognostication and market resilience, or the surprisingly high percentage of privately educated white British men and London-based financial trading companies at the Global Off-Grid Lighting Association, settler colonial relations here are not abstractions of structure, power, and interest, but 'the lived predicaments, uncertainties, and quandaries that arise in particular moments, events, actions, and situations' (to quote Zigon and Throop once more). Wood refuses to extract or disentangle William's deeply rendered ethical world from the multiple ethical worlds with which it sits in uncomfortable adjacency and overlap.

How, then, are we to start to see and feel and analyse at these ethical crossroads? For instance, how are we to heed the calls of the Wyoming coal miners to look beyond the light switch or the hybrid designation on a car to *see* them and their labour? Perhaps we can follow Walsh in recognizing that the social thickness of the Malagasy charcoal supply chain is also present in our reliance on Wyoming coal miners and Colorado oil workers for energy-intensive lifestyles in the United States and beyond. At the very least we can see – through exploding bat lungs in Tehuantepec and 'bottom of the pyramid' profiteering in Hyderabad – that a call for wind or solar is neither a panacea nor an end to politics. The goal perhaps, as mirrored in the form of this response, is to dwell as fully as possible in diverse ethical worlds while reaching for the empirical, ethnographic, and indeed ethical connections between them, lest we risk repeating the worst past of our discipline, in imagining 'qualities of internally homogeneous and externally distinctive bounded objects, [thereby creating] a model of the world as a global pool hall in which the entities spin off each other like so many hard and round billiard balls' (Wolf 1982: 6). To begin to see and feel and analyse at ethical crossroads is in part to note, then, a false analytic choice: again, structure, power, and interest are too often arrayed *against* close ethnographic attention to individual and relational ethical worlds. And yet they are in fact nothing more than ethical worlds themselves – luxury hotels and retirement accounts of kin; annual conferences where white supremacy[6] reigns; or the kinds of land claims possible in settler colonial societies – equally amenable to ethnographic attention.

Sticking with the ethnographic provocation of this volume, however – to attend closely to the ethical worlds of energy dilemmas – we might well ask *how*, by what social processes, might people, differentially, come to see and feel and analyse ethical crossroads? Mattingly, citing Faubion (2010; 2011) and Zigon (2007; 2009; 2011), asks anthropologists, 'to preserve a special space for a kind of ethical reflection and self-creation that offers more possibility for creative and potentially transformative modes of self-making' (2012*a*: 305).

> While differing in key respects, [Faubion and Zigon] demarcate a space for the 'dynamic' or 'break down' ethical moment in which the very norms and morals by which one ordinarily lives are themselves problematized and become objects of reflection, drawing inspiration from Foucault's discussion of 'problematization' in their work. Thus, Faubion is concerned to distinguish between what he calls the 'dynamic' aspects of self-creation and its 'more homeostatic and reproductive aspects' – the 'themitical' (2011: 20). 'The dynamic scene is one in which the typically subliminal themitical normativity of everyday routine is in suspension … The scene of crisis is a scene of the unfamiliar or of disturbance, in which the experience of the disruption or of the failure of the reproduction of routine is also the impetus of thought and action' (2011: 81-2) (Mattingly 2012*a*: 305).

The scene of a crisis, the unfamiliar, or a disturbance that provokes both the failure of routine and pathways to new forms of self-making – certainly, anthropogenic climate change can and will be this. It already is to the communities of Kivalina, Tuvalu, or the thousands of Maghrebian migrants fleeing twinned horrors of poverty and climate-change-related drought and famine. But because the Anthropocene is, in many ways, not yet this kind of tangible crisis for the daily lives recounted in this special issue, I want to conclude by drawing our attention to two crises – the 2008 financial meltdown and the protests around the Dakota Access Pipeline – to think both about how ethical ruptures happen in practice and about how some ethical worlds, more than others, are always already in (often violent and unwanted) relation with adjacent ethical worlds.

First, on the transformative possibilities of ethical rupture (of the kind invoked by Mattingly, Zigon, and Faubion) in the wake of the 2008 financial crisis.[7] Andrew was a securities lawyer in his mid-forties whom I met in the Alternative Banking Group of Occupy Wall Street. White, male, in a heterosexual marriage, and a life-long Republican, Andrew had been working in mortgage-backed securities (MBS) for nearly twenty years by the time I met him in 2012. He had long understood his work in ethical terms, and he differentiated MBS from financial practices which, in his estimation, did not create value. He conceived of securities as a tool that made the mortgage market more efficient, which in turn lowered costs to home buyers and democratized home ownership. Indeed, Ho (2009) and Zaloom (2012) both point out that those who work in finance consider it an ethical field, defined not by greed or reckless immorality, but by individual and collectively held visions of social purpose. Andrew inhabited these ethical fields and worked conscientiously on their behalf, but when it all came crashing down, he felt both personally responsible and terrified: 'I didn't have any idea what I was going to do or how I was going to support my family'. Andrew's intimate experience of the crash shows the anguish that accompanies such profound rupture, but also, again in Mattingly's words, the situated emergence of 'ethical reflection and self-creation that offers more possibility for creative and potentially transformative modes of self-making'. As Andrew's ethical field melted around him, he chose to make the tools of his expertise newly available for contestation and alternative mobilizations, thus his participation in Occupy Wall Street (and, I might add, his abandonment of the Republican Party). Here, then, is an example of crisis as an event that ruptures ethical sensibilities, in part via the ways in which it lays bare forms of ethical interference and contradiction: mortgage-backed securities were in fact kicking mostly Black and Latina/o people out of their homes, to Andrew's horror (see also Appel 2014a). His richly textured ethical world, in other words, was someone else's profound violation, and not because of structure, power, or interest (lest I sound like a broken record) but because of the empirical overlaps of the ethical worlds we unevenly inhabit.

Finally, then, laterally back to energy dilemmas via the Dakota Access Pipeline, and the question of which ethical worlds, more than others, are always already in (often violent and unwanted) relation with adjacent ethical worlds.

> Thousands of Water Protectors from more than three hundred Native nations, as well as allied supporters from a range of social movements, gathered at the Standing Rock Sioux Indian Reservation in Cannon Ball, North Dakota during 2016 to halt the construction of the Dakota Access Pipeline (DAPL). The DAPL threatens to cross under the Mni Sose (the Missouri River), which is the fresh-water supply for millions of humans and countless nonhuman relations. By blocking settler access to capital through direct action, the enactment of political counterclaims to the land and river through ceremony and legal challenges in US courts, #NoDAPL front-line protectors are directly challenging the fossil-fuel industry's centrality in colonial accumulation and demonstrating that

**Figure 1.** DAPL protesters in the Standing Rock Sioux Indian Reservation in Cannon Ball, North Dakota. (Original photo by Revolution Messaging, available at *https://www.flickr.com/photos/146636742@N07/ 31067462281/in/album-72157675631448300/*, licensed for use in the public domain.)

**Figure 2.** DAPL protesters occupy construction equipment, with members of the Morton County Sherriff's Department standing by. (Original photo by Desiree Kane, available at *https://ru.m.wikipedia .org/wiki/Файл:%22Happi%22_American_Horse_direct_action_against_DAPL,_August_2016.png*, used with permission of a Creative Commons licence.)

climate change is indelibly linked to historic and ongoing colonialism and Indigenous erasure and elimination (Dhillon & Estes 2016).

While we all inhabit ethical worlds and craft reflexive ethical practices within them, these worlds do not sit equally, as if side by side. While for some of us – Andrew and his commitment to the ethics of finance – rupture may be the impetus to new thought and action, for others of us – the Standing Rock Sioux and other indigenous peoples in this case – violent rupture in the face of other ethical worlds has been the groundwork for centuries. Through the narratives of Wyoming coal miners or Colorado's oil workers or Alberta's broke small businessmen or even Andrew, we can perhaps begin to imagine the ethical worlds of the Morton County Sherriff's Department (tasked with violently controlling Standing Rock protesters) or DAPL's various investors (Sunoco Logistics, Energy Transfer Partners, Phillips 66).

Just as with Andrew and the ethics of finance more generally, we may be able to trace out equally thick and immersive ethical worlds of these sheriffs or investors, but we cannot imagine their simple equality with the Standing Rock Sioux. Rather, they coexist, unequally (see also Fassin 2013). And as with finance, across the global political economy of energy, ethical worlds do not merely coexist as much as they overlap, intersect, interfere, and impinge. They are co-productive of one another. Thus, the North Dakota-based geophysicist who reminded High of a bumper sticker that said: 'Please God, Just Give Me One More Oil Boom. I Promise Not to Blow it Next Time' (High, this volume, p. 39) might well address Mason's ethical worlds of consultants, or the hedge funds that were squeezing William and Challenge Energy. Global oil prices are not a 'larger context' but forged in a suite of powerful and overlapping ethical worlds.

But of course, the lines of connection are not always so clear, nor are the unequal positions always so stark as #NoDAPL presents. For instance, how are we to answer Howe's question 'Is the betterment of a global climate – through the tools of renewable power – to be prioritized over localized ecological spaces where that energy is produced and conveyed?' But to follow lines of connection between ethical worlds, to understand how the multiplicity of ethical worlds press upon one another, we have research, we have ethnography, we have our capacity to hold multiple ethical worlds in the same analytic space. Ultimately, in other words, we do not have to pick one or the other; we do not have to choose between textured accounts of deeply held ethical worlds or the histories and power imbalances through which they emerge and are enacted.

Methodologically and theoretically, we do not have to choose, but instead we can see histories and power imbalances *themselves* as contemporary and fraught ethical scenes: water cannons directed at #NoDAPL protesters; the Global Off-Grid Lighting Association; the felicitous PowerPoint speculating on the futures price of coal. And if, methodologically and theoretically, we do not have to choose, politically and socially *we cannot choose*. A full commitment to new global energy arrangements requires that we attend both to lived experiences of energy dilemmas and to the ways that those experiences give shape to the lives and ethical possibilities of millions of other human and more-than-human ethical worlds.

## NOTES

[1] See Mattingly & Throop (2018) for a review of this literature.

[2] There is a growing literature on the relationship of the ethical turn to the question of politics. See Mattingly & Throop (2018) for an overview and see also Ortner (2016).

[3] There is a helpful discussion in some of the literature in the ethical turn (see Mattingly 2012*b*; Zigon & Throop 2014) about the Durkheimian conflation of the moral and the social (or the social *as* moral) that persists in much anthropology.

[4] For extant ethnographic work that troubles the assumed relationship between renewable energy and 'the good', see Argenti & Knight (2015); Harris (2010); Jepson, Brannstrom & Persons (2012); Pasqualetti (2011); Phadke (2011).

[5] On settler colonial relations in Canada, see Simpson (2016*a*; 2016*b*; 2017).

[6] Here I use Ansley's definition of white supremacy: 'a political, economic, and cultural system in which whites overwhelmingly control power and material resources, conscious and unconscious ideas of white superiority are widespread, and relations of white dominance and nonwhite subordination are daily reenacted across a broad array of institutions and social settings' (1989: 1024).

[7] This discussion is taken from Appel (2014*a*; 2014*b*).

## REFERENCES

Ahmed, S. 2017. *Living a feminist life*. Durham, N.C.: Duke University Press.

Ansley, F.L. 1989. Stirring the ashes: race, class and the future of civil rights scholarship. *Cornell Law Review* **74**, 993-1077.

Appel, H. 2014*a*. Finance, figuration, and the Alternative Banking Group of Occupy Wall Street. *Signs: Journal of Women and Culture in Society* **40**, 53-8.

——— 2014*b*. Occupy Wall Street and the economic imagination. *Cultural Anthropology* **29**, 602-25.

*Journal of the Royal Anthropological Institute (N.S.), 177-190*
© Royal Anthropological Institute 2019

————, A. MASON & M. WATTS 2015. The oil archive, expertise, and strategic knowledges [introduction]. In *Subterranean estates: life worlds of oil and gas* (eds) H. Appel, A. Mason & M. Watts, 91-3. Ithaca, N.Y.: Cornell University Press.

ARGENTI, N. & D.M. KNIGHT 2015. Sun, wind, and the rebirth of extractive economies: renewable energy investment and metanarratives of crisis in Greece. *Journal of the Royal Anthropological Institute* (N.S.) **21**, 781-802.

BENIOFF, M. & K. SOUTHWICK 2004. *Compassionate capitalism: how corporations can make doing good an integral part of doing well.* Franklin Lakes, N.J.: The Career Press.

BISHOP, M. & M. GREEN 2008. *Philanthrocapitalism: how giving can save the world.* New York: Bloomsbury.

DHILLON, J. & N. ESTES 2016. Standing Rock, #NoDAPL, and Mni Wiconi. *Cultural Anthropology* website (available on-line: *https://culanth.org/fieldsights/1010-standing-rock-nodapl-and-mni-wiconi,* accessed 23 January 2019).

FASSIN, D. 2013. On resentment and *ressentiment*: the politics and ethics of moral emotions. *Current Anthropology* **54**, 249-67.

FAUBION, J.D. 2010. From the ethical to the themitical (and back): groundwork for an anthropology of ethics. In *Ordinary ethics: anthropology, language, and action* (ed.) M. Lambek, 84-103. New York: Fordham University Press.

———— 2011. *An anthropology of ethics.* Cambridge: University Press.

HARRIS, J. 2010. Going green to stay in the black: transnational capitalism and renewable energy. *Race & Class* **52:2**, 62-78.

HARTMAN, S.V. 1997. *Scenes of subjection: terror, slavery, and self-making in nineteenth-century America.* Oxford: University Press.

HO, K. 2009. *Liquidated: an ethnography of Wall Street.* Durham, N.C.: Duke University Press.

HUGHES, D. 2017. *Energy without conscience: oil, climate change, and complicity.* Durham, N.C.: Duke University Press.

JEPSON, W., C. BRANNSTROM & N. PERSONS 2012. 'We don't take the pledge': environmentality and environmental skepticism at the epicenter of US wind energy development. *Geoforum* **43**, 851-63.

LAMBEK, M. (ed.) 2010. *Ordinary ethics: anthropology, language, and action.* New York: Fordham University Press.

LATOUR, B. 2004. *Reassembling the social: an introduction to actor-network-theory.* Oxford: University Press.

MATTINGLY, C. 2012a. Moral selves and moral scenes: narrative experiments in everyday life. *Ethnos* **78**, 301-27.

———— 2012b. Two virtue ethics and the anthropology of morality. *Anthropological Theory* **12**, 161-84.

———— & J. THROOP 2018. The anthropology of ethics and morality. *Annual Review of Anthropology* **47**, 475-92.

ORTNER, S. 2016. Dark anthropology and its others: theory since the eighties. *Hau: Journal of Ethnographic Theory* **6**, 47-73.

PASQUALETTI, M.J. 2011. Opposing wind energy landscapes: a search for common cause. *Annals of the Association of American Geographers* **101**, 907-17.

PHADKE, R. 2011. Resisting and reconciling Big Wind: middle landscape politics in the New American West. *Antipode* **43**, 754-76.

RALPH, L. 2014. *Renegade dreams: living through injury in Gangland Chicago.* Chicago: University Press.

ROBBINS, J. 2013. Beyond the suffering subject: toward an anthropology of the good. *Journal of the Royal Anthropological Institute* (N.S.) **19**, 447-62.

SIMPSON, A. 2016a. The state is a man: Theresa Spence, Loretta Saunders and the gender of settler sovereignty. *Theory & Event* **19**: 4 (available on-line: *https://muse.jhu.edu/article/633280,* accessed 29 January 2019).

———— 2016b. Whither settler colonialism? *Settler Colonial Studies* **6**, 438-45.

———— 2017. The ruse of consent and the anatomy of 'refusal': cases from indigenous North America and Australia. *Postcolonial Studies* **20**, 18-33.

WOLF, E. 1982. *Europe and the people without history.* Berkeley: University of California Press.

ZALOOM, C. 2012. The ethics of Wall Street. *Cultural Anthropology* website (available on-line: *https://culanth.org/fieldsights/363-the-ethics-of-wall-street,* accessed 23 January 2019).

ZIGON, J. 2007. Moral breakdown and the ethical demand: a theoretical framework for an anthropology of moralities. *Anthropological Theory* **7**, 131-50.

———— 2009. Within a range of possibilities: morality and ethics in social life. *Ethnos* **74**, 51-76.

———— 2011. *HIV is God's blessing: rehabilitating morality in neoliberal Russia.* Berkeley: University of California Press.

———— & C.J. THROOP 2014. Moral experience: introduction. *Ethos* **42**, 1-15.

## Conclusion : éthique de l'énergie et mondes éthiques

*Résumé*

Que se passe-t-il lorsque les effets de nos actions éthiques se répercutent au-delà, souvent loin au-delà, des phénomènes à la première ou deuxième personne ? Que se passe-t-il lorsque l'univers éthique si richement structuré d'une personne porte profondément atteinte à l'éthique d'une autre ? L'énergie constitue un terrain empirique particulièrement utile pour réfléchir aux questions posées par les mondes éthiques. Ceux-ci relèvent des contextes supra-individuels et au-delà-du-présent dans lesquels nous créons notre éthique quotidienne, autant que des vastes géographies et chronologies dans lesquelles les effets de nos pratiques éthiques se ramifient. Les mondes, champs ou paysages éthiques ne se limitent pas à des expériences à la première ou à la deuxième personne. Ils se recoupent, interfèrent les uns avec les autres, souvent de très loin, sur plusieurs générations, et certainement pas de façon équilibrée. Les pratiques éthiques des domaines les plus puissants se répandent, envahissent et modèlent celles d'autres domaines éthiques. Qu'est-ce que cela implique de commencer à voir, à ressentir, à analyser à ces croisées des chemins éthiques ? Et surtout, qu'implique la reconnaissance que la structure, le pouvoir et l'intérêt, trop souvent dressés contre l'examen ethnographique attentif des expériences individuelles et partagées, ne sont pas des « forces supérieures » mais d'autres mondes éthiques, que l'on pourrait tout aussi bien soumettre à l'attention ethnographique ?

# Index

activists, 10, 14, 20, 63; anti-coal, 17
American Petroleum Institute, 34
Anthropocene, 49, 110, 114, 163, 166, 173,
  186
anthropology, and compassionate
  capitalism, 48; and morality, 11, 51; and
  oil, 15–17; of energy, 10, 11, 14–15, 18, 19,
  51, 92, 93, 161, 163; of the good, 51, 55, 183
Appel, Hannah, 7, 10, 12, 16, 20, 23, 41, 69,
  75, 98, 177–190
Argentina, 17, 93
Austin, Diane, 17, 93
Australia, 16, 60, 165

biofuels, 18, 92
Bourdieu, Pierre, 125–127
Boyer, Dominic, 14, 18, 19, 94, 173
Brandtstädter, Susanne, 13, 33
Brint, Stephen, 133
Buffett, Warren, 85

Calderón, Felipe, 161
*campesinos*, 14, 164
Canada, 21, 184; oil boom, 72–73, 74, 83;
  orphaned wells, 67–90
Canadian Association for Petroleum
  Producers (CAPP), 71
capitalism, 17, 31, 48, 75; compassionate,
  48; humanitarian, 48, 55, 58, 183;

philanthrocapitalism, 48, 183
capitalization, 75, 86
Capitalocene, 49, 63
carbon emissions reduction, 18, 54, 163,
  182
charcoal, 9, 12, 15, 22, 53, 97, 177, 180; as
  artisanal energy, 111–113; eucalyptus, 118,
  119, 120, 121; green, 12, 22, 57, 117–121, 178,
  180; importance, 109–111; kilns, 112;
  ordinary ethics, 114–117; trade, 115–117
Chávez, Hugo, 146–147
Christian faith, 32, 37–41, 43, 178; Oilfield
  Christian Fellowship, 37–39
class, 17, 21, 62, 78, 92, 101, 178, 182
climate change, 10, 12, 17, 19, 20, 36, 41, 62,
  98, 100, 101, 114, 163
Clinton, Hillary, 100
coal, 15, 93, 178; and gender, 17; and race,
  17; as commodity, 97; as gift, 91, 93,
  97–99, 101, 102
coal miners, and unionism, 104; as energy
  providers, 94–97
coal mining, 9, 17; Wyoming, 15, 21–22,
  91–107, 178, 180–181, 187
Colombia, 14, 94, 155
consultant experts, 15, 16, 32, 74, 124–139,
  177, 178, 183–184, 188
corporate assets, 70–71